Mission: IMPEACHABLE

K. Alan Snyder

Mission: Impeachable
by K. Alan Snyder

Printed in the United States of America
ISBN 1-931-232-11-3

Allegiance Press
344 Maple Ave. West, #302
Vienna, VA 22180
703-691-7595

"Let us conduct ourselves and this inquiry in such a way as to vindicate the rule of law.

Let us conduct ourselves and this inquiry in such a way as to vindicate the Constitution.

Let us conduct ourselves and this inquiry in such a way as to vindicate the sacrifices of blood and treasure that have been made across the centuries to create and defend this last best hope of humanity on earth, the United States of America."

— Congressman Henry Hyde, September 11, 1998

Contents

Foreword

Some books are for the present, and some are for the future. *Mission: Impeachable* is for both. Historians a century from now will turn to this book to understand more about the personalities and principles of the House Managers, but readers now can gain nuggets of insight. For example, the chapter on James Rogan rebuts stereotypes concerning the management style of Tom DeLay and shows why Newt Gingrich backed off from involvement in the impeachment debate.

John F. Kennedy won a Pulitzer Prize almost half a century ago for his book *Profiles in Courage*. Alan Snyder has produced an equally valuable work that, because of its sympathy toward the House managers as well as its scholarly nature, is unlikely to receive such honor or as great an audience. But it should because *Mission: Impeachable* is a surprisingly good read about surprisingly courageous men: surprising because, in an age of focus groups, the House Managers agreed to fight for what almost surely was a lost cause.

More, in an era of sound bites, the House Managers focused on explaining principles that required more than two seconds or even two minutes to understand because they had taken at least two millennia to develop. These determined Congressmen went into the Senate chamber knowing that even in—especially in—a post-modern age, it was vital to speak about and fight for principles of justice and honesty.

James Rogan, quoted in the chapter about him, explains why he kept a diary during impeachment proceedings: "I don't really think anybody is going – one hundred years from now—[to] remember my name. They'll remember the fact that Clinton was impeached. But I wanted them to have an accurate record . . . because I knew that there were going to be revisionist histories going to work on this before it even was completed." He said that he planned to give his diary to the National Archives someday.

To the historians and students a century from now who are reading this: Search for that diary—and read through this book. In 1998 and 1999, when the president of the United States had lied under oath, a few, a happy few, a band of brothers risked their reputations in an attempt to bring him to justice. If in the year 2100 the United States still is the land of the free and the home of the brave, it will because of the courage you see described in these pages and the courage of others in the 21st century who also refused to take the easy road.

Dr. Marvin Olasky
Senior Fellow, the Acton Institute for the
Study of Religion and Liberty

Preface

"Self righteous." "Holier than thou." The words resounded throughout the Supreme Court chamber, the disdain with which they were spoken seemingly at odds with the ambience of this venerable courtroom. One naturally expected civility in the almost-reverential atmosphere, not such discordant notes.

I was sitting in the second row, listening to the keynote speaker for an academic conference on constitutional history. His words were anything but academic. I do not recall the exact theme of his talk, but the scornful adjectives he uttered were only a passing reference, not the main topic. To whom was he referring? The targets of his indignation were the House Managers who had argued the case for impeachment before the Senate in the recently completed trial of President William Jefferson Clinton.

After the talk, conference participants enjoyed a splendid dinner at the Court. Waiters with white gloves provided individual attention. The food was superb; its presentation was faultless. Once again, civility reigned.

Yet I could not shake what I considered to be disturbing words and an even more disturbing attitude that had inspired them. On the bus trip back to the conference center, I continued to ponder the discrepancy that presented itself: the establishment of the Court to uphold the rule of law, yet the use of the Supreme Court chamber to deride those who claimed to be standing for that very principle. Were the House Managers merely self-righteous hypocrites who paraded their morality for public consumption, or were they sincere? Were they "holier than thou" or truly concerned about the rule of law and the dangers of allowing the guilty to go unpunished?

Later that evening, I finished a book I had brought with me—*The American Leadership Tradition* by Marvin Olasky. I was impressed by the author's use of biography to elucidate the characters of the individuals profiled in his book. He had succeeded in modifying my opinion of some of those leaders. Andrew Jackson, Grover Cleveland, Theodore Roosevelt—I now had a different perspective on each of them.

The next morning, it occurred to me that the same could be accomplished in a book about the House Managers. I knew that many books were going to be written about this impeachment trial—the historical precedents for impeachment, the reasons for its inclusion in the Constitution, the exact meaning of "high crimes and misdemeanors," the "spin game" played by the President's defenders—but how many would focus on the Managers themselves? How many would use the biographical model for trying to understand the Managers' motivations for proceeding with the case against the President? The idea for this book was birthed that morning.

I believe it is important for readers to know the presuppositions of any writer. None of us writes from a purely objective perspective. We are all influenced by what we believe to be truth. Christian apologist Francis Schaeffer once noted,

> People have presuppositions, and they will live more consistently on the basis of these presuppositions than even they themselves may realize. By *presuppositions* we mean the basic way an individual looks at life, his basic world view, the grid through which he sees the world. Presuppositions rest upon that which a person considers to be the truth of what exists. People's presuppositions lay a grid for all they bring forth into the external world. Their presuppositions also provide the basis for their values and therefore the basis for their decisions.[1]

My presuppositions are first and foremost biblical in orientation. The grid through which I see the world—my basic worldview—is grounded upon biblical principles. These principles form the basis for my values, my decisions, and my analysis of right and wrong. These principles also inform my understanding of the role of civil government, placing me on the conservative side of the political spectrum. Naturally, then, I am predisposed to "take the side," so to speak, of the House Managers.

But I am also an academic. The training I receive in academia requires that I follow the evidence wherever it may lead. I must be honest and cannot, in good conscience, misrepresent the facts. Properly understood, there is no dichotomy here. My Christianity and my academic training require the same standard. Academic integrity rests upon moral integrity, which I believe flows from biblical faith. Consequently, when I undertake any research and writing project, I must be true to that faith. Political conservatism must become secondary; the truth must have priority.

So I enter upon this endeavor with a commitment to the truth, with a sincere desire to follow the evidence, and with the hope that I can make a contribution to the study of character in civil government.

Preface Endnotes

[1] Francis Schaeffer, *How Should We Then Live? The Rise and Decline of Western Thought and Culture* (Old Tappan, NJ: Fleming H. Revell Co., 1976), 19.

Introduction

Alexander Hamilton, writing in defense of the proposed Constitution in 1788, described the nature of any impeachment process. He forthrightly stated that the Senate, in judging matters of impeachment, would be dealing with "those offenses which proceed from the misconduct of public men, or, in other words, from the abuse or violation of some public trust." These would be "political" offenses, he noted, and he had no illusions about how a trial focusing on political matters would impact both those involved and the general public:

> The prosecution of them [political offenses], for this reason, will seldom fail to agitate the passions of the whole community, and to divide it into parties more or less friendly or inimical to the accused. In many cases it will connect itself with the pre-existing factions, and will enlist all their animosities, partialities, influence, and interest on one side or on the other; and in such cases there will always be the greatest danger that the decision will be regulated more by the comparative strength of parties than by the real demonstrations of innocence or guilt.[1]

Hamilton was prescient. Any witness to the Clinton impeachment trial could have written those same words, regardless of political sympathies. Whether Republican or Democrat, conservative or liberal, all would have to admit that the trial agitated passions and that participants in the trial, and the nation as a whole, divided into parties over the accusations and the accused. Most certainly, those parties were aligned with pre-existing factions, and some will claim that the verdict had far more to do with the comparative strength of those factions than with actual innocence or guilt.

the focus as stated above. After examining each Manager separately, the next chapter is devoted to the results of the 2000 elections. Did the House Managers, or the Republican Party as a whole, suffer at the hands of their constituents as a result of their actions? Finally, the conclusion offers my verdict on the rationale for the Managers' insistence on the President's removal from office. Were their actions essentially principled, or did partisanship bias the message? What should we think about the views and characters of the men who presented the case before the Senate?

Character is an issue that should not be relegated to an insignificant corner of our political discourse. It should be central to all political discussion. As America's second President, John Adams, remarked, "Public Virtue cannot exist in a Nation without private, and public Virtue is the only Foundation of Republics."[5] For the continuance of this republic, it is essential that its citizens be concerned with both private and public character—in its President and in its elected representatives.

Introduction Endnotes

1 Alexander Hamilton, James Madison, and John Jay, *The Federalist Papers*, #65, with an introduction by Clinton Rossiter (New York & Scarborough, Ontario: New American Library, 1961), 396-97.

2 Closing Argument of Hon. Henry Hyde, Senate Impeachment Trial of President Clinton, 8 February 1999; available at http://www.house.gov/judiciary/hyde0208.htm; accessed 27 May 1999.

3 Closing Argument of White House Counsel Charles Ruff, Senate Impeachment Trial of President Clinton, 8 February 1999; available at http://www.washingtonpost.com/wp-srv/politics/special/clinton/stories/defensetext020899.htm; accessed 27 May 1999.

4 Definitions for both principle and partisan come from the *New Webster's Dictionary of the English Language: Encyclopedic Edition* (New York: Belair Publishing, 1980).

5 John Adams to Mercy Warren, *Warren-Adams Letters*, Vol. 1, 1743-1777 (The Massachusetts Historical Society, 1917), 222; quoted in Verna M. Hall, comp., *The Christian History of the American Revolution: Consider and Ponder* (San Francisco: Foundation for American Christian Education, 1976), 604.

CHAPTER ONE

Why Impeachment?

The Date: *May 16, 1868*

The Place: *The Senate Chamber, Washington, DC*

The Event: *The first vote on articles of impeachment brought by the House of Representatives against President Andrew Johnson*

The Senate galleries were packed with spectators. An impeachment drama unfolded below on the Senate floor. Would Andrew Johnson become the first President to be removed from office for alleged high crimes and misdemeanors?

Eleven articles of impeachment had been brought against President Johnson. The first eight charged him with illegally removing Secretary of War Edwin Stanton from office, a violation of the Tenure of Office Act passed by Congress the previous year. The ninth article was for his violation of the Command of the Army Act, another 1867 act, which had virtually stripped the President of his direct control of the Army. The final two articles concerned Johnson's treatment of Congress. Article eleven declared that Johnson had impugned the authority of Congress because he considered it "a Congress of only part of the States, thereby denying and intending to deny, that the legislation of said Congress was valid or obligatory upon him . . . except in so far as he saw fit to approve the same."[1] The senators had decided that article eleven would be the first test of the strength of the House Managers' arguments. The vote would take place on this day.

The House of Representatives had passed its impeachment resolution on February 24. In a rather convoluted procedure, that resolution had passed prior to the writing of the specific charges that would be presented at the impeachment trial. The eleven impeachment articles were not approved until nearly a week later. The articles were presented to the Senate on March 4, and the debate over trial procedures began promptly the next day. The trial itself, over which Chief Justice Salmon P. Chase presided, started on March 30.[2]

The House chose seven Managers to make the case for impeachment in the Senate. Benjamin F. Butler, a former Union Army general who was universally hated by Southerners for his strict occupation policies in New Orleans, led the Manager team. His opening statement, which lasted three hours, was merely a portent of things to come. The trial arguments continued until May 4, with Manager John Bingham taking nearly three days to summarize the Managers' case against the President. When he concluded, the galleries responded with loud applause and cheers—an interruption that lasted so long that the galleries had to be cleared in order for the proceedings to continue.[3] It is presumed that the cheers were for the *case* that was being made, not for its *conclusion*.

As Chief Justice Chase took his chair at noon on May 16, the tension in the chamber heightened. Would the Senate, for the first time in American history, remove a sitting President from office? No one knew for sure because the vote would be close. By most counts, the Managers were one vote shy of the two-thirds needed for a successful removal. All eyes were on Kansas Senator Edmund Ross, the only Republican who had not yet committed himself publicly one way or the other.

Just two days earlier, Ross had received a telegram from his home state that read, "Kansas has heard the evidence, and demands the conviction of the President." It was signed by "D. R. Anthony, and 1,000 others." Ross responded, "I do not recognize your right to demand that I shall vote either for or against conviction. I have taken an oath to do impartial justice . . . and I trust I shall have the courage and honesty to vote according to the dictates of my judgment and for the highest good of my country." Not to be outdone, Mr. Anthony and his "1,000 others" retaliated, "Your telegram received. . . . Your motives are Indian contracts and greenbacks. Kansas repudiates you as she does all perjurers and skunks."[4]

The roll call began. Ross had been warned by fellow Radical Republicans that a "no" vote would end his political career. When his name was called, Ross stood and quietly cast his vote—for acquittal. His vote effectively ended the impeachment proceedings. When two more votes were held ten days later, the tally for both was identical: one vote short of conviction. The constitutional drama ended "without a formal vote ever having been taken upon eight of the articles presented."[5]

Some newspaper editorialists decided that Ross could best be compared to Benedict Arnold, Jefferson Davis, or Judas Iscariot. As predicted, his political career did end swiftly; he lost his reelection bid.

Edmund Ross—a man of principle? In a letter to his wife one week after his momentous vote, Ross declared, "This storm of passion will soon pass away, and the people, the whole people, will thank and bless me for having saved the country by my single vote from the greatest peril through which it has ever passed, though none but God can ever know the struggle it has cost me."[6]

Certainly he stood against his own party, eschewing partisanship. But were there other reasons for his stand? Did his control of patronage in Kansas lead him to vote for acquittal, thereby using leverage against the President to appoint Ross's friends to government posts? Over the next two months, President Johnson appointed five of Ross's friends and his brother to federal jobs.[7] An argument can be offered for both interpretations. Yet, regardless of Ross's motive, the result was the same: Andrew Johnson completed his term as President of the United States.

The Date:	*July 27, 1974*
The Place:	*The House Judiciary Committee, Rayburn House Office Building*
The Event:	*The Committee vote on the first article of impeachment against President Richard Nixon*

Chairman Peter Rodino had thought his Judiciary Committee would vote on the first article of impeachment on Friday, July 26, but the wrangling over the specificity of the charges had continued into the next day. He also had to contend with spectators in the hearing room who had disrupted the proceedings by calling for President Nixon's impeachment for "war crimes" against the people of Vietnam and Cambodia. The offenders had to be removed from the room.[8]

This day, Saturday, July 27, was the culmination of an ordeal stemming from the break-in at Democratic National Headquarters in the Watergate complex on June 17, 1972. The vote was on the charge that President Nixon had used "the powers of his high office . . . in a course of conduct or plan designed to delay, impede, and obstruct the investigation of . . . illegal entry; to cover up, conceal and protect those responsible; and to conceal the existence and scope of other unlawful covert activities."[9]

The debate on this article waged throughout the day, but it was obvious that before this day ended, the thirty-eight members of the Committee were going to have to take a stand on this particular article of impeachment. It was difficult even for some of the Democratic members, particularly those who were identified with the conservative wing of the party. Walter Flowers of Alabama soberly read his prepared text, a speech that brought a hush to the hearing room:

> There are many people in my district who will disagree with
> my vote here. Some will say that it hurts them deeply for me to

vote for impeachment. I can assure them that I probably have enough pain for them and me. I have close, personal friends who strongly support President Nixon. To several of these close friends who somehow, I hope, will hear and see these proceedings, I say that the only way I could vote for impeachment would be the realization, to me anyway, that they, my friends, would do the same thing if they were in my place on this unhappy day and confronted with all of these same facts that I have. And I have to believe that they would, or I would not take the position that I do.[10]

The roll call proceeded, this time not just before a gallery of spectators, as was the case with Andrew Johnson, but before a nationwide television audience. The final tally was 27-11 in favor of the article. All twenty-one Democrats had voted for it; six of the seventeen Republicans supported it also. Although not an overwhelming bipartisan vote, enough Republicans had agreed with the article to make it more than merely a Democratic vendetta against a President they did not like.

Congressman Rodino had served in the House for twenty-five years; he was in his first term as chairman of the Judiciary Committee. He did not break into a partisan gloat after recessing for the evening. He even ignored the reporters who clamored to speak with him. Those who saw him afterward portrayed him as glassy-eyed and uncommunicative. Staffers were expecting some dramatic or historic statement. Instead, "Rodino mumbled something incoherent and walked past them into his little office. He shut the door, picked up the telephone and dialed his wife in Newark. He told her it was over. She replied that she knew, that she had watched him on television and was very proud of him. He broke down and cried."[11]

That vote became the watershed event of the two-year national nightmare. Two more impeachment articles passed the Committee on Monday, and on the same day, the President turned over more of the subpoenaed Oval Office tapes. They included the "smoking gun" conversation in which he ordered the CIA to interfere with the FBI investigation of the

Watergate break-in. All Republican support for him disintegrated. The President of the United States resigned from his office on August 9, 1974.

The Date: *December 19, 1998*

The Place: *House of Representatives Chamber, Washington, DC*

The Event: *Full House vote on impeachment articles against President Clinton drafted and approved by the Judiciary Committee*

Two days of debate were drawing to a close. The debate had been intense and partisan, just as the Judiciary Committee hearings had been for the past month. Democrats denounced the impeachment articles. Even if the President had made unwanted sexual advances toward Paula Jones when he was governor of Arkansas and subsequently lied about it in a deposition in her civil case, and even if he had covered up a sexual relationship with White House intern Monica Lewinsky, misleading and/or lying to a grand jury in the process, these were not impeachable offenses because they were private actions. Not true, said Republicans, because he went beyond private acts to commit perjury and obstruct justice, using his office inappropriately for personal benefit. The lines were sharply drawn.

Speaker-designate Bob Livingston took the floor. Livingston had recently been a target of pornographer Larry Flynt's investigation to show that Republicans were hypocritical in their denunciation of the President's sexual misdeeds. Livingston, after having been publicly accused, admitted to marital infidelities. Yet, as he stood on the House floor on this day, he challenged the President whose actions, he said, had damaged the nation for nearly a year. "You have the power to terminate that damage and heal the wounds that you have created," he declared. "You, sir, may resign your post. And I can only challenge you in such fashion if I am willing to heed my own words." Livingston then shocked his House colleagues:

> I was prepared to lead our narrow majority as Speaker, and I believe I had it in me to do a fine job. But I cannot do that job or be the kind of leader that I would like to be under current circumstances, so I must set the example that I hope President Clinton will follow.
>
> Mr. Speaker, I will not stand for Speaker of the House on January 6, but rather I shall remain as a back bencher in this Congress that I so dearly love for approximately six months into the 106th Congress, whereupon I shall vacate my seat and ask my Governor to call a special election to take my place.[12]

Members on both sides of the aisle expressed concern that Livingston had felt forced to take such a drastic step. Democrats saw it as "a developing sexual McCarthyism," in the words of Jerrold Nadler of New York. David Bonior of Michigan, the minority whip, decried the "politics of personal smear" that was "degrading the dignity of public officials."[13] They saw the cases of Bill Clinton and Bob Livingston as equivalent.

Henry Hyde, however, begged to differ. "Something is going on repeatedly that has to be stopped. That is a confusion between private acts of infidelity and public acts, where as a government official, you raise your right hand and you ask God to witness to the truth of what you are saying. That is a public act. Infidelity, adultery . . . is a private act."[14] Although President Clinton and Congressman Livingston had both been unfaithful to their wives, only President Clinton, Republicans argued, had perjured himself before a grand jury.

The vote was called. Two of the four proposed articles of impeachment passed. The President was formally charged with providing perjurious, false, and misleading testimony to a grand jury in connection with the Independent Counsel's probe and with obstructing justice in the civil

suit filed against him by Paula Jones. With only five Democrats supporting the impeachment articles, the partisan appearance that had been
dominant for the entire year was maintained.[15]

Congressman Livingston's plea for the President to follow his example
made no apparent impression on Mr. Clinton. Instead, shortly after the
impeachment vote, the President's Chief of Staff, John Podesta, minority
leader Richard Gephardt, Vice President Al Gore, and the President
himself appeared on the South Grounds of the White House to remark
on the day's proceedings. Congressman Gephardt called for an end to
"the politics of personal destruction." Vice President Gore called it "the
saddest day I have seen in our Nation's Capital" and deplored "excessive
partisanship" that "unlocked a form of vitriol and vehemence that hurts
our nation." The President commented,

> I thank the few brave Republicans who withstood enormous
> pressure to stand with them [the Democratic leadership] for
> the plain meaning of the Constitution, and for the proposition
> that we need to pull together, to move beyond partisanship, to
> get on with the business of our country. . . .
>
> We must get rid of the poisonous venom of excessive parti-
> sanship, obsessive animosity, and uncontrolled anger. That is
> not what America deserves. That is not what America is
> about.[16]

Unbowed and undaunted, the President and his defense team prepared
for the upcoming Senate trial.

The Date:	*February 8, 1999*
The Place:	*The Senate Chamber, Washington, DC*
The Event:	*The House Managers' Closing Arguments*

Since January 14, the House Mangers had been trying to make their case, not only to the Senate, but also to the American public. Yet public opinion polls had not shifted; Americans still did not want their President removed from office. It did not appear that any Senators had changed their minds. It was becoming painfully evident that not even one Democrat would break partisan ranks and vote for an article of impeachment. Each Manager had had his say in the closing arguments. Congressman Hyde concluded the remarks for his colleagues.

He was glad to come "to the end of this melancholy procedure" and defended the integrity of his fellow Managers. Cynicism, he felt, had been "our most formidable opponent," acting like "an acid eating away at the vital organs of American public life. It is a clear and present danger, because it blinds us to the nobility and the fragility of being a self-governing people." And nothing, he said, "begets cynicism like the double standard—one rule for the popular and the powerful and another for the rest of us." His final plea to the Senators was "Let right be done" to set a good example for the youth of America. Hyde continued,

> Once in a while I do worry about the future. I wonder if, after this culture war is over, this one we are engaged in, an America will survive that is worth fighting for to defend.
>
> People won't risk their lives for the UN, or over the Dow Jones averages. But I wonder, in future generations, whether there will be enough vitality left in duty, honor and country to excite our children and grandchildren to defend America. . . . And now let us all take our place in history on the side of honor and, oh, yes: Let right be done.[17]

On February 12, the Senate voted on the two articles of impeachment. On the article alleging perjury, forty-five Senators voted guilty, fifty-five not guilty. On the article alleging obstruction of justice, the vote split fifty-fifty. Sixty-seven votes were required for removal from office. On neither article did a Democrat vote guilty. The President had decried "excessive partisanship," yet only Republicans were willing to break from the party position on these votes. One might reasonably question where the greater partisanship resided.

Why impeachment?

To impeach means to bring an accusation against someone and charge that person with wrongdoing. In politics, it means to accuse a public official of misconduct in office. Impeachment, per se, does not remove someone from office; it is merely an accusation. The impeachment must then be heard and judged by the proper authority.

In the United States Constitution, the House of Representatives brings the formal accusations of impeachable offenses. The Senate then judges the accusations. If the President is the one accused, the Chief Justice of the Supreme Court presides over the trial. Two-thirds of the Senators must agree with the accusations for any official to be removed from office. Another sanction may be a prohibition against holding another federal position. The Congress can go no further than this, but the person convicted and removed from office still may have to face civil or criminal charges in the judicial system, an undertaking that is separate from the impeachment process.[18]

The most significant issue, of course, is what constitutes an impeachable offense. The Constitution says specifically, "The President, Vice President and all civil officers of the United States, shall be removed from office on impeachment for, and conviction of, treason, bribery, or other high crimes and misdemeanors."[19]

There is no real debate over the nature of treason or bribery, but the phrase "high crimes and misdemeanors" always has sparked considerable controversy.

One of the most authoritative early American commentators on this subject was Supreme Court Justice Joseph Story who, in his 1840 *Familiar Exposition of the Constitution*, tackled the issue by embracing a combination of common sense and historical precedent. Story clearly did not believe that impeachment and removal from office required the breaking of a law. "If we say," he wrote, "that there are no other offenses, which are impeachable offenses, until Congress has enacted some law on the subject, then the Constitution, as to all crimes except treason and bribery, has remained a dead letter, up to the present hour. Such a doctrine would be truly alarming and dangerous. Congress has unhesitatingly adopted the conclusion that no previous statute is necessary to authorize an impeachment for any official misconduct." Further, he noted, "In the few cases of impeachment, which have hitherto been tried, no one of the charges has rested upon any statutable misdemeanors."[20] Story's view, then, was more than simply an opinion; early American impeachment practices confirmed it.

Constitutional scholar Raoul Berger's study of the history of impeachment, and particularly of the phrase "high crimes and misdemeanors," lends more support to Story's view. Berger notes that the phrase first appears in English history, not in criminal law, but in an impeachment. "Impeachment itself was conceived because the objects of impeachment, for one reason or another, were beyond the reach of ordinary criminal redress." He concludes that impeachment was a political, not criminal, weapon.[21] High crimes and misdemeanors were, therefore, "a category of *political* crimes against the state."[22]

The phrase never did find its way into the criminal law of England. Sir William Blackstone, writing during the American revolutionary era, considered a high misdemeanor principally as maladministration by public officials, unrelated to statutable crimes. He even reasoned that treason and bribery were political crimes, rather than statutable, primarily because they were offenses against the State, tied closely to corrupt administration of the State.[23] Alexander Hamilton, in *Federalist #65*, echoed Blackstone's view of the political nature of impeachable acts.

Berger also noted that James Wilson, signer of the Declaration of

Independence and the Constitution, and one of the first associate justices on the Supreme Court, clearly drew a line between impeachable offenses and violations of statutes: "Impeachments . . . come not . . . within the sphere of ordinary jurisprudence. They are founded on different principles, are governed by different maxims, and are directed to different objects; for this reason, the trial and punishment of an offense on impeachment is no bar to a trial of the same offense at common law."[24]

Berger concludes, "In sum, 'high crimes and misdemeanors' appear to be words of art confined to impeachments, without roots in the ordinary criminal law and which, so far as I could discover, had no relation to whether an indictment would lie in the particular circumstances . . . What lends a 'peculiar' quality to these crimes is the fact that they are not encompassed by criminal statutes or, for that matter, by the common law cases."[25]

One year after Berger published his book on impeachment, the House Judiciary Committee, during its investigation of President Nixon, issued a report on the constitutional grounds for presidential impeachment. Referred to as the Rodino Report, it confirmed Berger's findings.

Section Two of the Rodino Report noted that "at the time of the Constitutional Convention the phrase 'high Crimes and Misdemeanors' had been in use for over 400 years in impeachment proceedings in Parliament." It further pointed out that "from 1620 to 1649 over 100 impeachments were voted by the House of Commons" and that when high crimes and misdemeanors were cited, they "included both statutory offenses . . . and non-statutory offenses." In fact, the very first record of impeachment, in 1386, centered on the King's Chancellor breaking a promise he had made to Parliament—not quite a criminal offense in the law! Other impeachment charges in later centuries included "procuring offices for person[s] who were unfit, and unworthy of them," failure of an attorney general to prosecute cases after commencing the lawsuits, and "negligent discharge of duties and improprieties in office," the latter consisting of "browbeating witnesses and commenting on their credibility, and with cursing and drinking to excess."[26]

While there were few impeachments during the eighteenth century in

England, whenever they did occur, "high crimes and misdemeanors" appears in the charges. The Report's section on English parliamentary practice concludes that "the phrase 'high Crimes and Misdemeanors' was confined to parliamentary impeachments; it had no roots in the ordinary criminal law, and the particular allegations of misconduct under that heading were not necessarily limited to common law or statutory derelictions or crimes."[27]

The Report then analyzed the intent of the Framers of the Constitution and determined that they followed the English understanding of impeachment and the meaning of high crimes and misdemeanors. Quoting James Wilson in the Pennsylvania ratifying convention, the Report stated, "Far from being above the laws, he [the President] is amenable to them in his private character as a citizen, and in his public character by *impeachment*" (emphasis added).[28]

Finally, in Section Three, entitled "The Criminality Issue," the Report summarized its position and left no doubt that impeachments are not identical with criminal court cases:

> The post convention statements of and writings of Alexander Hamilton, James Wilson, and James Madison—each a participant in the Constitutional Convention—show that they regarded impeachment as an appropriate device to deal with offenses against constitutional government by those who hold civil office, and not a device limited to criminal offenses. . . .
>
> The American experience with impeachment . . . reflects the principle that impeachable conduct need not be criminal. Of the thirteen impeachments voted by the House since 1789, at least ten involved one or more allegations that did not charge a violation of criminal law. . . .
>
> Unlike a criminal case, the cause for the removal of a President may be based on his entire course of conduct in office. In particular situations, it may be a course of conduct more than individual acts that has a tendency to subvert constitutional government.

To confine impeachable conduct to indictable offenses may well be to set a standard so restrictive as not to reach conduct that might adversely affect the system of government. Some of the most grievous offenses against our constitutional form of government may not entail violations of the criminal law.[29]

This summary, and the investigation of impeachment history from which it originated, establishes the same point made by Joseph Story, James Wilson, and many others: impeachments are not based necessarily on outright violations of positive laws. There are other actions short of unlawful criminal activity that can lead to impeachment and removal from office.

It should be kept in mind that the Rodino Report was written by the Democratic majority at that time. The Republican majority in the Clinton impeachment used the Report as its basis for proceeding with the impeachment trial. One of the ironies of these two impeachment episodes is that Hillary Rodham, who would later become Hillary Clinton, was one of the staffers who contributed to the earlier Rodino Report.

Despite the Rodino Report's conclusions, many of President Clinton's congressional defenders took issue with the idea that impeachment and removal from office could be based on anything less than a criminal charge admissible in court. During the summations in the Judiciary Committee, for example, Abbe Lowell, the Democratic Counsel, declared,

Mr. Chairman, how did we get to perjury, which is what Article I suggests? Independent Counsel Starr's referral goes out of its way not to make a perjury charge, because that offense . . . is one of the hardest to prove . . . And as all the federal prosecutors who testified here said, this would never be a real case in a real court. So if lawyers can conclude that this would not be charged as a crime, how do you as lawmakers allow it to be charged as a high crime?[30]

When David Schippers, chief investigative counsel for the Committee, had his opportunity to respond later that day, he reminded the Committee of the distinction between indictable and impeachable offenses:

> Although the president's lawyers admit that his actions in the *Jones* case and in the Lewinsky matter were immoral—and I think they used the term "maddening acts"—they argue that they don't rise to the level of criminal activity, and certainly not to the level of impeachable offenses . . .
>
> . . . Some even suggested that a prosecutor wouldn't even consider an indictment based upon the evidence available here. Well, that remains to be seen.
>
> I doubt if any of those experts have read all the evidence that I have read, and we know that the prosecutors are in possession of that evidence, and perhaps much more. Whether to indict is their decision. And whether the offenses of President Clinton are criminally chargeable is of no moment whatever . . . It is a fundamental precept that an impeachable offense need not be a criminal act.[31]

Yet, despite Mr. Schippers's rejoinder, as Democratic members of the Committee made their closing statements, they continually referred to the necessity of the charges being indictable in a court of law. They seemed to ignore the history of successful and legitimate impeachment charges, claiming that the accusations against the President—perjury and obstruction of justice—did not rise to the constitutional level of impeachable offenses because his actions were in the context of sexual indiscretions. They felt these were private matters that did not impact the public performance of his duties.

Jerrold Nadler, for instance, commented, "Perjury is a serious crime, and if proven should be prosecuted in a court of law . . . Perjury on a private matter, perjury regarding sex, is not a great and serious offense against the nation. It is not an abuse of uniquely presidential power. It does not threaten our form of government. . . . The case is not there. The proof has not been put forward. The conduct alleged, even if proven, does not rise to the level of an impeachable offense."[32]

Robert Scott of Virginia scolded the Committee for turning "a deaf ear to hundreds of years of precedent and to the Constitution that has kept this country strong and unified." Yet, according to the Rodino Report, which looked exhaustively at the issue of precedent, charges such as the ones brought against President Clinton were well within the guidelines of former impeachments.

Mel Watt of North Carolina recalled Mr. Schippers's words about the bar of impeachment:

> He said, ". . . if you don't impeach as a consequence of the conduct that I have just portrayed, then no House of Representatives will ever be able to impeach again." He went on to say, "the bar will be so high that only a convicted felon or a traitor will need to be concerned."
>
> My friends, that's what the rule of law says, that you can . . . impeach a president only when that standard is met.[33]

Congressman Watt, with these comments, apparently concluded that the only way a President could be impeached was if he had committed a felony or treason. Congressman Watt's standard is different from the historical standard of impeachment.

Maxine Waters of California lectured the Committee: "We have heard members of Congress describe the president's actions as 'sickening,' 'reprehensible,' and 'unacceptable.' However, the Constitution does not allow for the impeachment of a president because we are upset by his personal behavior."[34] Yet personal behavior, outside the parameter of statutable offenses, always has been considered fodder for impeachment.

The debate shifted from the Judiciary Committee to the full House on December 18-19, 1998. The comments remained the same. Steny Hoyer of Maryland said, "It has not amounted to treason. It is not a case of bribery. And, as so many scholars of all political and philosophical stripes have testified, it does not amount to high crimes and misdemeanors."[35] According to Sheila Jackson Lee of Texas, "I believe not one of us in these chambers . . . would ask for the resignation of a Member so charged. . . . Nevertheless, the majority is recklessly attempting to make impeachable offenses of purely private acts, in direct attack on the Framers' intent that impeachment was for great and dangerous offenses against the Constitution."[36] Major Owens of New York asked, "On the basis of the charges before us, what prosecutor anywhere in America would press forward with this case and demand for such a harsh punishment?"[37]

Some members even saw something more sinister in Republicans' motives to remove President Clinton from office. "Let us not be confused," instructed Jesse Jackson, Jr., of Illinois. "Today Republicans are impeaching Social Security, they are impeaching affirmative action, they are impeaching women's right to choose, Medicare, Medicaid, Supreme Court Justices who believe in equal protection under the law for all Americans. Something deeper in history is happening than sex, lying about sex and perjury."[38] Given that Vice President Gore would have taken over the presidential duties if President Clinton had been removed from office, one can only speculate how that would have hurt any of the causes Congressman Jackson listed as being "impeached."

One Congressman combined all the objections into his speech. Edward Markey of Massachusetts opined,

> We are permitting a constitutional coup d'état which will haunt this body forever. A constitutional clause intended to apply to a Benedict Arnold selling out his country will now be expanded to cover every personal transgression. Every future president, Democrat or Republican, will be subject to harassment by his political enemies. . . .
>
> When we talk to people . . . on the streets, they believe that the high crime against the Constitution is their families being cheated out of their government's ability to work on things that affect their families: Medicare, social security, the democratization of access to jobs and education. . . .

GOP used to stand for "Grand Old Party." Now it just stands for "Get Our President."[39]

Republicans, meanwhile, relying in large part on the authority of the Rodino Report—a Democrat-crafted document—pressed forward with the impeachment vote. When two articles passed, the next task was to choose the Members who would make the case to the Senate.

The Manager Team

The role of a House Manager in an impeachment is to prosecute the case. He is to present the evidence, much as a prosecutor does in a courtroom. Prosecutorial experience, consequently, is a major factor in the choice of a Manager. It is also necessary to have someone who is thoroughly familiar with the facts that have led to the impeachment articles. Naturally, in the case of the impeachment of President Clinton, Members who served on the Judiciary Committee would be the first considered. Thirteen Managers were chosen—all from the Committee, all white males, all lawyers.

Henry Hyde of Illinois, who had served in Congress since 1974 and who had become chairman of the Judiciary Committee after the 1994 elections, was the obvious choice of the Republican leadership to take charge of the House Manager team. He had guided the Committee through its vote on impeachment and had been the final speaker for the pro-impeachment position in the House debate. "When the chief law enforcement officer trivializes, ignores, shreds, minimizes the sanctity of the oath," Hyde summarized, "then justice is wounded, and Members on that side [Democratic side] are wounded and their children are wounded. I ask Members to follow their conscience and they will serve the country."[40]

Hyde was particularly concerned about the Congress's credibility as it considered the President's impeachment. "Keep your eyes open and your mouth shut" were his words of advice to the Judiciary Committee. "We will not drive this investigation. I want it to move by its own momentum. We will cling mightily to that standard."[41]

In September 1998, *Salon*, an internet-based magazine, ran an article exposing a thirty-year-old sexual affair in Hyde's past, which ended five years before he became a Congressman. Hyde immediately released the following statement: "The statute of limitations has long since passed on my youthful indiscretions. . . . The only purpose for this being dredged up now is an obvious attempt to intimidate me, and it won't work. I intend to fulfill my constitutional duty and deal judiciously with the serious felony allegations presented to Congress in the Starr report."[42] In this statement, Hyde clearly was outlining the contrast between an old infidelity to his wife and the President's recent acts that went beyond infidelity and affected the very manner by which the law is carried out in the nation.

The rest of the Manager team was chosen from the Judiciary Committee primarily because they were the House Members who were most familiar with the documentation of the charges.

The selection of Georgia's Bob Barr for manager was perhaps the most controversial. Congressman Barr introduced an impeachment inquiry in November 1997, two months prior to the revelations about Monica Lewinsky. Even before this news broke, Barr was concerned about White House abuses of power in earlier scandal allegations. Barr's task in the trial was to show how President Clinton specifically violated the laws concerning perjury and obstruction of justice.

Larry Flynt targeted Barr. Flynt paid an undisclosed sum of money to Barr's former wife in exchange for "seven pages of sordid allegations against her husband."[43] These included adultery, driving her to an abortion clinic to have an abortion, and declining to answer questions about the adultery in a legal deposition.[44] Yet Barr's congressional career has included a pro-life record next to none. When pressed on the refusal to answer questions under oath, he maintained that a refusal to incriminate oneself is not the same as the crime of perjury—which was the accusation against the President.[45]

Although the other eleven Managers also came under intense scrutiny from those who were attempting to showcase hypocrisy in the accusers, only Hyde and Barr hd sufficient questions in their background to provide grist for the political talk shows. In Hyde's case, the episode was in the distant past, so it fell by the wayside. Members from both sides of the aisle asserted their belief in the man's integrity. For Barr, the battle was greater, but those who believed the President ought to be removed from office still saw a distinction between the accusations against the Congressman and those against the President. Besides, even if all the allegations against Congressman Barr could be proven, did that alter the seriousness of the charges against President Clinton? In what way should the former invalidate the latter? The impeachment articles stood on their own, regardless of the faults of those pressing for prosecution.

Ed Bryant of Tennessee was part of the Republican Revolution in the 1994 elections, when, for the first time in forty years, the Republicans controlled the House of Representatives. Although soft-spoken and not given to standing before the cameras, he provided much of the quiet resolve behind the impeachment process after being selected as a Manager. Bryant was chosen to question Monica Lewinsky for the video-taped deposition presented to the Senate.

Steve Buyer of Indiana entered Congress two years before the Republican Revolution, thus switching in 1994 from minority to majority status. A Gulf War veteran, Buyer was better known for his work on behalf of the military. His task during the trial was to "discuss why the offenses attack the judicial system, which is a core function of the Government, and how perjury and obstruction of justice are not private acts."[46]

As with Buyer, Charles Canady of Florida won election to the House for the first time in 1992. His devotion to constitutionalism led Congressman Canady to the House Judiciary Committee, where he also served as Chairman of the Subcommittee on the Constitution. Before the Senate, Canady explained why the charges against the President rose to the level of "high crimes and misdemeanors" under the Constitution.

Chris Cannon, a blunt, strongly conservative representative from a "safe" Utah seat, was a relative newcomer to Congress, taking his seat after the 1996 election. "My task," declared Congressman Cannon before the Senate, "is to clarify what the law states pertaining to obstruction of justice, and what legal precedent is applicable to the charges against William Jefferson Clinton."[47]

Representing Cincinnati, a district that had had three Democratic members of Congress prior to his first election in 1994, Congressman Steve Chabot was taking an electoral risk by participating on the Manager team. "I knew that there could be political consequences," Chabot later acknowledged, "but I wasn't really worried about that. I felt it was my duty."[48] Explaining the law of perjury was his assigned task.

Congressman George Gekas of Pennsylvania was a sixteen-year veteran of the House when he undertook the role of House Manager, and he was not without impeachment experience, having served as a Manager in the impeachment trial of federal judge Alcee Hastings. "My chief tenet in this whole thing," Gekas asserted, "was the preservation of the three branches of government. . . . What the President did with respect to the falsehoods under oath and the manipulation of the judicial process . . . all of that was an attack on another branch of government. I cannot to this day tolerate that."[49]

Best known for his pithy sound bites and wry sense of humor, Congressman Lindsey Graham of South Carolina, another member of the class of 1994, first caught the media's attention with his comment, "Is this Watergate or Peyton Place? I don't know."[50] In the Senate trial, he focused on the application of perjury and obstruction of justice as they apply to federal judges. "You couldn't live with yourself knowing that you were going to leave a perjuring judge on the bench. Ladies and gentlemen," he advised the Senate, "as hard as it may be, for the same reasons, cleanse this office."[51]

Congressman Asa Hutchinson, elected in 1996, held a unique position as a House Manager. He not only hailed from President Clinton's home state of Arkansas, but he also had successfully prosecuted the President's brother, Roger, while serving as a federal prosecutor. Then-Governor Clinton had commented at the time that the conviction had helped turn his brother's life around. Hutchinson's Senate presentation focused on evidence that demonstrated obstruction of justice.

Bill McCollum of Florida had been a House stalwart since 1981. As Chairman of the Subcommittee on Crime, McCollum had handled the hearings that investigated the government's actions in the Waco tragedy. "I bear no animosity towards President Clinton," declared Congressman McCollum to the Senate. "But I happen to believe that allowing a President who committed crimes of perjury and obstruction of justice and witness tampering to remain in office would undermine our courts and our system of justice."[52]

James Rogan of California took the greatest risk of any House Manager by accepting the appointment. Rogan, who took office in 1996, represented a district that includes Hollywood, a bastion of support for President Clinton. Many political liberals in the motion picture industry were out to ensure that Rogan would not return to Washington. Rogan was considered by many to have been the best legal mind on the team. Henry Hyde relied on him to be one of the final speakers, to help wrap up the case. When asked about the possibility of losing the upcoming election, he responded, "I was told at the time it would probably cost me my re-election. . . . That would make me nervous if I approached this job in a totally secular view . . . [but] I am here because the Lord has given me the privilege of serving my country in Congress. It's a temporary privilege; I don't get to keep this forever. It doesn't belong to me. I have no claim to it."[53]

Congressman James Sensenbrenner, unlike Rogan, was from a "safe" Wisconsin seat. He also had impeachment experience. Along with Henry Hyde, Sensenbrenner introduced the 1987 impeachment resolution that led to the removal of federal judge Alcee Hastings. In his opening statement to the Senate in the Clinton trial, Sensenbrenner noted, "We hear much about how important the 'rule of law' is to our nation and to our system of government. Some have commented this expression is trite.

But, whether expressed by these three words, or others, the primacy of law over the rule of individuals is what distinguishes the United States from most other countries and why our Constitution is as alive today as it was 210 years ago."[54]

These thirteen gentlemen, representatives of the American people, made the arguments before the Senate that President Bill Clinton needed to be removed from office. Did they do so from personal conviction that this was the *right* action to take, based upon principle, or did they operate primarily from partisan motives, placing *Republican* interests above the interests of the nation? Let's look at each of these Mangers individually to determine the answer to that question.

Chapter One Endnotes

1 "Presidential Impeachment Proceedings: Andrew Johnson," The History Place; available at http://www.historyplace.com/unitedstates/impeachments/johnson.htm; accessed 15 February 2000.

2 William H. Rehnquist, *Grand Inquests: The Historic Impeachments of Justice SamuelChase and President Andrew Johnson* (New York: William Morrow & Company, Inc., 1992), 217-24.

3 Ibid., 218-19, 224-26.

4 Ibid., 231-32.

5 Ibid., 235.

6 David Greenberg, "Andrew Johnson: Saved by a Scoundrel," *Slate*, 20 January 1999; available at http://slate.msn.com/historylesson/99-01-20/historylesson.asp; accessed 15 February 2000.

7 Ibid.

8 Howard Fields, *High Crimes and Misdemeanors: The Dramatic Story of the Rodino Committee* (New York: W. W. Norton & Company, Inc., 1978), 249.

9 Articles of Impeachment Adopted by the Committee on the Judiciary, 27 July 1974; available at http://vcepolitics.com/wgate/impart1.htm; accessed 16 February 2000.

10 Fields, 269.

11 Ibid., 274.

12 Merrill McLoughlin, ed., *The Impeachment and Trial of President Clinton: The Official Transcripts from the House Judiciary Hearings to the Senate Trial*, with an introduction by Michael R. Beschloss (New York: Times Books, 1999), 205.

13 Ibid., 206.

14 Ibid.

15 Ibid., 207.

16 All comments available at the White House publications webpage at http://www.pub.whitehouse.gov/uri-res/I2R?urn:pdi://oma.eop.gov.us/1998/12/19/4.text.2; accessed 29 May 2000.

[17] Closing Argument of Hon. Henry Hyde, Senate Impeachment Trial of President Clinton, 8 February 1999; available at http://www.house.gov/judiciary/hyde0208.htm; accessed 27 May 1999.

[18] U. S. Constitution, art. 1, secs. 2-3.

[19] Ibid., art. 2, sec. 4.

[20] Joseph Story, *A Familiar Exposition of the Constitution of the United States* (1840; reprint ed., Lake Bluff, IL: Regnery Gateway, 1986), 109.

[21] Raoul Berger, *Impeachment: The Constitutional Problems* (Cambridge: Harvard University Press, 1973), 59.

[22] Ibid. , 61.

[23] Ibid., 61-62.

[24] Ibid., 80.

[25] Ibid., 62-63.

[26] "Constitutional Grounds for Presidential Impeachment," Report by the Staff of the Impeachment Inquiry (Washington: US Government Printing Office, 1974), section 2.

[27] Ibid.

[28] Ibid.

[29] Ibid., section 3.

[30] McLoughlin, *The Impeachment and Trial of President Clinton*, 111.

[31] Ibid., 135.

[32] Ibid., 143.

[33] Ibid., 145.

[34] Ibid., 148.

[35] Ibid., 175.

[36] Ibid., 177.

[37] Ibid., 181-82.

[38] Ibid., 184.

[39] Ibid., 186.

[40] Ibid., 206.

[41] "Henry Hyde," The Associated Press Political Service: AP Candidate Bios, 30 November 1998.

[42] "This Hypocrite Broke Up My Family," *Salon*, September 1998; available at http://salonmagazine.com/news/1998/09/cov_16newsb.html; accessed 11 May 1999.

[43] J. R. Moehringer, "Rep. Barr Inspires Loyalty, Loathing in Home District," *Los Angeles Times*, 19 January 1999, A15.

[44] Ibid.; Marie Cocco, "A Pro-Lifer's Deceptions Raise the Barr of Hypocrisy to New Heights," (Newark, NJ) *Star-Ledger*, 17 January 1999, 4.

[45] Moehringer.

[46] Opening Statement of Hon. Stephen E. Buyer: The Offenses Charged in the Articles of Impeachment Attack the Judicial System, Senate Impeachment Trial of President Clinton, 16 January 1999; available at http://www.house.gov/judiciary/buyer011699.htm; accessed 12 April 1999.

[47] Opening Statement of Hon. Chris Cannon: Overview of the Law of Obstruction, Senate Impeachment Trial of President Clinton, 15 January 1999; available at http://www.house.gov/judiciary/cannonsenate.htm; accessed 16 April 1999.

[48] Congressman Steve Chabot, interview by author, tape recording, Washington, DC, 8 February 2000.

[49] Congressman George Gekas, interview by author, tape recording, Washington, DC, 29 February 2000.

[50] Graham Judiciary Committee Statement on Opening an Inquiry of Impeachment Against President Clinton, 5 October 1998; available at http://www.house.gov/judiciary/graham.htm; accessed 28 April 1999.

[51] Opening Statement of Hon. Lindsey Graham, Senate Impeachment Trial of President Clinton, 16 January 1999; available at http://www.house.gov/judiciary/graham011699.htm; accessed 12 April 1999.

52 Opening Statement of Hon. Bill McCollum, Senate Impeachment Trial of President Clinton, 15 January 1999; available at http://www.house.gov/judiciary/mcsenate.htm; accessed 16 April 1999.

53 Congressman James Rogan, interview by author, tape recording, Washington, DC, 8 February 2000.

54 Opening Statement of Hon. James Sensenbrenner, Senate Impeachment Trial of President Clinton, 14 January 1999; available at http://www.house.gov/judiciary/sensenate.htm; accessed 16 April 1999.

CHAPTER TWO

Henry Hyde:
Let Right Be Done

The silver-haired figure sitting behind his desk sighed and paused. He seemed to be contemplating the portion of the Capitol visible from his office window. The question posed to him was "Do you regret having been involved with all this?" The answer finally came—slowly, deliberately, cautiously—as he searched for just the right words to express how he felt. "In one way, I regret it profoundly," he began. "It drained a lot of the joy. And that's the word that I felt as a Member of Congress. I have always literally loved my work, coming to work, participating in the cut and the thrust of legislation, helping constituents. It's all been a glorious adventure. The personal attacks that I had to undergo that were very harmful to me divested this enterprise of a lot of that sunshine and joy that I previously experienced."[1] Clearly, Henry Hyde, Illinois Congressman and a pillar of the House since 1974, widely respected by both parties until his leadership role with the House Managers, did not consider the Clinton impeachment the zenith of his political career.

Yet, despite the pain his involvement caused, Hyde believed he really had no choice:

> I viewed my role as Chairman of the House Judiciary Committee and the recipient of all this evidence as one of doing my duty, onerous though it was. We all want to be loved. We all want to be liked. We all want to be respected.

And going against public opinion is not anything you do lightly. But I could not see any honorable way to evade proceeding with hearings in our committee and letting them go where the facts led us, being true to my oath of office, to my concept of why I was in Congress. It wasn't just to have the enjoyment and the fun of debating legislation; it was to do my duty, as I saw it. This was something that I felt as a matter of duty. So, I think I have been hurt by personal attacks . . . but . . . knowing what I know, I would have no other course but to do what we did. And I'd do it again.[2]

In his twenty-four years in the House prior to the impeachment proceedings, Henry Hyde had built a solid reputation with friend and foe alike. *The Almanac of American Politics* described Henry Hyde as "One of the most respected and intellectually honorable members of the House," who "acts from deep belief more than political calculation." They further explained, "His stands [on issues] seem to stem from deep religious beliefs combined with a trial lawyer's combative instincts, a respect for rule combined with a certain compassion."[3]

Another political source called him "Articulate, smart. . . . No matter who is the sponsor of a conservative initiative, Hyde is likely to be its most impressive spokesman, waiting for flawed liberal arguments and then pouncing with all the wit and sarcasm he once used as a Chicago trial lawyer."[4] An Illinois columnist noted, "Hyde has often made his mark as one of the best matches of the U.S. House. . . . Whenever he speaks in the well of the House, Democrats and Republicans flock out of the cloakrooms to hear him express his ideas with wit and elegant phrasing."[5] One liberal leader commented, "He's a conservative, but a thoughtful conservative. Every once in a while we get a chance to work together. He is a wonderful ally and formidable opponent."[6] A newspaper from his district editorialized, "Hyde is a respected congressman. . . . He is able to disagree without being disagreeable while holding a position. This is the substance of politics and politics is the art of getting things done in a democracy."[7] And one network news reporter had gone so far as to say,

"What you've got to realize is that Henry Hyde is one of the smartest men who ever walked. So no matter what he has to do, he knows how to do it."[8]

Despite the praise of colleagues and reporters throughout most of his career, Hyde, as head of the Manager team, went from respected statesman to partisan ideologue in the eyes of some. Or at least that was the portrait that critics of the impeachment painted. How true was this new image?

Background: Pre-Impeachment

Henry Hyde, born in Chicago in 1924, has been an Illinois resident most of his life. He left the state to attend Duke University and then to serve in the Navy from 1944 to 1946 during World War II, stationed in the South Pacific, New Guinea, and the Philippines. After the war, he received his bachelor's degree from Georgetown University in 1947, then he returned to his native state to obtain a law degree from Loyola University in 1949. When he was admitted to the bar in 1950, he entered private practice, specializing in litigation.

Hyde's political career began with election to the Illinois House in 1967, where he also served one term as Republican majority leader. Hyde's parents had been Democrats; he left that Party because he believed it dealt too softly with the Soviet Union. He went straight from being a state legislator to a national Congressman in the election of 1974 and has won re-election ever since.

When he came to Congress, Hyde's name soon became linked with the abortion debate. In 1976, he pushed successfully for an amendment forbidding the use of federal dollars in paying for or encouraging abortions. Although the Hyde Amendment, as it has since been called, was buffeted by challenges at the beginning, and attempts to water it down, it still remains essentially intact.[9] His championing of the pro-life cause made him a hero in its ranks, but he remained modest about his role: "Somebody once said that we can't be great, but we can attach ourselves to something that is great. I'm a spear-carrier in the opera. And way in the back, I might add."[10]

Hyde's attack on abortion has continued unabated. When the partial-birth abortion debate began, he was in the forefront once again. On the House floor, in 1996, he stated,

> Mr. Speaker: In his classic novel *Crime and Punishment*, Dostoyevsky has his murderous protagonist Raskolnikov complain that "Man can get used to anything, the beast!"
>
> That we are even debating this issue—that we have to argue about the legality of an abortionist plunging a pair of scissors into the back of the neck of [a] tiny child whose trunk, arms, and legs have already been born, and then suctioning out his brains—only confirms Dostoyevsky's harsh truth. . . .
>
> The justification for abortion has always been the claim that a woman can do what she wants with her own body. If you still believe this 4/5th's delivered baby is a part of the mother's body, your ignorance is invincible.[11]

Although Hyde began with the direct effect abortion had on the babies, he moved to its application to society at large. "It isn't just the babies that are dying for the lethal sin of being unwanted," he argued. "We are dying, and not from the darkness, but from the cold: the cold-ness of self-brutalization that chills our sensibilities and allows us to think that this unspeakable act is an act of 'compassion.'" Anyone voting for partial-birth abortion no longer had the right ever to use the word "compassion" again, in his view. Furthermore, the whole procedure was "a lethal assault against the very idea of human rights, and destroys, along with a defenseless little baby, the moral foundation of our democracy. Democracy," he reminded his audience, "isn't after all, a mere process—it assigns fundamental values to each human being—the first of which is the unalienable right to life."[12]

Hyde concluded,

One of the great errors of modern politics is the unavailing attempt to separate our private consciences from our public acts. It can't be done. At the end of the 20th century, is the crowning achievement of our democracy to treat the weak, the powerless, the unwanted as things to be disposed of? If so, we haven't elevated justice—we have disgraced it. . . .

I am not in the least embarrassed to say that I believe that one day each of us will be called upon to render an account for what we have done, and what we have failed to do, in our lifetime. And while I believe in a merciful God, I would be terrified at the thought of having to explain, at the final judgment, why I stood unmoved while Herod's slaughter of the innocents was being reenacted here in my own country.[13]

That last paragraph provides insight into why Hyde is so committed to dealing with abortion. His Catholic faith informs him about the sanctity of human life made in God's image, and he believes that he will be called upon to give an account for how he treated the innocent unborn. For him, there is no separation of faith from politics. He proclaims himself "amazed" that anyone can create a dichotomy between religious beliefs and general conduct. Religion, he says, provides "guidelines for people to adjust their behavior or to conform their behavior to what they believe is the divine will. And so, I must say that the religious Henry Hyde is the same as the political Henry Hyde. I like to think I make an effort to be guided by those religious precepts which have animated my life in general."[14]

He considers his linkage of faith with politics to be distinctly American: it reflects the Declaration of Independence and "the thinking of our founders and framers." Hyde believes that "one of the most fundamental mistakes" in American thinking today is a false idea of separation of church and state. All it really means historically, he comments, is that "there should be no national church." He points out that one of the first acts of the first Congress was to hire a chaplain. "I think we have lost a great deal through the scurrilous efforts to disassociate ourselves from any religious thought," he explains.[15]

The above excerpt concerning partial-birth abortion also highlights something else: Hyde's rhetorical skills. He is considered by most to be one of the premier orators in Congress. As a *Congressional Quarterly* report from the late 1980s acknowledged, "Watching him in action, it is easy to see flashes of the Chicago trial lawyer he once was. He speaks with wit, passion and deep conviction about the conservative causes he holds dear, and displays a delight in rhetorical engagement that is matched by only a few other members. . . . Whoever is nominally responsible for initiatives backing President Reagan's policies on Nicaragua or arms control, it is Hyde who tends to offer the most compelling arguments in their favor." And Hyde loves making the arguments. "Conflict and disputation," he told the *Congressional Quarterly* reporters, "are the heart and soul of drama, the heart and soul of literature and the heart and soul of the legislative process—if we're not all to die of boredom." [16]

The Iran-Contra Affair, which plagued President Reagan's second term, was a challenge for Hyde. A Republican Administration stood accused of breaking the law by selling arms to Iran and allowing the proceeds to be sent to Nicaraguan opponents (Contras) of the Communist Sandinista government. Hyde, as a minority member of the Judiciary Committee, took part in the televised hearings. He acknowledged that the activities of Colonel Oliver North and others did go against the Boland Amendment, which had been attached to an appropriations bill. In the July 14, 1987, hearing, he told Colonel North that lying to Congress and "operating the contra support operation out of the White House was wrong."[17] He even urged one of President Reagan's counsels, David Abshire, to encourage the President to use his State of the Union message to take full responsibility for the Administration's mistakes and to apologize to the American people. As Hyde said at the time, "If the President wants credit for the good things that have happened on his watch, he can't decline responsibility for errors and mistakes."[18]

When the Committee issued its report, Republicans, Hyde among them, wrote their own minority report. In it, Republicans agreed that the

President and his staff had made mistakes, but they also recognized that President Reagan had acknowledged the mistakes and took action "to correct what went wrong." The report clearly detailed the difference between these mistakes and the larger issues:

> The bottom line, however, is that the mistakes of the Iran-contra affair were just that—mistakes in judgment, and nothing more. There was no constitutional crisis, no systematic disrespect for "the rule of law," no grand conspiracy, and no Administration-wide dishonesty or coverup. In fact, the evidence will not support any of the more hysterical conclusions the committee's report tries to reach.[19]

Hyde wrote his own supplement to the report. He stressed that there were national security issues in play that acted as a counterbalance to the Congress's Boland Amendment: "A dominant theme of these hearings has been vigorous condemnation of those who allegedly violated the letter or the spirit of the Boland Amendments, or who lied to Congress or were not forthcoming in their testimony about Central American policy. The rationale for these transgressions—the need for secrecy to protect lives, the sensitivity of negotiations with Iran about hostages, combined with the notorious inability of Congress to keep a secret—were summarily rejected by most of the committee's members." Near the end of his supplement, Hyde concluded,

> We ought to admit, frankly, that we are, as a nation, deeply divided at these basic choice points. It is one of the great failures of the Reagan Administration that it has not forced these questions out into the open of our public life so that they could be debated civilly and frankly, rather than surreptitiously. Perhaps the providential paradox of our present situation is that these absolutely fundamental questions have been brought to the surface anyway, chiefly through the testimony of Lt. Col. Oliver North.[20]

In short, Hyde saw a conflict in policy in which mistakes were made by his fellow Republicans, and he saw a need for secrecy in the manner in which certain aspects of foreign policy were carried out. What he did not see was an assault on the Constitution or an attempt to subvert the legal system. When, as Chairman of the Judiciary Committee, he proceeded with the impeachment inquiry against President Clinton, some were quick to tag him with the hypocrite label. Democrat Maxine Waters scolded, "You have done a 360-degree turn. I'm a little disappointed. Never in my wildest imagination did I think that you would have such a conflict in views about perjury and lying."[21]

Hyde emphatically rejected that interpretation. Perjury had to occur in a court of law; it was not synonymous with holding back sensitive information from Congress: "I said 'context is everything,' and I stand by that. Trying to save Central America from a Castro takeover required some clandestine operations, and they required sometimes withholding information."[22] Hyde supported President Reagan's effort to "keep the anti-communist forces in the field." The freedom of the Western Hemisphere was Hyde's concern: "I thought the stakes were very high. . . . But the Democrats never saw it that way. The Democrats, again, in their effort to get Reagan and to get the Republicans, hamstrung every effort made to resist the Sandinistas."[23]

In Hyde's view, the Clinton impeachment issues were far different than those at stake in the Iran-Contra Affair: "In the Clinton matter, it was a *personal* misconduct—something very base and hardly as noble as the effort to protect freedom in Central America. So there's no comparison between the activity under question in the Clinton matter and in the Reagan matter. Reagan himself never was charged with telling lies or perjury or covering up conduct."[24] In other words, President Clinton's conduct had nothing to do with policy; he was merely trying to cover up his own behavior. He also was charged with lying to a grand jury, which struck at the heart of the judicial system.

Congressman Hyde did have to deal with one accusation of scandal against him prior to the impeachment hearings. He had been an outside director for the Clyde Federal Savings and Loan Association in Illinois. That corporation went into receivership in 1990, six years after Hyde had resigned from his directorship. The Resolution Trust Corporation, in 1993, sued twelve of the former officers and directors, Hyde included.[25] He fought his inclusion in that lawsuit for four years, claiming he had no role in the demise of the institution.

Ultimately, the suit was settled out of court, and Hyde was not obligated to pay back anything. Critics thought that perhaps he had received special treatment because of his position, but Hyde denied it. He steadfastly clung to his innocence, saying, "I'm the victim of a lawsuit that never should have been brought. I'm not paying a nickel."[26] He was prepared to go to trial, if need be, to clear his name, but that proved unnecessary. "I have learned only too painfully what the abuse of governmental power can do to someone's life and career," he commented later.[27]

Impeachment in the House

"I'm in a position where I'm contending with the president of the United States, and I must be destroyed."[28] That is how Henry Hyde characterized his situation prior to opening the Judiciary Committee's investigation into President Clinton's alleged wrongdoing. Neither was he eager to enter into the fray: "God, I'd like to forget all of this. I mean, who needs it?" But, in the end, he could not look the other way. "I'm frightened for the rule of law. I really believe that notion that no man is above the law."[29]

The Judiciary Committee has been part of Henry Hyde's life ever since he came to Washington after the 1974 elections. As a lawyer, he felt that he would be comfortable with the matters on which the Committee focused. For most of those years, he was right. When Republicans took the majority in the House in the 1994 elections, he became Chairman of the Committee, the first time any Republican had been able to do so since the early 1950s. As Chairman, his involvement in the impeachment inquiry preceded that of his fellow Managers. He became the voice of the

Judiciary Committee from the beginning.

Hyde venerates the institutions of the Congress and sees his position as Chairman of the Judiciary Committee as a trust from the past. "Henry is haunted by the ghost of this place," commented Manager Lindsey Graham. "He feels as if all those who have come before him are looking at him and saying, 'Don't let us down.'" In an unveiling of a portrait of Hyde in the Committee hearing room in October 1998, at the outset of the impeachment inquiry, he already seemed to feel the weight of his responsibility. He confided to the assembled group, "I came here thinking I could change the world. Now my ambition is to leave the room with dignity."[30]

The Judiciary Committee's active role began with the delivery of the Starr Report to the Congress in September 1998. That delivery also initiated Hyde's continual contact with the press as the official spokesperson for the Committee. In a press release of September 9, he addressed the "solemn duty" that confronted the Committee and the need for "a heroic level of bipartisanship." He promised to work closely with the Democrats on the Committee, then added, "Politics must be checked at the door, party affiliation must become secondary, and America's future must become our only concern. I will not condone, nor participate in, a political witch hunt. If the evidence does not justify a full impeachment investigation, I will not recommend one to the House. However, if the evidence does justify an inquiry, I will fulfill my oath of office and recommend a fuller inquiry."[31]

The next day, speaking before the House Rules Committee, Hyde repeated most of the previous day's statement, but respecting his call for bipartisanship, he offered the optimistic view that while this would "prove to be a lofty challenge," he nevertheless believed that "the gravity" of the representatives' responsibilities would "overwhelm the petty partisanship that lingers in us all." At the end of his statement, he talked of the sacredness of an oath, which meant "a solemn calling on God to witness to the truth of what you are saying." He quoted Sir Thomas More who was beheaded by Henry VIII for refusing to ignore his conscience: "When you take an oath, you hold your soul in your hands, and if you break that oath, you open up your fingers and your soul runs through them and is lost." He hoped the image would be burned on the minds of his colleagues:

> I believe with all my heart that each of us took that oath of office seriously, and that we will so conduct ourselves that when this ordeal is over, we will have vindicated the rule of law and brought credit to this institution in which we are privileged to serve.[32]

Hyde opened his remarks to the full House on September 11 with the words of historian Thomas Macauley: "Laws exist in vain for those who do not have the courage and the means to defend them." The inference was obvious, but he drove home the point that the circumstances and the requirements of the Constitution demanded that the Congress "vindicate the rule of law." Fashioning the type of rhetoric that drew even his opponents to his speeches, Hyde invoked the sacrifices of earlier times: "We have pledged a trust to those patriots who sleep across the river in Arlington Cemetery and in American military cemeteries around the world: we have pledged that their defense of freedom and the rule of law will not have been in vain."[33]

Hyde extended the timeline into the future as well: "We have also pledged a trust to the Americans of the 21st century: we have pledged to hand over to them, intact and unsullied, the rule of law in a constitutionally-ordered democracy." Nor did the Chairman want his colleagues to forget their duty toward those who elected them: "And we have pledged a trust to our fellow Americans with whom we share this moment in history: our neighbors, who have sent us to this Congress to serve the common good through the rule of law." Again, drawing upon history, Hyde quoted Theodore Roosevelt, who declared, "No man is above the law and no man is below it, nor do we ask any man's permission when we require him to obey it."[34]

Already, prior to the opening of hearings, the Republican argument was sct: an appeal to the rule of law and to the idea that no one, not even the President of the United States, can thumb his nose at it. The American principle always had been that this nation would not tolerate arbitrary power in the hands of its elected officials. Republicans wanted that bedrock concept laid down at the start.

Hyde then decided to attack two potential problems: apathy and lack of understanding of the consequences of dismissing this principle:

> We are, sometimes, too cavalier in our attitude toward the rule of law. It is something we take for granted. Yet we live in a century which, in blood and tears, in pain and sorrow, has vindicated the contention of the Founders of this Republic and the Framers of its Constitution, that the rule of law is the only alternative to tyranny, or to the anarchy that eventually leads to tyranny.[35]

The rule of law had progressed throughout history, Hyde contended, primarily because man is a spiritual being "created with intelligence and free will, a moral agent, capable of freedom, and capable of ordering freedom to the pursuit of goodness, decency, and justice." The question before the House was whether the Members were committed to maintaining this principle. If so, Hyde declared, they would have to set aside their partisan differences: "Because we are servants of the Constitution, because we too are subject to the rule of law it enshrines, no partisanship in the matters before us will be worthy of us." Intending to stir the hearts of his listeners, Hyde concluded,

> Thus we, too, are under judgement in these hearings: the judgement of the people; the judgement of history; the judgement of the moral law.
>
> Let us conduct ourselves and this inquiry in such a way as to vindicate the rule of law.
>
> Let us conduct ourselves and this inquiry in such a way as to vindicate the Constitution.
>
> Let us conduct ourselves and this inquiry in such a way as

to vindicate the sacrifices of blood and treasure that have been made across the centuries to create and defend this last best hope of humanity on earth, the United States of America.[36]

If the Chairman thought his appeal would melt away all resistance, it did not take long to dispel that notion. By September 23, Hyde had to issue another statement in response to Democratic complaints. First, the Democrats wanted specific deadlines for the hearings. Hyde felt that artificial deadlines were inappropriate because they may not provide enough time to review the Starr Report fully. He also suspected that once a deadline was set, stalling tactics would go into effect, thus nullifying a true inquiry.

Additionally, he was disturbed by what he called the confusing mixed messages he was receiving from the other side of the aisle. Democrats wanted an expeditious process, he explained, but Republicans were being attacked for moving too quickly. They said that the Committee had all the materials it needed to wrap up the investigation in thirty days, but they simultaneously declared that more materials from the Independent Counsel's office were necessary before the matter could be fairly resolved. They said they wanted to follow the Watergate precedent (which took nine months), but they demanded a timetable that the Watergate investigators rejected. Further, Hyde noted, "the White House continues to assert quite falsely that the Committee's actions are being dictated by the Speaker. Nothing could be further from the truth. Any statements to the contrary are merely political spin intended to undermine the credibility of the Committee's process."[37] Consequently, before the Committee had opened its hearings on the possibility of a formal inquiry, the Chairman knew already that he had a tough road ahead in his quest for bipartisanship.

Reflecting back on the role of partisanship in the process, Hyde offered the opinion that the Committee had become more partisan over the years: "I think younger people, younger men and women, bring energy and a sort of idealism to their work. But they also bring a heightened partisanship, I've noticed. Older, more mature legislators understand the human condition a little better, are more tolerant, and have had more experience with contradictory points of view—conflict. The younger people have an intolerance, and that heightens the partisan nature of the debate."[38] But it was obvious to him where most of that spirit of partisanship resided:

> The partisanship, in my humble opinion, was (and they're never charged with it) on the Democratic side. Many Democrats—many, if not most—were condemnatory and embarrassed by Clinton's conduct. I talked to many of them. . . . But they did not want to have him removed from office because they felt that would weaken their claim to the throne—their power. And power was what it was all about. . . .
>
> At all costs, including, in my judgment, damage to the rule of law, they were not going to yield. None of them did in the Senate and in the House. Senator Byrd, who was a symbol of the Democratic rectitude in the Senate, made public statements that the President had lied under oath, but he couldn't bring himself to vote guilty on the impeachment.[39]

There were glimmers of bipartisanship. The full House voted on September 18, 363-63, to send the Starr Report to the Judiciary Committee and to release the information therein to the public. When the Committee met on October 5 to consider whether to open an inquiry, Chairman Hyde, in his opening statement, acknowledged that the country was weary of the situation, as were the members of the Committee. But he reminded his colleagues that they had taken an oath to "perform all of our constitutional duties, not just the pleasant ones."[40] Twice in his statement he quoted from Peter Rodino, who had chaired the Watergate hearings, thus drawing parallels between the events. He was determined to show that the current Committee was merely following its predecessor's procedures.

The impeachment's opening phase ended on October 8 with a full House vote on whether to proceed with an inquiry. Hyde did his best to encourage Democratic support in a floor statement prior to the vote. He realized, he said, that Members were pulled in many directions, but he appealed to them to follow their consciences: "We must listen to that still small voice that whispers in our ear, duty, duty, duty."[41]

Furthermore, he wanted Democrats to know that he understood their concerns. "Many on the other side of the aisle worry that this inquiry will become an excuse for an open-ended attack on this Administration," he said. Drawing upon his own experience as a long-time member of the minority party, he added, "I understand that worry. During times when Republicans controlled the Executive Branch and I was in the minority, I lived what you are living now." He pledged fairness, an expedited search, and a commitment to work with his "Democratic friends." Above all, he reiterated his determination "to look every day for common ground and to agree where we can. When we must disagree, we will do everything we can to minimize those disagreements. At all times, civility must be the watchword for Members on both sides of the aisle." He warned, "Too much hangs in the balance for us not to rise above partisan politics."[42] The vote was 258-176, with only thirty-one Democrats joining the Republican majority. Bipartisanship was losing ground quickly.

The loss of Republican House seats in the November elections provided a basis for many Democrats and media commentators, and some Republicans, to say that the impeachment was a dead letter. They looked upon those results as a public rejection of the Republican determination to go forward with the investigation. "There was enormous pressure," Hyde remembers. "The press began to take sides and question the motives of all of us who were confronted with the law." But Hyde believed he had to fulfill his constitutional duty: "We were confronted with his [Starr's] referral, which consisted of eighteen cartons of tape recordings and videocassettes and transcripts and under oath— testimony under oath—plus his report, which indicated eleven separate instances of conduct by the President, which, in the opinion of the Independent Counsel, amounted to impeachable offenses. So we had to do something with it. It was put on our table, and we reviewed it very carefully, and with Democratic presence. Our next move was to move for a hearing before the Committee. We reviewed the material, and it's 60,000 pages. We concluded that it deserved a hearing by the Committee."[43]

Immediately, the Democrats criticized the majority decision not to call witnesses. Later, some of the Republicans commented that witnesses should have been called, but Hyde believed there was no need:

> It didn't seem to me and to us that we should have to reinvent the wheel, so to speak, and call these witnesses again to have them repeat what they had already repeated under oath before the grand jury. So we relied on the transcripts that were under oath. . . .
>
> We invited witnesses from the Democrats. We said, "Call anybody you want." They declined to call witnesses until at one point where they suddenly decided to call and ask for witnesses and then picked a lot of academicians. There were no fact witnesses. The facts, as charged, seemed to be conceded by the Democrats. Throughout this entire proceeding, they never really questioned the facts.[44]

Another Democrat criticism was Hyde's refusal to set a date for ending the hearings. Hyde did not relish getting involved in the first place, so why was he reluctant to go along with a request that would have ensured the matter would be expedited? His explanation was that the Committee did not yet know if Ken Starr would be sending more information. Other investigations by the Independent Counsel's Office were still ongoing— the nine hundred FBI files of Republicans that had found their way to the White House and the firing of the White House travel office employees. Only when Starr testified before the Committee on November 19 and told the Congressmen that he was closing those other investigations without referrals did Hyde feel it was proper to consider a closing date. While that decision may be open to critique, in light of Hyde's distaste for the whole affair, the belief that he wanted to chair interminable proceedings lacks credibility.

As the Committee opened its formal impeachment inquiry on November 19, the Chairman had the first word. He promised that if President Clinton wanted to testify, he would be given "unlimited time to do so." In this opening charge to the members of the Committee, Hyde raised a number of questions and offered his view on why these proceedings were so important to the future of the country:

> What is the significance of a false statement under oath? Is it essentially different from a garden-variety lie? A mental reservation? A fib? An evasion? A little white lie? Hyperbole?
>
> In a court proceeding, do you assume some trivial responsibility when you raise your right hand and swear to God to tell the truth, the whole truth, and nothing but the truth?
>
> And what of the rule of law—that unique aspect of a free society that protects you from the fire on your roof or the knock on your door at 3 a.m.? What does lying under oath do to the rule of law?
>
> Do we still have a government of laws and not of men? Does the law apply to some people with force and ferocity while the powerful are immune? Do we have one set of laws for the officers and another for the enlisted? Should we?
>
> These are but a few questions these hearing are intended to explore. And just perhaps, when the debate is over, [and] the rationalizations and the distinctions and the semantic gymnastics are put to rest, we may be closer to answering for our generation the haunting question asked 139 years ago in a small military cemetery in Pennsylvania—whether a nation conceived in liberty and dedicated to the proposition that all men are created equal can long endure.[45]

As the hearings progressed, Hyde tried to conduct them civilly. On December 1, a day devoted to discussion of the crime of perjury, some of the experts did not agree with the Republicans' application of the perjury law to what the President had done. When the afternoon session ended, Hyde thanked the witnesses with the following words: "Even when you disagreed with us, which is most of the time, you helped us. You're here because you're darn good citizens and you want to contribute to this awful task we are grappling with, and you have made a great contribution."[46] Those are hardly the words of a rabid partisan.

One week later, after the White House provided a list of fourteen witnesses it wanted to present at the hearings, Hyde consented. Although Congressman John Conyers, the ranking minority member, thanked Hyde for allowing the witnesses to appear, he took the occasion to criticize the process. "The independent counsel had four years to investigate the president," he complained. "This committee has had four months. The White House is now getting two days." He called the legal case against the President "a house of cards" and disparaged the resistance of Republicans to censure motions. "If the American people ever wanted strong evidence that the extremists are still in control of this process, then that is it," he charged.[47] Yet even when accused of extremism, Chairman Hyde did not lose his composure.

As the Committee vote on the articles of impeachment approached, each member of the Committee had the opportunity to make an opening statement. Hyde used his time to emphasize once again why impeachment was necessary. He began with a clarification of the proposed charges:

> Perjury is not sex, obstruction is not sex, abuse of power is not about sex. It's important to understand that none of the proposed articles include allegations of sexual misconduct. The president is not accused of marital infidelity because such conduct is essentially private.
>
> But when circumstances require you to participate in a formal court proceeding and under oath mislead the parties and the court by lying, that is a public act and deserves public sanction. Perjury is a crime with a five-year penalty.[48]

The Democrats, however, seemed to be using the "so-what defense," arguing that even if the President had done everything alleged, his lies "do not rise to the level of impeachment." For some, according to Hyde, impeachment seemed to be somewhat like beauty: it was in the eye of the beholder. But he could not hold that view. His view, which was "not a vengeful one," nor "vindictive," nor "craven," was ultimately "a concern for the Constitution and a high respect for the rule of law." The President's lies were not occasional, but multiple. "We have calculated lawlessness which takes us for fools," Hyde argued.[49]

Turning to the issue of fairness, he offered this apologetic:

> I have been relentlessly accused of being unfair. I can only say I have tried. I have tried and I have tried. We have labored under an artificial time constraint, but one that I adopted back before the election, when the spirit of the age was "Get this over with. Get this behind us. The country doesn't want this to be dragged out over the next coming year."
>
> I bought into that. I agreed it was in the interests of the country, the president, and the Congress to move this along as fast as we could. And I believed we could finish it by the end of the year. That was naïve, and there are so many things left undone because of time constraints.
>
> But now that the election is over, and now that the Democrats—and by the way, we did not want to do anything just before the election, for fear of being accused of trying to politicize our activities, so we held back—but now that the Democrats have picked up some seats, we hear the phrase "lame duck Congress." Well, we can't have it both ways. We're trying to finish this decently, honorably, fairly, within time constraints, because I don't want this to spill over into next year. I don't want this to be an endless process. I think it's in the interests of the country to finish it, and we have tried our level best. And I have tried to grant every request the Democrats have made. Maybe we haven't succeeded, but I have certainly tried.[50]

An examination of the passage reveals a certain amount of frustration with the Democrat opposition. Hyde demonstrably was agitated by the accusations of unfairness when he believed he had done his best to guarantee the opposite. Although he did not use the words hypocrisy or partisanship, clearly he felt that those traits dominated, even before the matter got to the House floor. He reminisced later:

> People believe what they want to believe. Saul Bellow said something that is utterly true: "A great deal of energy can be invested in ignorance when the need for illusion is great." Boy, did that fit this situation. They wanted to believe passionately that we were right-wing religious fanatics; bitterly partisan; willing to do any dirty trick possible; that Ken Starr was a despicable demon and that this poor man [Clinton], just because he has a certain sexual exuberance, was being crucified by partisan Republicans. They wanted to believe that so badly that they have an *enormous* capacity for self-deception. They really do. And if it was convenient, they believed it.[51]

He rejected the accusation that this was a vote to overturn the results of two presidential elections. With more than a hint of sarcasm, he noted that if President Clinton were to be impeached, Bob Dole would not succeed to the office. "We vote for our honor," Hyde concluded, "which is the only thing we get to take with us to the grave."[52]

Prior to the full House vote on impeachment, Hyde suffered another public indignity. Actor Alec Baldwin, appearing on the television program *Late Night with Conan O'Brien*, in a "comedy" skit, claimed that President Clinton had the country's support and that if this were other countries, "all of us together would go down to Washington and we would stone Henry Hyde to death. We would stone him to death . . . And we would go to their homes and we'd kill their wives and children. We would kill their families." Hyde's reaction was one of frustration: "To kill my family because you disagree with me? To laugh about that? There are people out there, sick people, just waiting for a push."[53] Jack Valenti, head of the Motion Picture Association of America, chastised Baldwin for his comments, noting that he had "crossed the line": "This was to go stone somebody and kill his family. However it was said it's not something you use as a joke, it's not something you parody. This is incendiary." Baldwin did write a letter of apology to Hyde, but the episode is indicative of the emotions stirred by the impeachment proceedings.[54]

Hyde, as Chairman of the Judiciary Committee, led off the debate in the full House on December 18. Much of what he shared was not new; he was simply restating the case. Yet he did try to hone in on the crux of the matter when he stressed near the beginning of his statement that "the matter before the House is a question of *lying under oath. This* is a public act. This is called 'perjury.' The matter before the House is a question of the *willful, premeditated, deliberate, shameless corruption* of the nation's system of justice. Perjury and obstruction of justice cannot be reconciled with the Office of the President of the United States. That, *and nothing other than that,* is the issue before us" (emphasis added).[55]

He spoke of the compact between the President and the people being broken, of the President as the "trustee of the nation's conscience," and of the weakening of the Constitution by tolerating perjury and justifying it with the "so-what" defense. Hyde then launched upon a historical review of the rule of law from the Ten Commandments and the Mosaic Law, to the Roman legal system, to the Magna Carta. He invoked the memory of 1776, when the Founders pledged their sacred honor to defend the rule of law, and segued to the Civil War, which again touted the rule of law. The historical panorama ended with the twentieth-century struggle against totalitarianism, which he called "the worst tyrannies in human history." The rule of law, Hyde continued, "is no pious phrase from a civics textbook. . . . The rule of law is like a three-legged stool: one leg is an honest judge, the second leg is an ethical bar, and the third is an enforceable oath. All three are indispensable to avoid political collapse."[56] President Clinton's perjury and obstruction of justice, therefore, regardless of how petty some Members thought it was, had the effect of undermining the entire system of government, if allowed to go unchecked.

Hyde repeated his oft-used phrase that no man can be above the law, but he put it in context when he said that the "no man" applied "no matter how highly placed, no matter how effective a communicator, no matter how gifted a manipulator of opinion polls or winner of votes." He was not expecting perfection, he conceded, but the idea that no one is above the law was "a rock-bottom, irreducible principle of our public life." He continued,

> There is no avoiding the issue before us. We are, in one way or another, establishing the parameters of permissible presidential conduct. . . . We cannot have one law for the ruler and another for the ruled.
>
> This was, once, broadly understood in our land. If that understanding is lost, or if it becomes seriously eroded, the American democratic experiment and the freedom it guarantees is in jeopardy. . . .
>
> What we are telling you today are not the ravings of some vast right-wing conspiracy, but a reaffirmation of a set of values that are tarnished and dim these days, but it is given to us to restore them so our Founding Fathers would be proud.
>
> It's your country—the President is our flag bearer, out in front of our people. The flag is falling, my friends—I ask you to catch the falling flag as we keep our appointment with history.[57]

Hyde was the first to speak; he also was the last. As the vote neared on December 19, he noted that most Democrats knew that the President was a "serial violator of the oath." That was why they were looking for an alternative such as censure to show their disapproval. But, according to Hyde, censure was simply "impeachment lite." They wanted to censure him so there would be "no real consequences, except as history chooses to impose them."[58] Censure, though, he argued, was not the proper recourse. Only impeachment would do.

Convincing the Senate

Probably no one on the House Manager team knew better than Hyde how much of an uphill battle he and the others were facing. A Congressman can learn a lot in twenty-four years, and he knew the politics of this particular situation. The opinion polls gave the President high job approval ratings, the Democrats were voting as a block regardless of the evidence, and the Republican Senators were, by and large, skittish about how it all looked. They would have preferred to move on to other business. In a procedural meeting with Senate leaders in January, Hyde heard fellow Republicans undercut the entire impeachment procedure. Senator Pete Domenici of New Mexico let Hyde and three of his Manager team—Bryant, Rogan, and Hutchinson—know that they would "never get sixty-seven votes to remove the President from office." Domenici added, "You don't want to hear this, but it's true."[59] In a later meeting, Senator Ted Stevens of Alaska was even more direct:

> Henry, come on. You want to put all this stuff in, you want to spend all this time, you want to go through this dog and pony show—there's no way you're going to get sixty-seven votes no matter what you do. . . . Henry, I don't care if you prove he raped a woman and then stood up and shot her dead—you are not going to get sixty-seven votes.[60]

How does one proceed in the face of such obstacles? Certainly it took courage to remain faithful to the task, knowing all the while that your audience, both in the Senate Chamber and on television, wished the whole episode would just go away. The Managers were too much like a national conscience, and the nation resented being reminded of right and wrong.

Hyde later acknowledged that pursuing the impeachment made no political sense: "In the face of the polling numbers, which were heavily supportive of the President, in the face of popular support for keeping him in office and not proceeding, not impeaching him, it was at some considerable political risk that we proceeded to do what we felt was our duty under the law and under the Constitution, to bring these matters to the floor of the House and to have a vote."[61]

Some may argue that the Managers doggedly stayed on course because of their personal loathing for the President. Hyde firmly rejects that interpretation and points to what he considers the source of the mischaracterization—the White House itself:

> One of the defenses, one of the *very* successful spins from the White House was that we were Clinton haters and that we were blinded by his successes as President and we would stop at *nothing* to destroy him. This was the animating spirit behind Mrs. Clinton's consigning us to a 'vast right-wing conspiracy.' None of that was true. All of us have a lawyer's respect for the Office of President, a lawyer's respect for the rule of law, and, politically, it would be no gain for us to precipitate the removal of President Clinton and observe the enthronement of President Gore (emphasis added).[62]

Not only did Hyde not hate Bill Clinton, but he actually admired him in some ways. He thought one of the saddest parts of the entire process was the President's dissipation of what could have been a good Presidency. "It's all down the drain," Hyde reflected, "because of personal, tremendous lack of judgment and other things one could say. But I bear the man no ill will at all. I think he's a tragic figure, frankly."[63] One hears grief, not hatred, in Hyde's comments.

In spite of the accusations and the odds against them, the Managers did proceed, and it was Henry Hyde's duty to lead this team. On the first day of the Managers' presentations, Hyde's only responsibility was to provide an overview of how the Managers would offer their case. But he did take the occasion to remind the Senators of their responsibility:

> To guide you in this grave duty you have taken an oath of impartiality. With the simple words "I do," you have pledged to

put aside personal bias and partisan interest and to do "impartial justice." Your willingness to take up this calling has once again reminded the world of the unique brilliance of America's constitutional system of government. We are here, Mr. Chief Justice and Distinguished Senators, as advocates for the Rule of Law, for Equal Justice Under the Law and for the sanctity of the oath.[64]

One wonders how many Senators caught the irony of the situation: they were judging whether the President had taken his oath of office seriously while simultaneously being charged to take theirs seriously. The unspoken assertion, of course, was that if they did not remove President Clinton from office, they would not have fulfilled their oath of impartiality.

After all the other Managers made their presentations, Hyde had the final word in this opening round. He repeated much of what he had said before the House, but there were some additions and different emphases. He reminded the Senators that their judgment "should rise above politics, above partisanship, above polling data." He again spoke of the sacred honor that was so important to the Founders and wondered if we still had the same concern: "Every school child in the United States has an intuitive sense of the 'sacred honor' that is one of the foundation stones of the American house of freedom. For every day, in every classroom in America, our children and grandchildren pledge allegiance to a nation, 'under God.' That statement, that America is 'one *nation under God*,' is *not* a prideful or arrogant claim. It is a statement of humility: all of us, as individuals, stand under the judgment of God, or the transcendent truths by which we hope, finally, to be judged. So does our country."[65]

Hyde had talked about the broken covenant in his House presentation. In this Senate speech, he chose to dwell longer on that subject. Whenever the President takes the oath of office, he enters into a covenant, Hyde asserted. President Clinton had mentioned a "new covenant" with America in his early days in the Oval Office. So, said Hyde, let's take the President at his word "because a covenant is about promise-making and promise-keeping. For it is because the President has defaulted on the promises he made—it is because he has violated the oaths he has sworn—that he has been impeached." This broken covenant has further ramifications, he argued. The President represents America in world affairs. If our representative is a perjurer who cannot be trusted, then in the eyes of other nations, "America can no longer be trusted." Hyde continued on the subject of trust:

> *Trust*, not what James Madison called the "parchment barriers" of laws, is the fundamental bond between the people and their elected representatives, between those who govern and those who are governed. *Trust* is the mortar that secures the foundations of the American house of freedom. And the Senate of the United States, sitting in judgment in this impeachment trial, should not ignore, or minimize, or dismiss the fact that the bond of trust has been broken, because the President has violated both his oaths of office and the oath he took before his grand jury testimony. [66]

Fully aware that an attempt had been made to portray the Managers as hypocrites because of private indiscretions in their own pasts,[67] Hyde then addressed that issue. He admitted that each person presenting the case was cognizant of the ways in which they had failed to live up to their own standards throughout their lives. "None of us comes before you claiming to be a perfect man or a perfect citizen," Hyde explained, "just as none of you imagines yourself perfect." They were flawed human beings, yet "flawed human beings must, according to the rule of law, judge other flawed human beings." He continued,

> But the issue before the Senate of the United States is not the question of its own members' personal moral condition. Nor is the issue before the Senate the question of the personal moral condition of the members of the House of Representatives. The issue *here* is whether the President of the

United States has violated the rule of law and thereby broken his covenant of trust with the American people. This is a *public* issue, involving the gravest matter of the *public* interest. And it is not affected, one way or another, by the personal moral condition of any member of either house of Congress, or by whatever expressions of personal chagrin the President has managed to express.[68]

In his summary, Hyde felt bound also to defend the Managers against charges of being mean-spirited, frivolous, or irresponsible in prosecuting the President. "We have brought these impeachment articles," he stressed, "because we are convinced, in conscience, that the President ... lied under oath: that the President committed perjury on several occasions before a Federal grand jury. We have brought these articles ... because we are convinced, in conscience, that the President willfully obstructed justice, and thereby threatened the legal system he swore a solemn oath to protect and defend." To drive the point home and to remind the Senators once again of the importance of their responsibility, he continued: "These are not trivial matters. These are not partisan matters. *These are matters of justice*, the justice that each of you has taken a solemn oath to serve in this trial."[69]

Near the end of his comments, Hyde introduced an unusual piece of evidence into the case—evidence of the effect that the President's behavior already was having on the country. It was a letter to Hyde from a third-grade boy saying that he thought the President should have to write an essay for telling lies. The boy had to write one when his father had punished him for lying. A postscript from the father stated, "Part of his [the son's] defense of his lying was that the President lied. He is still having difficulty understanding why the President can lie and not be punished."[70] Hyde concluded,

> Mr. Chief Justice and Senators—
> On June 6, 1994, the 50th anniversary of the American landing on the beaches of Normandy, I stood among the field of

white crosses and Stars of David. The British had a military band of bagpipes playing Amazing Grace. I walked up to one cross to read a name, but there was none. All it said was "Here lies in Honored Glory a Comrade in Arms Known but to God." How do we keep faith with that comrade in arms?

Go to the Vietnam Memorial on the National Mall and press your hands against some of the 58,000 names carved in the wall—and ask yourself how we can redeem the debt we owe all those who purchased our freedom with their lives. How do we keep faith with them?

I think I know. We work to make this country the kind of America they were willing to die for. That's an America where the idea of sacred honor still has the power to stir men's souls.

I hope that a hundred years from today, people will look back at what we have done and say, "They kept the faith."[71]

After the presentations by the President's lawyers, the Senate set aside two days for Senators to ask questions. Senator Trent Lott of Mississippi, the Majority Leader, posed one that was read by Chief Justice Rehnquist: "Do you have any comment on the answer given by the President's counsel with regard to the views of the American people?" Hyde responded by quoting Edmund Burke, who had been asked the same question once. Burke's response had been that although a representative of the people "owes the highest degree of fidelity to his constituents, . . . he doesn't owe his conscience to anybody." Representatives of the people are not to weigh their mail every day and vote accordingly, Hyde argued: "Our work here is not an ongoing plebiscite. We are elected to bring our judgment, our experience and our consciences here with us." He believed firmly that "there are issues of transcendent importance that you have to be willing to lose your office over." For him, the issues of abortion, national defense, and equal justice under law were worth such a cost:

Equal justice under the law is what moves me and animates me and consumes me, and I'm willing to lose my seat any day in the week rather than sell out on those issues.

Despite all the polls and all the hostile editorials, America is hungry for people who believe in something. You may disagree with us, but we believe in something.[72]

With the verdict of the trial becoming increasingly obvious, particularly after Senator Robert Byrd's motion to dismiss the impeachment articles, Hyde took advantage of one friendly question from a Republican Senator to air his frustrations. "By dismissing the articles of impeachment before you have a complete trial, you are sending a terrible message to the people of the country," he warned. "You are saying, I guess perjury is okay, if it is about sex. Obstruction of justice is okay, even though it is an effort to deny a citizen her right to a fair trial." He concluded, "I know, oh, do I know, what an annoyance we are in the bosom of this great body. But we are a *constitutional* annoyance, and I remind you of that fact" (emphasis added).[73]

On February 8, after all the arguments, pro and con, had been made, Hyde had the last word before the Senate vote. "We are blessedly coming to the end of this melancholy procedure," he began. "But before we gather up our papers and return to the obscurity from whence we came"—a self-deprecating comment that elicited laughter from the Senate—"permit, please, a few final remarks."

He thanked Chief Justice Rehnquist first "for the aura of dignity that he has lent to these proceedings." Then he turned to the President's lawyers. This could have been the opportunity to offer a scathing partisan attack, but he chose instead a lighter touch: "They have conducted themselves in the most professional way. They have made the most of a poor case, in my opinion. There is an old Italian saying—and it has nothing to do with lawyers, but to your case—that 'you may dress the shepherd in the silk, he will still smell of the goat.'"[74] More laughter ensued.

After some heartfelt comments about the Managers and the staff working for them,[75] Hyde returned to the issue weighing on everyone in the room. The Managers had presented their case with fervor, he noted, but that did not mean they had any lack of respect for the Senators. In fact, in the minds of the Managers, their "most formidable opponent" was not the opposing counsel or the opposing political party; rather, it was the cynicism in people who believed that all politics and, by association, all politicians, were corrupt. "That cynicism is an acid eating away at the vital organs of American public life," Hyde claimed. "It is a clear and present danger, because it blinds us to the nobility and the fragility of being a self-governing people." Would the Senate vote, he asked, enlarge that cynicism? It would if the Senators decided to allow the President to continue in office; it would set up a double standard.[76]

In his speeches, Hyde regularly uses stories to help make his points. To the Senators, at this critical juncture in the impeachment trial, he drew upon the story of a boy in England who had been kicked out of the Royal Naval College for allegedly forging someone else's signature on a postal money order. The boy said he was innocent. The incident, portrayed in a play and in a movie called *The Winslow Boy*, escalated until it finally reached the desk of King Edward VII. When the King read the petition from the boy's lawyer, he was impressed by the reasoning, and despite the fact that the case had been lost in every court, he reversed the verdict, writing across the front of the petition, "Let right be done." Hyde proclaimed, "I have always been moved by that phrase. I saw the movie; I saw the play; and I have the book. And I am still moved by that phrase, 'Let right be done.' I hope when you finally vote that will move you, too."[77]

Hyde expressed surprise that one of the President's lawyers had said that the Managers wanted to win "too badly." Had they committed perjury in their drive to oust the President? Had they obstructed justice or claimed false privileges? Had they hidden evidence under someone else's bed? Had they encouraged false testimony? "That is what you do if you want to win too badly," he reasoned. The Senators should have had no problem grasping the inference. Hyde doubted that there could be too many people on the entire planet who did not believe that President Clinton had lied under oath or had obstructed justice; therefore, Hyde concluded that "the real issue doesn't concern the facts, the stubborn facts, as the defense is fond of saying, but what to do about them."[78]

Democrats seemed to want to do *something,* as long as it was not impeachment. Hyde said he was "dumbfounded" when he looked at the censure resolutions that the Democrats were circulating. They mirrored exactly what the Managers were saying. He quoted from one that had been printed in the *New York Times:*

> Then they say:
> "The President deliberately misled and deceived the American people and officials in all branches of the U.S. Government."
> This is not a Republican document. This is coming from here.
> "The President gave false or misleading testimony and impeded discovery of evidence in judicial proceedings."
> Isn't that another way of saying obstruction of justice and perjury?
> "The President's conduct demeans the Office of the President as well as the President himself and creates disrespect for the laws of the land. Future generations of Americans must know that such behavior is not only unacceptable but bears grave consequences including loss of integrity, trust and respect."
> But not loss of job.[79]

To Hyde, these strong words indicated that the Democrats agreed with the Managers. Yet they were unwilling to do what the Constitution called for in such circumstances. "Do you really cleanse the office as provided in the Constitution, or do you use the Airwick of a censure resolution? Because any censure resolution, to be meaningful, has to punish the President, if only his reputation. And how do you deal with the laws of bill of attainder? How do you deal with the separation of powers? What kind of a precedent are you setting?" Hyde questioned.[80] Constitutionally, their cure was worse than the disease.

Hyde then pondered the fate of America. "Once in a while I do worry about the future," he confessed. "I wonder if, after this culture war is over, this one we are engaged in, an America will survive that is worth fighting for to defend. People won't risk their lives for the U.N., or over the Dow Jones averages. But I wonder, in future generations, whether there will be enough vitality left in duty, honor and country to excite our children and grandchildren to defend America." The Senate's decision, he warned, would play a large role in the future trend of American culture and politics: "Wherever and whenever you avert your eyes from a wrong, from an injustice, you become a part of the problem."[81]

How was he to summarize everything that the Managers had said up to this point? In his final appeal to the Senate, Hyde tried to put it all in a nutshell:

> If you agree that perjury and obstruction of justice have been committed, and yet you vote down the conviction, you are extending and expanding the boundaries of permissible Presidential conduct. You are saying a perjurer and obstructer of justice can be President, in the face of no less than three precedents for conviction of Federal judges for perjury. You shred those precedents and you raise the most serious questions of whether the President is in fact subject to the law or whether we are beginning a restoration of the divine right of kings. The issues we are concerned with have consequences far into the future because the real damage is not to the individuals involved, but to the American system of justice and especially the principle that no one is above the law.[82]

Not one Democrat voted for removal from office.

Reflections

A *Chicago Tribune* poll taken after the impeachment showed that a third of DuPage County voters had a lower opinion of Hyde than before the impeachment. One Hyde admirer lamented, "Henry Hyde's career was hurt more than Bill Clinton's. By taking this job, his political career got stomped on. If he wanted to move up in politics, I think he's made too many enemies on the other side to do that." Death threats became commonplace; he had to go everywhere with two bodyguards. [83]

William Schneider, resident fellow with the American Enterprise Institute and political analyst on CNN, offered this commentary: "He looks like a zealot. His decision to go right ahead with this on a partisan basis won't do his legacy any good. The word partisan will forever be attached to his name." Another academic, Stephen Hess of the Brookings Institution, passed this verdict: "I don't think he's going to get high marks in history. It seems clear that various strategies he attempted to get from here to there weren't very successful. He didn't do his thing very well."[84]

Yet not everyone felt that way. In the week after the Senate trial, Hyde's congressional office was so inundated with flowers that staffers had to take bouquets home to make more space for those still arriving. One woman asked him to sign an autograph for her unborn grandchild—sort of a political treasure for the future. A neighbor in the building where Hyde lives in his district "slipped a note under his door on behalf of his deceased father, whose death-bed wish was to thank Hyde for protecting the Constitution." Less than a month after the end of the trial, Hyde spoke at the Lincoln Day Banquet in Ohio's Fifth Congressional District. The host for the dinner chose to introduce him as "Congressman Henry Hyde—hero." The introduction led to a prolonged standing ovation. One of the attendees, Charles F. Kurfess, former speaker of the Ohio House, exclaimed, "The welcome he got here tonight and this huge turnout is a statement of the respect for the position he found himself in and how he handled it."[85]

Hyde knows that the American people, generally, backed the President and not the Managers, but he is thankful for those who did show their support. "We got over 300,000 pieces of mail, 75 percent of which were favorable to us," he remembers. "Some very touching letters, I can assure you. Very touching. A whole section from the Library of Congress wrote us and signed their names—one department over there—that they supported us and admired us for protecting and defending the Constitution. It was real interesting."[86]

When asked what he hopes the United States can learn from this impeachment experience, his answer started again with a sigh and a pause. Then he said,

> I think respect for the rule of law and understanding that honor and integrity are at the heart of our democracy and that leaders ought to hold fast to principle. Our democracy has to prove itself again and again. It's just as good as the people who govern. Cynicism is self-defeating. We need our best people to be attracted to public service. If we continue to demean them, for whatever purposes, we're damaging self-government.[87]

The rule of law—honor—integrity—principle—self-government. Henry Hyde lives in a world where these words dictate how people act. He might be tempted to say that, far too often, Washington, DC, is not part of that world.

Chapter Two Endnotes

[1] Congressman Henry Hyde, interview by author, tape recording, Washington, DC, 8 February 2000.

[2] Ibid.

[3] Quoting *The Almanac of American Politics, 1994*; available at http://www.house.gov/hyde/hydebio.htm; accessed 11 May 1999.

[4] Quoting *Politics in America 1994, The 103rd Congress* in ibid.

[5] Quoting Tom Roeser in the *Chicago Sun-Times* in ibid.

[6] Quoting Ralph Neas, executive director of the Leadership Conference on Civil Rights in *Insight Magazine*, January 1994, in ibid.

[7] Quoting the *Wheaton (Illinois) Journal*, October 1993, in ibid.

[8] Quoting Cokie Roberts in *The New American Politician*, 1998, by Burdette Loomis, in ibid.

[9] *Congressional Quarterly Weekly Report*, 2 October 1993, 2649.

[10] Jacqueline Calmes and Rob Gurwitt, "Profiles in Power: Leaders without Portfolio," *Congressional Quarterly Weekly Report*, 3 January 1987, 11.

[11] Henry J. Hyde, "Calling on Our Better Angels," *The Human Life Review* 22:4 (1 September 1996): 25.

[12] Ibid.

[13] Ibid.

[14] Hyde interview.

[15] Ibid.

[16] Calmes and Gurwitt, "Profiles in Power."

[17] "Iran-Contra Hearings: The Committee's Turn: Speeches to North," *The New York Times*, 14 July 1987, A12.

[18] David E. Rosenbaum, "Supporters Say President Owes Apology on Iran," *The New York Times*, 15 January 1987, A1.

[19] "Reports of the Iran-Contra Committees: Excerpts From the Minority View," *The New York Times*, 17 November 1987, A6.

[20] Lee H. Hamilton and Daniel K. Inouye, *The Iran-Contra Affair: Supplemental and Additional Views: Chapter 10, Views of Hyde*; available at http://www.elibrary.com; accessed 24 June 1999.

[21] "Never Condoned Lying Under Oath, Hyde Says," *The Los Angeles Times*, 9 December 1998, A20.

[22] Ibid.

[23] Hyde interview.

[24] Ibid.

[25] Albert R. Karr, "RTC Sues Ex-Aides of Illinois S&L Over Negligence," *The Wall Street Journal*, 28 April 1993, A6.

[26] Elaine Hopkins, "Hyde Vows to Avoid Settlement," *Journal Star (Peoria, IL)*, 16 February 1997.

[27] Matt O'Connor, "Hyde Blasts Federal Officials for Lawsuit: US Lawmaker Settles S&L Case, Blames Congress," *Chicago Tribune*, 6 March 1997, 1.

[28] Jonathan Weisman, "Impeachment's Man in the Middle," *The Baltimore Sun*, 15 November 1998, 1A.

[29] Ibid.

[30] John F. Dickerson, Wendy Cole, and Elaine Shannon, "A Nice Guy in a Nasty Fight: A Man of Courtliness and Character, Henry Hyde Must Above All Show that the Republicans Are Fair," *Time*, 12 October 1998, 34.

[31] Hyde Statement on Referral of Report from Office of Independent Counsel, 9 September 1998; available at http://www.house.gov/judiciary/090998.htm; accessed 28 April 1999.

[32] Hyde Statement to House Rules Committee, 10 September 1998; available at http://www.house.gov/judiciary/091098.htm; accessed 28 April 1999.

[33] Hyde Floor Statement on Referral Resolution, 11 September 1998; available at http://www.house.gov/judiciary/091198f.htm; accessed 28 April 1999.

[34] Ibid.

[35] Ibid.

[36] Ibid.

[37] Statement by House Judiciary Committee Chairman Henry Hyde, 23 September 1998; available at http://www.house.gov/judiciary/092398.htm; accessed 28 April 1999.

[38] Hyde interview.

[39] Ibid.

[40] Opening Statement on Resolution of Impeachment Inquiry, Hon. Henry Hyde, 5 October 1998; available at http://www.house.gov/judiciary/opening.htm; accessed 28 April 1999.

[41] Floor Statement by Henry Hyde, 8 October 1998; available at http://www.house.gov/judiciary/100898.htm; accessed 28 April 1999.

[42] Ibid.

[43] Hyde interview.

[44] Ibid.

[45] Text of Opening Statement Made Thursday by the House Judiciary Committee Chairman, Rep. Henry Hyde, 19 November 1998; available at http://www.washtimes.com/investiga/investiga13.html; accessed 16 April 1999.

[46] McLoughlin, *The Impeachment and Trial of President Clinton*, 66.

[47] Ibid., 67.

[48] The Impeachment Hearings: Opening Statements: Chairman Henry Hyde, 11 December 1998; available at http://www.washingtonpost.com/wp-srv/politics/special/clinton/stories/hydetest121198.htm; accessed 1 April 1999.

[49] Ibid.

[50] Ibid.

[51] Hyde interview.

[52] The Impeachment Hearings: Opening Statements: Chairman Henry Hyde, 11 December 1998.

[53] Colin Bessonette, "Q&A On the News," *The Atlanta Journal and Constitution*, 6 June 1999, 2A.

[54] Lisa de Moraes, "Valenti to Baldwin: Cool It, Smart Alec!" *The Washington Post*, 21 December 1998, C07; "Late-Night Alec Baldwin Skit Criticized," *The Arizona Republic*, 20 December 1998, E4.

[55] Statement of the Honorable Henry J. Hyde Before the U.S. House of Representatives: Resolution on the Impeachment of the President, 18 December 1998; available at http://www.house.gov/judiciary/101370.htm; accessed 16 April 1999.

[56] Ibid.

[57] Ibid.

[58] McLoughlin, *The Impeachment and Trial of President Clinton*, 206.

[59] David Schippers, *Sellout: The Inside Story of President Clinton's Impeachment* (Washington, DC: Regnery Publishing, Inc., 2000), 14.

[60] Ibid., 22-23.

[61] Hyde interview.

[62] Ibid.

[63] Ibid.

[64] Opening Statement of Hon. Henry Hyde, Senate Impeachment Trial of President Clinton, 14 January 1999; available at http://www.house.gov/judiciary/hydesenate.htm; accessed 16 April 1999.

[65] Summary Presentation of Hon. Henry Hyde, Senate Impeachment Trial of President Clinton, 16 January 1999; available at http://www.house.gov/judiciary/hyde011699.htm; accessed 12 April 1999.

[66] Ibid.

[67] These episodes are described in chapter one, "Why Impeachment?" There is no need to repeat the specific accusations in this chapter.

[68] Summary Presentation of Hon. Henry Hyde, Senate Impeachment Trial of President Clinton, 16 January 1999.

[69] Ibid.

[70] Ibid.

[71] Ibid.

[72] Questions and Answers, Senate Impeachment Trial of President Clinton, 23 January 1999; available at http://www.nytimes.com/library/politics/ 012499impeach-qtext.html; accessed 31 March 1999.

[73] Peter Baker, *The Breach: Inside the Impeachment and Trial of William Jefferson Clinton* (New York: Scribner, 2000), 336.

[74] Closing Argument of Hon. Henry Hyde, Senate Impeachment Trial of President Clinton, 8 February 1999.

[75] Quoted in the introduction to this work.

[76] Closing Argument of Hon. Henry Hyde, Senate Impeachment Trial of President Clinton, 8 February 1999.

[77] Ibid.

[78] Ibid.

[79] Ibid.

[80] Ibid.

[81] Ibid.

[82] Ibid.

[83] Dina ElBoghdady, "Back Home, Hyde's Still in Charge," *The Detroit News*, 24 February 1999, A1. The article also noted, "But Hyde's supporters dismissed the *Tribune* poll as inaccurate and misleading. Of the 450 voters polled in DuPage County, they said, only 201 of them were in Hyde's district. Even if he did represent all the poll respondents, it's no surprise one-third of them would disapprove of his performance since he captured two-thirds of the vote in November."

[84] Laura Janota, "How Will History Judge Hyde's Role? Future Generations May Cast Congressman in Role of Bad Guy, Experts Say," *Daily Herald (Arlington Heights, IL)*, 14 February 1999.

[85] Joe Hallett, "Hyde Gets a Hero's Welcome; Top Prosecutor Says He's Weary of Scandal Talk," *The Columbus Dispatch*, 7 March 1999, 4A.

[86] Hyde interview.

[87] Ibid.

CHAPTER THREE

Bob Barr:
Pugnacity and Principle

As one walks into Congressman Bob Barr's Capitol Hill office, a plaque on the left wall, just above the couch, attracts one's attention. On the plaque is this quote from Theodore Roosevelt:

> *No man is above the law*
> *and no man is below it.*
> *Nor do we ask any man's permission*
> *when we require him to obey it.*

Congressman Barr considers that quote to be a model for his own conduct in public office. He received the plaque from a fellow Georgian while he served as U.S. Attorney for the Northern District of Georgia during President Reagan's second term. It was a gift of appreciation for Barr's successful prosecution of *Republican* Congressman Pat Swindall. The prosecution enraged the state's GOP establishment; Congressman Newt Gingrich, at that time, even lobbied for Barr's ouster from the U.S. Attorney's office.[1] As Barr recalls, the case "was over, essentially, the very same issue [as that of President Clinton's]: a high public official violating the law, violating the public trust, really in very much the same way. Lying before a federal grand jury is something that ought not to be tolerated regardless of party affiliation. I've always believed that."[2]

Barr's action in that case certainly was not partisan, and his comment is a direct appeal that the law be applied fairly to everyone, even members of one's own political party. Yet Barr, more than any other Manager, stirs strong partisan emotions, often exhibited through angry rhetoric. A mere ten minutes searching Internet sites yielded the following comments from Barr critics:

"Bob Barr is an Obnoxious Right-Wing Midget."

"Bob Barr is a White Racist Gun Freak."

"Bob Barr: American Tyrant."

"House of Crooks Presents: Bob Barr."

"Letter to Hillary Clinton: Bob Barr Is One Dangerous, Frightening Dude."

"Bob Barr Fights Our Rights."

"Bob Barr Is a Fraud and a Fake."

One site claimed that a poll put Barr at number one on a list of least-admired Americans. The audience for this poll is questionable; all of the names on the least-admired list just happen to be political conservatives or those who have aided the conservative cause (e.g., Paula Jones), except for NBC newsman Tim Russert and cult leader and mass murderer Charles Manson.[3] Perhaps Russert was included because Rush Limbaugh has made positive comments about him. Manson, curiously enough, ranked only number twenty, well behind all the conservatives. This "sample" audience admired Charles Manson more than Bob Barr.

Barr definitely is outspoken. He backs down for no one. Some of the comments on those Internet sites were generated from homosexual activists and devotees to the pagan religion of Wicca, two constituencies with which he has fundamental disagreements. Other Barr critics point to his private life—divorced twice and accused of encouraging one of his former wives to have an abortion—and level the charge of hypocrisy.[4] Barr has responded that he "never suggested, urged, forced or encouraged anyone to have an abortion" and that he never perjured himself in a court proceeding.[5] There is some indication that Barr did switch to a pro-life stance prior to his election to Congress. Once he became pro-life, though, his record on that issue has been perfectly consistent. "That's where the rubber meets the road," noted Georgia Right-to-Life legislative director Carolyn Garcia, "and Congressman Barr has met that test."[6]

The primary reason for the Larry Flynt-sponsored accusation about Barr's treatment of former wives was, of course, to convince the public that Barr had no moral authority to stand in judgment of President Clinton. But Barr, remarking on the Flynt charge more than a year later, drew a distinction:

> What we are talking about, again [in the Clinton case], was perjury and obstruction of justice: acts committed by a public official in his public capacity about public events and in the context of a public institution. Nothing that any of the Members of the Judiciary Committee on the Republican side were so-called accused of, whether it was charges leveled against Chairman Hyde, charges leveled against myself, charges leveled against Dan Burton in his capacity as Chairman of the Government Reform and Oversight Committee—none of those actions and those charges had anything whatsoever to do with public acts by public officials about public matters in public forums.[7]

Even as Henry Hyde told the Senate during the impeachment trial, "None of us comes before you claiming to be a perfect man or a perfect citizen," yet "flawed human beings must, according to the rule of law, judge other flawed human beings."[8]

Life Before the Impeachment

Although now a Congressman from Georgia's Seventh District, Barr has lived in many places, both in the United States and elsewhere. Barr, the second of six children, was born in Iowa City. The Barr family followed Bob Barr, Sr., to locales such as Baghdad, Tehran, and Lima as he served in the Army Corps of Engineers. The senior Bob made an impression on his son: "To my father, truth was something sacred, and that without it, society could not function."9

Bob, Jr., received his undergraduate degree at the University of Southern California in 1970, his master's from Georgetown in 1972, and his law degree from Georgetown in 1977. Barr served as a CIA intelligence analyst for seven years before making Georgia his final destination. He became a criminal defense lawyer and began working in Georgia Republican politics. His first attempt at political office, a 1984 run for the Georgia legislature, failed, but with the recommendation of then-Georgia Senator Mack Mattingly, he received the appointment as U.S. Attorney. 10

Barr's tenure as U.S. Attorney for the Northern District of Georgia ran ` from 1986 to 1990, when he resigned to run the Southeastern Legal Foundation, a conservative organization founded in 1976 to advocate limited government, individual economic freedom, and the free enterprise system by tackling cases directly affecting those issues.11

In 1992, Barr tried again for elective office, battling Paul Coverdell for the Republican nomination for U.S. Senator. Again, he fell short. He had not yet established his credentials with the Right-to-Life movement or social conservatives in general. Typical of the comments at the time was that of Ralph Reed, who said, "We have no enthusiasm for the Coverdell candidacy, but we do not feel that Bob Barr has articulated a consistent stand on family issues such that he merits support."12

Since that election, Barr has increasingly cast his lot with social conservatives. Neither is he reticent to talk about religious faith. "Public officials ought to carry their religious beliefs into public service," he says. "I believe religious teachings in the Bible clearly provide the just basis for governing. We ought to not be afraid to recognize that."13 When George W. Bush related in a Republican presidential primary debate that the person he most admired was Jesus Christ, Barr was quick to support Bush against criticisms that he had inappropriately mixed religion and politics. "The spastic over-reaction to an honest, spontaneous remark from a political candidate illustrates in a very poignant way how much the media looks down on people who have the faith to believe in God and the courage to talk about that belief," Barr wrote in one of his weekly columns. "Of course," he continued, "advocates of a radically secular society conveniently forget the fact that it is impossible to establish a moral, ethical and effective government without a belief in God. Without some bedrock guiding principles, human behavior is simply shaped entirely by the circumstances of the moment, without clear or lasting concepts of right and wrong, or the order that comes only through such a system. The end result is that human social behavior in the absence of religious belief inevitably becomes less controlled and more harmful to others; which is, come to think of it, what we see happening in the world today."[14] The candidate that the Christian Coalition was hesitant to support in 1992 is now publicly identified with Christian conservative causes.

Finally, in 1994, Barr took his place in the House of Representatives as part of the Contract-with-America Republican takeover of the Congress. He received appointments to the Judiciary, Banking, and Government Reform committees. On the Government Reform Committee, he serves as chair of the Subcommittee on Criminal Justice, Drug Policy, and Human Resources.

Barr knew even before he arrived in Washington that he wanted a spot on the Judiciary Committee: "When I came up here in December of 1994 for our orientation, I made a point to go by and meet Henry Hyde, whom I had never met before. I knew of him by reputation, but I had never met him. My wife and I went in to see him, and I told him it would be an honor to serve on the Judiciary Committee and I would very much appreciate the opportunity to do that." Was that because the new Congressman already had a presidential impeachment in mind? Not at all, replies Barr. He says he did not begin to think about impeachment until the Government Reform Committee investigated campaign funding violations after the 1996 election.[15]

Impeachment aside, Barr made his mark almost immediately. "My constituents didn't send me up here to glad-hand and have a good time," he explained. "They sent me up here to get something done." One of Barr's Republican colleagues in the House, Mark Souder of Indiana, who has worked closely with and has supported Barr on issues, once noted, "Bob never throws a grenade when a nuclear bomb will work." Souder also is convinced that political calculation does not motivate his friend; rather, Barr acts on what he believes is right regardless of the political consequences: "Bob doesn't necessarily think how things are going to play out for him."[16]

Barr came to the forefront on the Waco investigation in 1995, emerging as the Republicans' "toughest interrogator of administration witnesses." Neither was he reluctant to cut off Attorney General Janet Reno twice because he did not feel she was answering the questions he had asked. Yet he insisted that he was not using the hearings to fix blame on the President. He just wanted to ensure that nothing like that would happen again: "Aside from who's responsible for what, it just sort of personified in some ways that we have some serious problems with the growth of the federal government, a government becoming too big and thinking it can do whatever it wants to do."[17]

Personal privacy issues, regulatory reform, tax relief, Social Security, national defense, and achieving a balanced federal budget have been Barr's priorities in Congress. Authorship of the Defense of Marriage Act in 1996, which denied federal recognition to same-sex marriages, earned him praise from social conservatives and made him the bane of gay rights activists.

Yet on privacy issues, Barr finds himself at times on the same side as the ACLU. Both opposed "the Clinton-FBI push for roving wiretaps that— on the basis of a single warrant—would allow law enforcement agencies to tap all phones in any home or business used by, or near, a targeted person." He also has fought "government access—without court order—to commercial and private business records," spoken out against a national identity card, and resisted a so-called "unique health identifier" for every American, which Barr fears would allow access to the "most intimate and private details of every American's health history."[18]

Most of his notoriety, however, came from his attempt to open an impeachment inquiry against President Clinton two months before the name Monica Lewinsky became part of public discourse. Why did he do it? Does this prove he is an extremist? Was he acting as a partisan, shoving aside impartiality for the sake of his party's political advantage? Barr commented later,

> I was not elected to this position to sit back and prove to the world that I'm impartial. I'm not impartial when it comes to my constituents, and I'm not impartial when it comes to the Constitution. I'm not impartial when it comes to standing for the rule of law and accountability. I'm very partial when it comes to those issues.
>
> What I saw throughout 1997 in the hearings that Dan Burton's Committee conducted, for example, and a lot of other evidence [that] was starting to come out and develop during 1998, was corruption—evidence of deep corruption in this Administration, and personally with this President. That was the basis for my original inquiry of impeachment that we filed on November 5, 1997, with, I think, a dozen and a half other Members of Congress. To me, there were very sound reasons to proceed with an impeachment. This notion that simply because a Member of Congress has reached a conclusion to proceed in a certain direction, [that this] disqualifies them from working to achieve that end, is just utter nonsense.[19]

On the issue of partisanship, Barr has this perspective:

> The way they phrase that argument, you can never win the argument with them. The fact of the matter is, I am a Republican. The fact of the matter is, the President is a Democrat. One can always simply state those facts and then just walk away from the issue and say, "See, I told you so. This is a Republican, this is a Democrat—of course it was partisan." But that's very superficial, and most people recognize that. Moreover, my personal history of dealing with these sorts of

issues I think clearly establishes that my concern is not a partisan concern. It never has and never will be. When I led the prosecution in my U.S. Attorney's Office of a Republican Member of Congress, that was hardly something that could be construed as partisan.[20]

After Barr introduced his inquiry resolution, the President himself weighed in on Barr as someone who had "always had a rather extreme view of these things." The resolution "blamed Clinton for intentionally obstructing congressional investigations, allowing illegal foreign campaign contributions to influence his decisions, using federal facilities and equipment for campaign purposes, and circumventing federal election laws." In his press conference announcing the resolution, the Congressman gave as his rationale that the time was right "to take a very measured step to reassert the rule of law in this country and to correct abuse of office and abuse of power and make the president accountable."[21]

Commentators criticized the Georgia Republican immediately, calling the effort "Don Quixote politics," "political vandalism," and "strictly partisan." Even Republican political analyst Laura Ingraham editorialized, "When Republicans lob impeachment grenades, they convey a guerrilla warfare mentality not suited to a majority party. It probably won't go much further, but it is succeeding in making Republicans look disjointed."[22] A scant two months later, however, Barr did not look as extremist as some were painting him.

By March 1998, he was not alone in his desire for impeachment, but still he was in the minority. His greatest hope was that it would not be the Lewinsky affair fueling an impeachment inquiry; Barr preferred that the inspiration for moving forward be other issues that the Independent Counsel had been investigating.[23] He knew he was viewed as an extremist by some, but he argued against that perception. "People don't understand what impeachment is," he noted. "Impeachment should not be thought of as—and was not intended to be—an extreme measure. It was the one tool, the only tool that was given to us by our founding fathers to correct an abuse of office by a high government official." What was happening in the Clinton Administration, he believed, was "not abuse of power by one or two people, but systemic abuse." Again, he denied that partisanship was his reason for pursuing this remedy: "My interest in an impeachment inquiry is motivated by what I truly believe is the national interest of the country. . . . We need to reassert the rule of law. We need to reassert that our public officials are accountable to the people. And we need to protect our national security. And it has nothing to do with politics."[24]

Impeachment in the House

As the Clinton scandal unfolded throughout 1998, the impetus for an impeachment inquiry grew. When the Independent Counsel's Office unloaded boxes of evidence upon the House in September and when the full House voted to send the Starr Report to the Judiciary Committee, Barr finally saw his quest becoming reality. The Committee held hearings in October to decide if an official inquiry should be initiated.

In his opening statement, Barr painted a picture of what no one could possibly want. "Imagine a place," he began, "where a dictator, a king, a prime minister or a president could walk into your home at any time and force you to accede to any demand, however unreasonable." That was the norm throughout history, yet America had set up a system based on the rule of law, which stood "as a stark exception to the historically prevalent notion that a ruler can take whatever he wants, whenever he wants it, from any subject." America now needed to be aware that this safeguard was slipping:

> As we so quickly forget in times of stability and prosperity, our system is a fragile one—a brief flicker of light in the otherwise dark march of human political history. If we drop our guard, even for a moment, and allow a president to demand citizens gratify his personal desires, and let him place himself

in the way of laws designed to prevent such conduct, that light will be greatly dimmed, if not snuffed out.[25]

He reminded the Committee that the Founding Fathers understood why it was so important to restrain power, incorporating into the Constitution protections against an overbearing government. The Clinton case was not complex, he argued. An American President demanded something from a citizen (i.e., Paula Jones), and when she refused, he used his office to smear her name and to attempt to keep her legitimate grievance from receiving redress in the courts of justice. "Instead of telling the truth to the court and a grand jury, the President lied. Instead of cooperating with the court, he obstructed its efforts. At this very moment," he added for emphasis, "government and private employees are working under his direct orders to block this committee's efforts." Barr then explained the significance of the case:

We are witnessing nothing less than the symptoms of a cancer on the American presidency. If we fail to remove this cancer, it will expand to destroy the principles that matter most to us.

Any system of government can choose to perpetuate virtue . . . or vice. If this President is allowed to use the presidency to gratify his personal desires, in the same way a corrupt county or parish boss solicits money for votes, future occupants will, sadly, do the same. If the proposition that perjury is sometimes acceptable is allowed to stand, in the blink of an eye, it will become acceptable in every case (after all, "equal protection of our laws" will be used to demand equal protection of perjury for all). Such a precedent would hang forever, as an albatross, around the neck of our judicial system. If we stand by while a President obstructs justice and destroys his enemies, our entire government will be contaminated with cynical disdain for the rule of law.[26]

The American presidency, Barr reminded his colleagues, is the most powerful political office in the world and is able to destroy billions of people because of the nation's military arsenal. Do we want someone in that office who abuses the power of that office? In this case, it might be just one individual who is being abused, but if a President will abuse one, might not he abuse many? This could devastate the United States, in Barr's view. "If we fail to address such charges, we will soon be left standing dazed and befuddled among the smoldering ruins of a great democracy," he warned. By "choosing temporal stability over permanent justice" and by "putting politics over principle," we will reap "diminished freedoms, lost lives, and ruined institutions." He reminded the Committee members that "History is littered with the wreckage of nations whose leaders buried their heads in the sand as adversity appeared on the horizon. The United States of America in 1998 must not suffer the same fate."[27]

Americans, Barr continued, have the right to seek redress in the courts without government officials blocking their access. They also have the right to point out improper conduct in their leaders without being threatened by those leaders' surrogates. "When those rights are taken away, as this President has done, we must say unequivocally, 'no sir, this you cannot do,'" Barr explained. He then challenged the Committee to keep principle foremost in its deliberations:

> These are the principles our committee must vindicate. A great weight rests on our shoulders today. As we run from press conferences to meetings to the House floor, it is easy to forget our most solemn responsibility—preserving the rule of law. If we accept that this debate is about sex and politics, rather than truth and justice, we have already failed in our responsibility. Anyone who has made it their goal to hide the truth, obstruct this process or use it for political gain, should summon up whatever tattered remains of honor they have left, stand up, and walk out of this room.[28]

That last statement was typical Barr bluntness. It put the Committee Democrats on notice that, in Barr's view at least, they could not close their eyes to the grave constitutional issues before them and still remain honorable. Barr then called upon the memory of American heroes and asked the assembled Committee members whether, if those heroes could somehow stand in the committee room that day, the members "could look into those faces, and tell them it really doesn't matter that the President abused his power, lied to the American people, perjured himself, and subverted the rule of law." His characteristic bluntness returned: "Anyone who can answer yes to that question doesn't have the right to sit here today."[29]

He concluded his comments by declaring to all present that opinion polls were not to be their guide. Rather, he insisted, "it is our job as legislators to diagnose threats to our democracy and eliminate them." He worried that they had delayed too long already and that the damage to the system could be too deep to heal. He reminded them that "the step we are taking today is one I urged over a year ago." Barr wanted them to know that his lone voice crying in the wilderness had not been the voice of an extremist, but of someone who had seen the problems others had refused to see. Barr concluded, "We must move forward quickly, courageously, fairly, and, most importantly, constitutionally, along the one and only path charted for us in the Constitution: impeachment."[30]

Did he experience pressure not to continue with the impeachment process after the 1998 congressional elections showed a loss for the Republicans? "There was tremendous pressure," Barr remembers. The pressure came from the media, from the Clinton Administration, and from "operatives" that Barr believed were working for the Administration, operatives who "orchestrated improper use of files and other information" on him and other members of the Judiciary Committee. Barr considered these actions to be "obstruction of Congress."[31]

Responding to the pressures can be an added pressure in itself. Did he, at any time, consider that perhaps the effort was not really worth all the trouble? Barr, in his usual direct manner, responded, "No. To me the more pressure you get on a political issue like this, it's a pretty good sign that that's all the more reason to press forward." In other words, he considered the pressure to be an indication that the Committee was on the right track. "In my view," he continued, "people don't engage in those sorts of tactics, one, unless they have something to hide; and two, unless they have a pretty clear belief or have concluded that you are likely to win. That's why there is so much pressure." He saw a direct correlation between the high level of opposition and the chances of a successful impeachment. If there was no chance for success, why was there so much opposition?[32]

Barr reflected further on the 1998 elections and their aftermath:

> I remember having some conversations with some media people in Atlanta the evening of the election of 1998, in which it was apparent that we were going to lose seats. The media people were sort of, on one hand, gloating over the fact that to them this meant the death knell of the impeachment effort. On the other hand, they were somewhat remorseful because, of course, it's good fodder for the news. They were sort of torn. There was sort of a common wisdom or common perception right after the election of 1998 that meant that the impeachment was dead. But I think, and perhaps if the Clinton Administration had just backed away at that point and had the President not taken this in-your-face attitude, they might have been more successful in defusing the issue. But I think their cocky, aggressive attitude in the wake of the election of 1998 caused a lot of our members to say, well, maybe there is something to this; we're not going to let them push us around on this. So I think the Clinton Administration hurt itself with the attitude that it took.[33]

Some Republican Judiciary Committee members were hesitant to continue the impeachment inquiry because of the election results, says Barr. He credits Henry Hyde with keeping them on course, calling him "a tremendous unifying force" and one who manifested "tremendous leadership and a tremendous example for us to move forward. He kept people together."[34]

When the inquiry began in November, Congressman Barr, in remarks to the Committee, again challenged his colleagues to take this investigation seriously. He knew it was not going to be an easy decision to pass articles of impeachment against a sitting President. He called it "the most serious constitutional action Congress can take short of declaring war" and told the other Committee members that none of them "should take this process lightly." Neither should they rationalize the President's actions nor remain willfully ignorant, although those options would certainly tantalize. The President, he countered, should be treated no differently than anyone else. Referring undoubtedly to the Democratic side, Barr said he was saddened that many of his colleagues who had "devoted their lives to fighting inequality and ensuring equal justice for all Americans" now seemed eager to overturn all those years of struggle just to "protect a President they favor." He warned that "the precedents we set in this matter will remain part and parcel of our legal system for years to come, damaging or benefiting each of us, regardless of the political party to which we belong."[35]

Abraham, the Old Testament patriarch, was willing to sacrifice his only son, Isaac, because he realized that there were principles that were higher than even the life of one person, Barr related. The same could be said of the present impeachment situation: the principles of the Constitution were higher than the presidency of one man. "If impeaching Bill Clinton is necessary to protect our Constitution and preserve the rule of law," Barr asked, "do we have the courage to do it?" Would the Democrats on the Committee be unwilling to prosecute Ken Starr if Starr had committed perjury? Barr also reminded the members that as a Republican prosecutor, he had jailed a Republican Congressman for perjury and obstruction of justice. Then he spoke of the magnitude of the offenses in question: "They are grave offenses that strike at the heart of our legal system; the principle that all who participate in our court proceedings must tell the truth is the most fundamental underpinning of our society."[36]

Barr then attacked the Democratic strategy in the inquiry. They wanted first to know the definition of "high crimes and misdemeanors" before looking at what the President had done. He considered that approach to be "the intellectual equivalent of debating how many angels can fit on the head of a pin or trying to determine whether a tree falling in the forest makes a noise if no one is there to hear it." While those might be interesting debates, they would bear "no relationship to the real world of legal or government proceedings." The vote for impeachment did not rest with legal scholars or historians, he maintained, but with the Congress:

> In the final analysis, I don't think there are many Members of Congress who can say directly, and with a straight face, that a President can commit numerous felonies and stay in office. Either all the lofty phrases we eagerly repeat at every opportunity mean something, or they don't. Either all Americans are equal under our law, or some Americans—a New Royalty— deserve special treatment. Either truth is the most valuable commodity in our legal system, or it is worthless.
>
> Let us use this unique opportunity to shape this debate, define the issues, and lead the process, rather than continue— as so many have—to react, respond, pontificate, and run out the clock. Our Constitutional clock, now a mere 211 years old, must be kept running. Our colleagues 25 years ago, and their impeachment staff, including Hillary Rodham, recognized the importance of this, and so must we.[37]

While the hearings proceeded, Barr faced another accusation: that he was a racist because he had spoken to a group called the Council of Conservative Citizens (CCC), a white supremacist organization. The accusation emanated from Harvard Law Professor Alan Dershowitz, who had clashed with Barr publicly in the Committee hearings. On December 1, when Dershowitz was a witness against the articles of impeachment, Barr had commented that there seem to be two Americas and that the "real" America understands what perjury is. This comment outraged Dershowitz, who said that the term "real America" was a code word for racism and bigotry. Barr's reaction? "That's the silliest thing I have ever heard," a statement that might have led Dershowitz to seek proof for his contention.

The speech to the CCC had been in June 1998, in Charleston, South Carolina. Barr said that he accepted the speaking engagement on the topic of impeachment at the request of the Republican national committeeman for that state. Further, he asserted that all he knew about the organization from the material he had received was that it was a grassroots conservative group, and that if he had known some of the group's views, he would not have attended.

After the speech became public information, Barr responded to the accusations by saying that he was unequivocally and "adamantly opposed to discrimination in any way, shape, or form."[38] He also commented that the group "does harbor some very unusual views that neither I nor any member of Congress endorses." The group's national chief executive rejected Barr's assertions, stating that Barr knew very well where the organization stood on the racial issue because the official had sent copies of its magazine to Barr's office. Another CCC official noted that Barr had been present, just prior to his speech, at a panel that made those views quite clear. Barr acknowledged that he had heard the panel, and that what he heard gave him "serious pause," but since he was scheduled to speak, he decided to do so and then leave. He also denied that he had seen any material outlining the organization's racist views.[39]

To Barr, the timing of this accusation was highly suspicious. It seemed to have the imprint of the White House, which, in his view, would go to any lengths to halt the impeachment proceedings. "It's more of the scorched-earth policy of attacking members of the committee being undertaken by the administration and its defenders," he claimed. "It is no coincidence that, days before a vote on impeachment, one of President Clinton's most ardent supporters is falsely accusing me of harboring racist views."[40] The attempt to paint him as a racist was "outrageous" and, Barr insisted, based only "on a brief appearance I made before a group in South Carolina to discuss the impeachment process." Barr concluded, "There appears to be no despicable conduct the president's defenders will not stoop to in order to protect him."[41]

Barr went one step further to put the matter behind him. He wrote to the Anti-Defamation League (ADL) and to the CCC, making clear his position on race. He denounced the CCC's racist views and urged them "to be more forthright with their speakers, rather than engaging in a disingenuous effort to legitimize these outlandish views by wrongly associating elected officials, such as myself and Senate Majority Leader Trent Lott." He told the ADL that if he "had been aware white supremacist views occupied any place in the Council of Conservative Citizen's philosophy," he "would never have arranged to speak." The ADL accepted the Congressman's statement and thanked him for setting the record straight.[42]

Barr had to wage this battle while simultaneously attempting to stay focused on the impeachment inquiry. Without one reference to the controversy swirling around him, he continued to speak forthrightly at the hearings. Just prior to the Committee vote on impeachment articles, he again offered his reasons for moving forward with the impeachment.

Daniel Webster, Barr noted, had been asked one time "to name the single most important gift America had given the world." Webster answered, "The integrity of George Washington." The contrast with President Clinton was obvious.

Barr continued by asking why people from all over the world were drawn to these shores. They were seeking the uniqueness of America—a uniqueness "built on and protected by one principle: the rule of law." Unfortunately, the phrase "rule of law" had been repeated so often that it was losing its meaning. Barr reminded the Committee of the importance of this principle:

> What is the rule of law? The rule of law finds its highest and
> best embodiment in the absolute and unshakable right each

one of us has to walk into a courtroom and demand the righting of a wrong. It doesn't matter what color your skin is, what God you pray to, how large your bank account is, or what office you hold. If you are an American citizen, no one should stand between you and your access to justice.[43]

Paula Jones's "absolute and unshakable right" to demand justice had been abridged by the President. It could have been anyone else whose right had been abridged—perhaps a member of the Judiciary Committee, or even one's husband, wife, child, or neighbor. "It just happened to be Paula Jones," Barr said.[44]

Since Barr had introduced his own impeachment inquiry resolution prior to the Lewinsky matter, he returned to his initial concerns, pointing out that the case the Committee was discussing was only "a small manifestation of President Clinton's utter and complete disregard for the rule of law." The President had made a habit throughout his years in office of thwarting investigations and obstructing Congress and the courts. "It may be decades," Barr predicted, "before history reveals the vastness of his abuse of power, or the extent of the damage it has wrought." He continued,

President Clinton apparently subscribes to the same theory Richard Nixon articulated in a 1977 interview with David Frost. Nixon said, "When the president does it, that means it is not illegal." That was dead wrong then, and it is dead wrong today—wrong, that is, unless one subscribes to the principle that the president is not only above the law, but that he is the law.[45]

Abuses of power had occurred throughout American history, Barr acknowledged, from segregation, to Japanese internment camps during World War II, to Watergate. Justice did not always triumph at the time, but ultimately prevailed, allowing the rule of law to survive, staving off potential tyranny. "And in each of these cases, America was guided by the law and the Constitution, not polls or focus groups," he declared, in a not-so-oblique contrast to the practices of the Clinton Administration. Barr then made his final appeal for articles of impeachment:

> We are living in an America in which we know that felons
> are prosecuted and are not allowed to remain in office. We live
> in an America in which rights prevail, wrongs must be righted,
> and indeed, we have to stand up today, tomorrow, and forever,
> for the rule of law, the Constitution, and accountability. Vote
> articles of impeachment, which are the one tool given to use
> by our Founding Fathers, to do precisely that, in precisely this
> circumstance, with precisely this president.[46]

When the full House took up the debate, Barr contributed his share, noting that four Democrats on the Judiciary Committee had never even looked at the materials sent to the Congress by the Independent Counsel's Office. Further, only one Democrat who was not on the Committee had bothered to look at the information. What did this mean? "Apparently, most Members on the other side are not interested in the evidence," Barr concluded.[47]

When John Conyers, ranking Democrat on the Judiciary Committee, later complained that the President had been subject to "entrapment," Barr responded that there was no such thing legally as entrapment for perjury or obstruction. Addressing the Speaker, he continued,

> I would say to the distinguished ranking member on the
> Committee on the Judiciary that when President Clinton or
> any person appears before a grand jury or before a court, they
> have three—count them—and only three choices: They can tell
> the truth, they can take the fifth amendment, or they can lie.
> President Clinton chose the last option, he lied.
>
> It is a legal impossibility for somebody to be forced to lie
> before a grand jury or in court, and that is the essence of what
> entrapment is. The president chose voluntarily to tell a lie; to

conduct perjurious, misleading, and untruthful statements. He cannot be forced to do that.[48]

The acrimony that existed in this divided House became even more evident when Patrick Kennedy, nephew of President John F. Kennedy, took offense when Barr, in his speech urging Clinton's impeachment, quoted President Kennedy. Outside the House chamber, Kennedy declared to Barr, "Anyone speaking to a racist organization has no right invoking the name of my uncle." When Barr addressed Kennedy as "young man," Kennedy again took offense and retorted, "I'm a duly elected member of this body." Barr's response, "I'm impressed—I'm duly impressed," led another Democrat to pull Kennedy away from the confrontation before it could escalate further.[49] Although the House voted for articles of impeachment, the poisoned political atmosphere was going to make the Senate trial of impeachment a trial in the other sense of the word as well.

Barr in the Senate

The entire Manager team felt hampered by the Senate rules for conducting the trial. Getting live witnesses on the Senate floor was essential for the success of their endeavor, the Managers believed, yet Senators were reluctant. Grumbled Barr, in one of the Manager meetings, "Let those Republican Senators stand up in front of the public and God and tell the world that they don't think we should be allowed to prove our case. Then let them go back to their states and try to explain why."[50]

Barr himself became a potential hindrance to the Managers' case. When Senators learned that he might be making one of the main presentations, they passed along the hint that such a move might kill the case from the start. The controversies surrounding him, and his early move for an impeachment inquiry even before the Lewinsky matter became public fodder, made him anathema to nearly all Democrats. Although Hyde was loathe to do so, he informed Barr that he would like him to be the point man for responding to any trial motions filed by the White House rather than serve on the evidence team. "Henry, I'll do whatever you want me to do," Barr responded.[51] This was a clear indication that Manager Barr was willing to lay aside his personal desires for the good of the overall effort.

Barr's new task in his Senate presentation was to detail the specific incidents in which President Clinton committed perjury and obstruction of justice. He asserted at the start that showing that the President's actions fit within the parameters of these crimes would not be difficult: "It is not a problem of fitting a round peg into a square hole. Quite the contrary. We have a case here in which the fit between fact and law is as precise as the finely tuned mechanism of a Swiss watch. The evidence that President William Jefferson Clinton committed perjury and obstruction is overwhelming. These are *Pattern Offenses*."[52]

The evidence Barr presented dealt with eight areas involving President Clinton's misconduct: his submission of a false affidavit in the *Jones* case; his perjury before the grand jury about that affidavit; his agreement to use cover stories to hide his relationship with Monica Lewinsky; his statements to Betty Currie intending to influence her testimony; his obstruction regarding the subpoena for his gifts to Lewinsky; his intensification of the Lewinsky job search through Vernon Jordan; his false statements to senior aides; and his sanction of the false statements made by his attorney about the affidavit during the *Jones* deposition. In his conclusion, Barr laid out the reasons why all this was so important to the future of the nation:

> What we have before us, Senators, and Mr. Chief Justice, is really not complex. Critically important, yes. But not essentially complex. Virtually every federal or state prosecutor—and there are many such distinguished persons on this jury—has seen such cases of obstruction before in their careers, probably repeated—a pattern of obstruction of justice compounded by subsequent perjury to cover it up.
>
> The President's lawyers will almost certainly try to weave a spell of complexity over the facts of this case. They will nit-pick

the time of a call, or parse a specific word or phrase of testimony, much as the President has done. We urge you, the distinguished jurors in this case, not to be fooled. Use *your* common
sense. *Your* reason. *Your* varied and successful career experiences.
Just as any juror in any jury box anywhere in America does each
day a court is in session. Just as does the average juror, so too
have each of you sworn to decide these momentous matters
impartially. Your oath to look to the law and our majestic
Constitution demand this of you. As this great body has done
so many times in the course of our nation's history, I am confident you will neither shirk from nor cast aside that duty.

. . . We ask you to strike down these insidious cancers that eat
at our system of government and laws. Strike it down with the
Constitution so it might not fester as a gaping wound; poisoning future generations of children; poisoning our court system;
and perhaps even poisoning future generations of political leaders. Just as Members of both Houses of Congress have been
convicted and removed from office for perjury and obstruction;
and just as federal judges have been removed by you from life
tenure for perjury and obstruction, so must a president; so,
sadly, should this President.[53]

The Managers had one final opportunity to make their case prior to
the Senate vote. On February 8, Barr gave his closing arguments. He
began with a quote from Ronald Reagan, one that he trusted would
direct the Senators to their duty and the need for principle to be their
guide. Reagan had said, in 1981, that some people derided the idea that
there could be simple, straight-forward answers to a nation's problems.
Those were people, said Barr, "who decried clarity and certainty of principle, in favor of vagueness and relativism." Barr then quoted Reagan and
concluded with his own words:

"They are wrong. There are no easy answers, but there are
simple answers. We must have the courage to do what is

morally right. Winston Churchill said that 'the destiny of man is not measured by material computation. When great forces are on the move in the world, we learn we are spirits—not animals.' And he said, 'There is something going on in time and space, and beyond time and space, which, whether we like it or not, spells duty.'"

Duty. A clear, simple concept. A foundational principle. Your duty is clearly set forth in your oath; your oath to do impartial justice according to the Constitution and the law.[54]

Would an appeal to principle and duty really help at this late hour? "Many are saying," Barr told his Senate audience, "with a degree of certainty that usually comes only from ignorance, that there's nothing I or any of us can say to you today, on the eve of your deliberations, to sway your minds. I beg to differ with them. . . . There is much, in urging a vote for conviction, that can be gained by turning to, and keeping in mind, President Reagan's words to America, to do duty." [55] But just what did Reagan and Barr mean by duty? His explanation of duty targeted the preoccupation that he felt the Senate, and the country as a whole, had with polls.

Duty, Barr maintained, had to be "unclouded by relativism" and "unmarred by artificiality." Further, it had to be "untainted by polls." Barr used the example of history in his attempt to convince the Senate to ignore the polls:

> Polls played no role in the great decisions, decisive decisions that made America a nation and kept it a free and strong nation. Polls likewise played no role in the great trials of our nation's history that opened schools equally to all of America's children, or that provided due process and equal protection of the laws for all Americans, regardless of economic might or political power. . . . Your duty, which I know you recognize today, is and must be based not on polls or politics, but on law and the Constitution. In other words, principle.[56]

At this point, Barr continued to focus tenaciously on the idea of principles as the foundation for the Senators' impeachment decision. Would they reaffirm the principles of the Constitution and the laws of the land? Would those principles be taken back from the "pallid hands of pollsters and pundits, and from the swarm of theorists surrounding these proceedings"? Would the Senators, he asked, take up those principles again, in the spirit of the Founding Fathers and "other true statesmen of America's heritage"?[57]

As his argument drew to a close, Barr tried to show that the case the Managers were making could not be described legitimately as merely partisan. He spoke of an immigrant from Eritrea, currently living in Atlanta, who clearly saw the principle at stake in these proceedings:

> The man whose words I quote is a man who watches this process through the eyes of an immigrant, Mr. Seyoum Tesfaye. I have never met Mr. Tesfaye, but I have read his works. He wrote, in the *Atlanta Journal and Constitution*, just 3 days ago, on February 5th, that this impeachment process "is an example of America at its best . . . a core constitutional principle that profoundly distinguishes America from almost all other nations." He noted, without hyperbole, that this process, far from being the sorry spectacle that many of the President's defenders have tried to make it, truly "is a hallmark of representative democracy," reaffirming the principle that "no man is above the law—not even the President."
>
> These are not the words of the House Managers, though they echo ours.
>
> These are not the words of a partisan.
>
> These are the words of an immigrant—a man who came to America to study, and has stayed to work and pay taxes just as millions of us do every day . . .
>
> Obstruction of justice and perjury must not be allowed to stand. Perjury and obstruction cannot stand alongside the law and the Constitution. By your oath, you must, like it or not,

choose one over the other, up or down, guilt or acquittal. I respectfully submit on behalf of the House of Representatives and on behalf of my constituents in the Seventh District of Georgia that the evidence clearly establishes guilt and that the Constitution and laws of this land demand it.[58]

Although Barr claimed that it was not too late to sway some minds, the final tally shows that his appeal apparently swayed no one.

The Aftermath

Some people may question Bob Barr's sincerity in his drive to oust President Clinton from office, choosing instead to believe that he simply hated the President and wanted Republicans to get the upper hand. Yet those who believe that must bear the burden of proof that he was motivated solely or primarily by partisanship. His words certainly do not lend themselves to that interpretation. When Mel Steely, a history professor at the State University of West Georgia, interviewed Barr for the Georgia Political Heritage Program, he came away saying, "My impression is that Barr was very serious about it. Barr is almost single-minded on that sort of thing. He felt this wasn't right." Steely added, "People generally see him as pursuing a vendetta. I don't see it as personal. . . . It's almost a dogged insistence that what's right is right and what's wrong is wrong."[59]

Barr continues to speak of the impeachment, and he does not shy away from his involvement. In December 1999, he provided his reflections on the subject in an article that appeared in *The Hill*. After listening to his fellow Managers make their case against President Clinton, Barr concluded that historians "would treat us far better than our contemporary critics." The President had no one to blame but himself, and he was the one—not the House Managers—who made sex the central issue. Congress had done its constitutional duty and had avoided "an extra-constitutional remedy like censure." He also was gratified that the Senate followed the process through to its conclusion, "even though the result of he trial was essentially set in stone before the first gavel sounded."[60]

The "most significant untold story," according to Barr, was how the impeachment process influenced President Clinton's own actions. For instance, Barr questioned whether the President got the nation involved in military actions to take attention away from the impeachment: "Did President Clinton kill citizens of other countries and put the lives of American servicemen and civilians at risk in order to divert or minimize the negative publicity of the impeachment process?" Historians, said Barr, need to look closely at that issue. Returning again to his "principle" theme, Barr stated, "By vindicating the principle that our nation's laws apply to all Americans, and by showing the world that a majority of our country's elected representatives believe in the rule of law and accountability, the House Managers performed an invaluable service that may not be fully appreciated for years to come, but I am convinced, will be."[61]

Barr does not regret his role as a Manager, yet he admits it was not a pleasant experience: "I think a lot of Henry Hyde's critics or Bob Barr's critics think that we just salivated over the chance to do this and relished it. Not at all. It was very, very taxing. . . . I'm very proud to have participated, but it was not something that was fun in any sense whatsoever." His only regrets have to do with what was not accomplished. He maintains a wish list: "I wish we had begun sooner and looked into some different issues, such as the campaign financing scandals and the foreign monies and laundering money through labor unions. I wish we had not waited necessarily so long for the Independent Counsel's report. Even though I would have handled some of those things differently, I'm very, very proud of what we did do in the House, the Managers in particular."[62]

In Barr's opinion, the United States can learn much from this impeachment experience:

> That if you have a group of people who are steadfast and courageous and do the right thing, the country benefits. On the other hand, if we allow crime to go unpunished, if we allow high public officials to be above the law and unaccountable, then it has a very, very detrimental impact on the daily

lives of Americans in ways that a lot of people didn't even realize at the time. We hear about it, I hear about it, from school
officials all the time. Problems that they're having to deal with
with their students today because of what Bill Clinton did and
what he is perceived as having been able to get away with.

We are seeing the repercussions already, and I think they're
going to be with us for a long time. . . . It's going to take an
awful long time to get our country back where it was before
Bill Clinton. It's not going to happen in one administration, or
maybe even in two.[63]

If it does happen, Bob Barr will feel that he has played an important role
in putting the nation back on the right track.

Chapter 3 Endnotes

1 Lloyd Grove, "Clinton's Public Enemy; Even Before Monica Lewinsky, Bob Barr Had Impeachment on His Mind," *The Washington Post*, 10 February 1998, E01.

2 Congressman Bob Barr, interview by author, tape recording, Washington, DC, 29 February 2000.

3 Smudge Report; available at http://infoseek.go.com/?win=_search&sv=M6&qt=Bob+Barr&oq=&url=http%3A//smudgereport.com/stories/leastadmired.html&ti=LEAST+ADMIRED+AMERICANS&top=; accessed 12 August 2000.

4 Details of this accusation are found in chapter one, "Why Impeachment?"

5 "White House, GOP Spar Over Flynt Charges," *The Sacramento Bee*, 13 January 1999, A8.

6 Marie Cocco, "A Pro-Lifer's Deceptions Raise the Barr of Hypocrisy to New Heights," *The Star-Ledger (Newark, NJ)*, 17 January 1999, 4. Garcia also commented, "I remember someone saying to me that there was an awareness about an abortion. And I think he wanted it to be known up front."

7 Barr interview.

8 Summary Presentation of Hon. Henry Hyde, Senate Impeachment Trial of President Clinton, 16 January 1999.

9 "Vote Marks Big Milestone for Barr," *Portland Oregonian*, 13 December 1998, A12.

10 Grove, "Clinton's Public Enemy"; Congress.Org Website; available at http://infoseek.go.com/?win=_search&sv=M6&qt=Congressional+Directory&oq=&url=http%3A//congress.org/&ti=Congress.Org+-+Your+Link+to+Congress&top=; accessed 14 August 2000.

11 Southeastern Legal Foundation Website; available at http://infoseek.go.com/?win=_search&sv=M6&qt=Southeastern+Legal+Foundation&oq=&url=http%3A//www.southeasternlegal.org/&ti=Main+Page+-+Southeastern+Legal+Foundation&top=; accessed 14 August 2000.

12 "Anti-Abortionists Not Thrilled with Coverdell or Barr in Senate Race," *The Associated Press Political Service*, 2 August 1992.

13 Barr interview.

[14] Bob Barr, "Some Christmas Thoughts on Religion and Politics," Weekly Column, 24 December 1999; available at http://www.house.gov/barr/wc_122499.html; accessed 12 August 2000.

[15] Barr interview.

[16] Grove, "Clinton's Public Enemy." Souder also said, "Bob has personal relationship problems with a lot of people. I have usually gotten along with him, though everybody has their ups and downs with him. His temperament rubs a lot of people the wrong way. But after I went on two Codels [congressional delegations] with him, and I saw him smile, I warmed up to him." When told about Souder's comments, according to Grove, Barr acknowledged it with a grin and replied, "I've heard that about me. Why don't you just say I'm a nice guy and leave it at that?"

[17] David Pace, "Barr Emerges as GOP Inquisitor in Waco Hearings," *The Associated Press Political Service*, 2 August 1995.

[18] Nat Hentoff, "Barr's Other Side," *The Washington Post*, 19 January 1999, A17.

[19] Barr interview.

[20] Ibid.

[21] David Pace, "Georgia Lawmaker Files Resolution for Clinton Impeachment Inquiry," *The Associated Press Political Service*, 6 November 1997.

[22] Skip Thurman, "One Man's Impeachment Crusade," *Christian Science Monitor*, 18 November 1997, 4.

[23] Bailey Webb, "Barr Still Plans Move to Impeach Clinton," *Marietta (Georgia) Daily Journal*, 3 March 1998.

[24] "Despite Little Support, Barr Presses for Impeachment," *The Associated Press Political Service*, 13 March 1998.

[25] Statement of Congressman Bob Barr, House Judiciary Committee, 5 October 1998; available at http://www.house.gov/judiciary/barr.htm; accessed 28 April 1999.

[26] Ibid.

[27] Ibid.

[28] Ibid.

[29] Ibid.

[30] Ibid.

[31] Barr interview.

[32] Ibid.

[33] Ibid.

[34] Ibid.

[35] Remarks by Rep. Bob Barr, Hearing on the History and Background of Impeachment, 9 November 1998; available at http://www.house.gov/judiciary/22407.htm; accessed 16 April 1999.

[36] Ibid.

[37] Ibid.

[38] David Pace, "Georgia Rep. Bob Barr Charged Friday that . . . ," *The Associated Press Political Service*, 11 December 1998.

[39] Thomas B. Edsall, "Barr Rejects Views of Group He Visited; He Says He Had No Idea of Stands," *The Washington Post*, 12 December 1998, A04.

[40] Ibid.

[41] Pace, "Georgia Rep. Bob Barr Charged Friday."

[42] "Rep. Bob Barr to ADL: Council of Conservative Citizens' White Supremacy Views Are Repugnant," Anti-Defamation League Press Release, 22 December 1998.

[43] The Impeachment Hearings: Opening Statements: Bob Barr, 11 December 1998; available at http://www.washingtonpost.com/wp-srv/politics/special/clinton/stories/barrtext121198.htm; accessed 1 April 1999.

[44] Ibid.

[45] Ibid.

[46] Ibid.

[47] McLoughlin, *The Impeachment and Trial of President Clinton*, 187.

[48] Ibid., 189-90.

49 Maria Recio, "Some Fear A New House Divided: The Exchange Between Bob Barr and Patrick Kennedy Reflects Growing Resentment Between the Parties," *The Fort Worth Star-Telegram*, 19 December 1998, 20.

50 Schippers, *Sellout*, 20.

51 Baker, *The Breach*, 296.

52 Opening Statement of Hon. Bob Barr, Senate Impeachment Trial of President Clinton, 15 January 1999; available at http://www.house.gov/judiciary/barrsenate.htm; accessed 16 April 1999.

53 Ibid. The text of Barr's conclusion given in this chapter is the language of his written presentation. During his delivery of the presentation, Sen. Tom Harkin (D-IA) interrupted with an objection to Barr's use of the term "jurors" when referring to the Senate. Chief Justice Rehnquist agreed that the term was not entirely accurate and told Barr to refrain from referring to the Senators as jurors. Barr finished his talk using the term "triers of fact." McLoughlin, *The Impeachment and Trial of President Clinton*, 257-58.

54 Closing Argument of Hon. Bob Barr, Senate Impeachment Trial of President Clinton, 8 February 1999; available at http://www.house.gov/judiciary/barr0208.htm; accessed 9 February 2000.

55 Ibid.

56 Ibid.

57 Ibid.

58 Ibid.

59 Richard Whitt, "7th District Race: Team Hopes Softer Barr Image Makes Voters Smile," *The Atlanta Journal and Constitution*, 3 October 1999, 3C.

60 Bob Barr, "How History Will View the Impeachment Managers," *The Hill*, 8 December 1999; available at http://www.house.gov/barr/o_120899.html; accessed 12 August 2000.

61 Ibid.

62 Barr interview.

63 Ibid.

CHAPTER FOUR

Ed Bryant:
The Need for Accountability

"One of my guys, Sam Brownback, who's a Senator, says that Washington is a veritable candy store. Anything you want, it's up here. Many a good man and, I guess, woman now, you could say, has come up here well intended and gets in that candy and sees everything that's out there and gets pulled into some things that they shouldn't." That is Ed Bryant's assessment of the quicksand that awaits many a legislator who finds his way into the Congress. It takes a special commitment to integrity and accountability to avoid that quicksand.[1]

How can it be avoided? Bryant has his own approach. When he is in Washington, he lives in a house with other legislators—Representatives and Senators—who have chosen to be accountable to one another. Both Democrats and Republicans live in the house. They help one another to shun the "candy store" in order to maintain integrity in public office. Bryant believes that he is supposed to set an example "of the way you can be a Godly person and serve in government. In doing that," he says, "you help restore people's faith in government."[2] Bryant characterizes himself as a "born-again Christian" who feels that he has "a duty to get involved and try to influence the process" in government.[3] Getting involved with the impeachment process, hard as it was for him at times, was one of those duties that he felt he could not set aside for the sake of expediency. In his view, the public needed its faith in government restored.

Bryant also regularly attends prayer breakfasts and Bible studies on

Capitol Hill, ranging in size from dozens of members to no more than a handful. For Bryant, his faith is fully integrated into his congressional responsibilities. As he informed one reporter,

> We seemed to be turning our backs on God. Who out there is really surprised our teen-agers are getting pregnant, using drugs, when that's the message we give them? We are reaping what we and prior generations have sown. . . .
>
> I don't see this as a religious movement in Washington. I see it as an introduction of new people who reflect their districts. We are trying to change the direction of the country, and we are trying to work within the system.[4]

Working within the system was how Bryant saw his role as a House Manager. Perhaps he also saw the Clinton situation as a bad harvest resulting from what previous generations had sown.

Life Before Congress

Ed Bryant is a native West Tennessean, born in 1948 in Jackson.[5] Currently, he lives in Henderson with his wife and three sons. He left Tennessee to attend the University of Mississippi, earning a history degree in 1970, followed by a law degree in 1972. Commissioned through ROTC, Bryant entered the Army after receiving his law degree and served as an officer in the Military Intelligence Branch. As a captain, he became part of the Judge Advocate General's Corps, which, he notes, was "a very different JAG Corps" than that which is portrayed by the television program of the same name. During his stint with JAG, he participated in "a lot of court martial cases, criminal cases." He completed his tenure at West Point, teaching constitutional law to cadets. "I had great army assignments," he recalls. [6]

Upon leaving the Army, he moved back to his home state and practiced law in Jackson from 1978 to 1991 with the firm of Waldrop and Hall. His specialty was civil defense cases: "I defended people who were sued. I had been representing certain insurance companies like Allstate and Farm Bureau and people like that. Whenever their insured got sued, they sent the package to me and I defended the case, took depositions, tried cases, and those kinds of things. That was my career."[7] His experience with such cases led him to work for tort reform legislation when he later became a Congressman.

Bryant's Christian faith and political involvement merged in 1988 when he became one of the Tennessee coordinators for Pat Robertson's quest for the Republican presidential nomination. Robertson's attempt fell short, but Bryant had no trouble supporting whomever the Republican Party nominated. As he noted at the time, "Even the least conservative of the Republicans is still a long way away from the most conservative of the Democrats."[8] While this may appear to some to be a statement of partisanship, it actually deals more with belief. Bryant sought the ascendancy of the conservative philosophy of government over the liberal brand.

Private law practice converted to public service in 1991 when President Bush appointed Bryant to the post of United States Attorney for the Western District of Tennessee. He supervised an office of about twenty-eight Assistant U.S. attorneys, handling "anything from drug dealers to bank robberies to white collar crime to bankruptcy fraud, as well as all the civil cases."[9] His office prosecuted the largest mass murder case in Tennessee history; it also ranked among the best offices in prosecuting criminals who used handguns while committing crimes. Bryant targeted abuse and fraud in Medicaid, Medicare, and other health-related programs and became one of the first U.S. Attorneys to set up an investigative task force to look into the problem.[10]

One of his high-profile cases was the prosecution of Democratic Congressman Harold Ford for bank fraud. Ford, the only black Tennessee Congressman, was displeased with the jury selected to hear his case because it consisted of eleven whites and only one black. He requested a jury instead from Memphis, where there would be greater racial parity among the members. The judge rejected the request because it was based on a racial criterion. By this time, Bill Clinton had become President, and his Justice Department sided with Ford. Bryant knew that he was going to be replaced eventually, but he was so distressed over the manner in which the Clinton Justice Department under Webster Hubbell was handling this particular case that he resigned his position in 1993.[11] Ford eventually was acquitted.

Some might say this was the genesis of Bryant's "hatred" of the President. He denies any such motivation, noting that his "dealings were more with Hubbell," with whom he also dealt at the Waco hearings. Speaking for the House Managers as a whole, Bryant commented, "I don't think anybody hated the President."[12] Further evidence that indicates he did not hold a grudge is his attitude toward Harold Ford, Jr., son of the former Congressman, who is now the successor to his father in Congress. Bryant has indicated that the younger Ford is doing an outstanding job, publicly proclaiming, "Harold has really made an effort to reach out and serve in a bipartisan fashion."[13] These are not the sentiments of a partisan with a chip on his shoulder.

The Congressional Record

In 1994, with 60 percent of the popular vote, Ed Bryant became a freshman Member of Congress, joining many other new Republicans in the takeover of the House. An ardent supporter of the Contract with America platform, he was one of the original sponsors of the National Security Revitalization Act and a co-sponsor of nearly all of the crime bills that emanated from that Contract. He was particularly strong in his support of the Effective Death Penalty Act, which curtailed what he considered to be frivolous appeals filed by death-row inmates.

His seat on the Agriculture Committee put Bryant in the middle of property rights issues, arguing against burdensome rules and regulations on property owners. He also worked on reforming the food stamp program. Revealing a streak of independence, he broke from the Republican position and pushed to block the program on the Federal level, preferring instead to allow states to operate their own food assistance endeavors. Although that bid failed, it revealed a concern for federalism in wanting to shift responsibility back to the states.

Bryant focused on internal reform as well, trying to keep Congress itself in check. Previous Congresses had passed a number of bills that had exempted the Congress from the requirements of the bills, although they applied to all other citizens. Bryant voted to reverse that action; Congress, thought Bryant, needed to live up to the standards that it imposed on others. In the debate over the balanced budget amendment, he voted for the version that would have required a three-fifths supermajority for tax increases. This fiscal conservatism has manifested itself in other ways. He has been the thriftiest member of the Tennessee congressional delegation. In his first term, he spent only 77 percent of the money allotted for his congressional office expenses.[14] In 1997, he voted against a raise in his own pay, although the bill passed anyway.[15]

Bryant supports the line-item veto, but when President Clinton used it to cut military spending at Fort Campbell in Tennessee, he thought it was inappropriate. "I feel like this is a new toy that he has and he feels like he's got to play with it. This one was a mistake on his part." Why was that? Critics might say it was because this particular veto cut away some pork that Bryant supported. Not at all, he responded: "The Fort Campbell money would have paid for a new vehicle maintenance shop to replace the existing 55-year-old facility—in such bad shape it lacks running water and has gaping holes in the walls that turn it into a 'whiffle ball' in the wintertime." Fort Campbell, noted Bryant, was important to national defense because it houses the 101st unit, "which is one of the first units to be called out." He would be in favor of the line item veto getting rid of pork, he commented, "but this is definitely not pork."[16]

Ethics in government has been one of Bryant's paramount concerns. In 1996, he had to face an ethical problem within his own Party when Speaker Newt Gingrich admitted that he had violated House ethics by misusing funds. While Bryant acknowledged that he had "a little problem" with what Gingrich had done, he did not believe that the Speaker realized at the time that his actions were violating the ethics rules. "We all make judgments that aren't the best sometimes," Bryant concluded. Knowing that Democrats would accuse Republicans of hypocrisy for voting to retain Gingrich as Speaker, Bryant said that he saw a clear distinction between what Gingrich had done and the actions of former Democratic Speaker Jim Wright, who resigned for ethical violations. "This is night and day to Speaker Jim Wright," Bryant commented. Wright had benefited financially from his actions; Gingrich had not.[17] Yet Bryant did vote to reprimand Gingrich and to fine him $300,000 for his violations. He hoped his vote, and the vote of the majority of Republicans, would show the public "that despite the philosophical differences between the two parties . . . we are able to cast aside those differences."[18] Republicans could penalize members of their own Party.

Even as the Clinton impeachment possibility heightened in mid-1998, Bryant drew attention to another ethics-in-government problem: financial conflicts of interest among federal judges. *The Kansas City Star* had published a series of articles revealing that many judges were presiding over cases against companies in which the judges themselves owned stock, a practice that is forbidden by federal law. Bryant and North Carolina Republican Congressman Howard Coble led the call for remedial legislation. "If they [judges] can't do a better job of policing themselves, then maybe it's time to change the law and make sure (they do)," Bryant declared. He was astounded that the newspaper's investigation had turned up fifty-seven lawsuits in which the judge had a conflict of interest. "I just can't believe there are 57 such cases where the judges did not come clean and recuse themselves. It violates the basic tenets of American justice," he complained.[19] Soon he would be even more concerned about American justice.

The House Impeachment

As the possibility of an impeachment loomed, reporters sought Bryant's views on the subject because of his seat on the Judiciary Committee. By September 1998, he made known his concern for the institution of the presidency. It had been so damaged by President Clinton's actions, Bryant believed, "that even if he survives the Starr investigation, Americans still will wonder if they can trust him." Although he did not call for the President's resignation, he thought Clinton should consider it and ask himself if it would be good for the country to stay on. "He has lost his moral leadership, his moral authority that all of us expect the president to have," Bryant explained. "This is the person who is going to send soldiers overseas and risk getting them killed. You want a president you can believe in, who is being honest with you (when he says) 'We really have to go to war, I'm not lying to you.' Unless you have that moral authority, then you suffer and the country suffers."[20]

Recognized by both parties as someone who usually avoids "partisan squabbles," Bryant was not eager to enter the controversy. "I've consciously tried to remain out of the fray," he disclosed. "I try to stay away from the national media. There is a line you can cross by talking too much and making strong statements. You could give someone a stick to hit you over the head with if you say too much." He decided not to take advantage of all the cameras that seemed suddenly to be omnipresent.[21]

He wished to be cautious, wanting to be fair with the evidence. "There's an old saying," he recounted, "that as prosecutors, our goal is not to get convictions, but to get justice. We have to weigh this . . . with an idea of achieving justice in the end . . . The president is someone I think should be held to a higher standard of truth-telling. But on the other hand, he is the president and you have to respect that and move very carefully, given the Constitution and our history."[22]

Bryant's active involvement in the impeachment began with the October Judiciary Committee hearings on whether to open an impeachment inquiry. "For some of my colleagues in Congress," Bryant noted in his Committee statement, "the issue simply boils down to the separation of the President's private life as opposed to his work as the Chief Executive Officer of our nation." But that was not the case. "This is not a matter of private affairs," he continued. "Nor is it a question of infidelity between the President and his wife. This is also not about politics or polls or the economy." Taking aim at the partisanship that seemed to dominate in the Congress, he added, "This is not about getting more Democrats or Republicans elected in November or the possibility of a President Gore. No, this is about seeking the truth."[23]

Would the Committee achieve bipartisanship? Bryant accepted the possibility that there would be a divide between the parties in their conclusions, but he maintained the hope that they all could "conduct this inquiry in a non-partisan manner." Drawing upon his own experience as a federal prosecutor and upon the precedent set by the Rodino Committee during the Nixon impeachment, Bryant urged his colleagues not to rush such an important task by imposing timetables on the inquiry:

> We must work hard to preserve the integrity of the judicial process. We must also set an example that truth is what we seek and lying, especially under oath, is not permissible. We have impeached judges for similar offenses; some Americans are behind bars for such offenses. So, we cannot simply ignore that portion of the Rule of Law, which states that no man is above the law. . . . We must and shall resolve this matter in a fair, non-partisan manner.[24]

Bryant also was a member of the Subcommittee on the Constitution, which held hearings on the history of impeachment. These hearings took place shortly after the 1998 elections, which did not go as well for Republicans as they had hoped, although they did maintain control of both the House and Senate. As the hearings approached, Bryant stated flatly that he did not consider the election results to be a referendum on impeachment. He declared that he was not going to be swayed either by the election results or by his party affiliation; instead, he was determined to weigh all the evidence before concluding whether the President had committed perjury: "I still don't think we have all the facts. I do think it is a serious matter when the President lies under oath in a court proceeding, whether it be a grand jury or a deposition. I think he would argue that he still didn't lie. To me, if it is proven that he did lie under those circumstances, it's awfully close to an impeachable offense." He added, "In the end, I hope not only I, but the whole committee, will do the right thing regardless of the politics and the pressures."[25]

In the subcommittee hearings, Bryant led off with a Mark Twain anecdote that he thought described the situation into which President Clinton had placed himself. "As we begin this process," he related, "I am reminded, in part, of the story where a businessman, notorious for his lack of integrity, announced to Mark Twain that before the businessman died, he intended to make the pilgrimage to the Holy Land, climb Mt. Sinai and read the 10 Commandments aloud at the top. 'I have a better idea,' Twain said. 'You could stay in Boston and keep them.'" Bryant continued, "Let there be no doubt. But for the conduct of this President, his own Attorney General's invocation of the Independent Counsel statute and the U.S. Constitution itself, none of us would be here today."[26] In other words, this was not Bryant's doing, nor that of the Republicans. They were simply following the law.

As he looked toward that day's testimony from expert witnesses on impeachment, Bryant knew there would not be unanimity. There would be discussions about private and public conduct, bribery and tampering with witnesses, and perjury. Tongue in cheek, he added:

> Or, maybe today, we will find somewhere in our great Constitution, the Congressional power we've been missing over the past two centuries to reprimand or censure the President. That will come in handy the next time he vetoes the partial birth abortion bill.
>
> At the end of this day, Congress will stand alone in its duty to uphold the Constitution and judge whether, if proven, the President, the Chief Law Enforcement Officer of the land, who appoints the Attorney General and her 93 U.S. Attorneys, who himself has the Constitutional duty to see that our laws are faithfully executed, and who himself takes an oath to faithfully execute his office and defend the Constitution, commits

several federal criminal laws with the effect of abusing the office of [the] Presidency and working grave injury to the judicial branch of government.

Specifically, as Edmund Burke said in 1795, "All that is necessary for evil to triumph is for good men to do nothing."[27]

Bryant had concluded that he did not desire to be numbered among those good men who did nothing.

When the time came for opening statements prior to the Judiciary Committee vote on articles of impeachment, Bryant chose to deal first with the constitutional issues. He reminded the other Committee members that the Constitution provided only one remedy—impeachment—for government officials who had violated the public trust. "As such," he lectured, "we must not invent, for the purpose of expediency, a remedy which does not exist. The House cannot and should not be able to reprimand, censure or fine the other two branches of government. . . . Rather, members must be prepared to vote their conscience on whether or not to impeach, that is to charge the president with an impeachable offense. This is our single role in this process."[28]

Neither was impeachment part of the criminal law, Bryant reminded his audience: "It's not governed by the rules of criminal procedure or court precedence and not necessarily the rules of evidence. Impeachment is truly a unique constitutional process combining elements of the legal and political systems."[29] Even Democratic Senator Robert Byrd supported his view, Bryant noted, because Byrd had stated that an impeachable offense did not necessarily have to be an indictable offense. Obviously, Bryant was hoping that the invocation of a revered Democrat might help convince some of the Democrats on the Committee.

Although Republicans clearly attempted to follow the example set by the Nixon impeachment, Bryant expressed concern over misapplication of the Nixon precedent:

Before we begin our evaluation of the charges, let's be clear that the standard we must attain in this House before we can impeach is not, and I repeat, is not the same case as that against President Nixon in 1974.

Some intimate that the Nixon case is the magic threshold, and anything less should not be considered for impeachment. That is simply, as the president's legal team put it, a misleading statement.

Analogize this situation to the prosecutor in a law court who fails to indict the bank robber who robbed five banks because the prosecutor had previously indicted a robber of 20 banks. As for our own evaluation, our first task is to ascertain the facts. The second task is to determine if the facts support an impeachable offense.[30]

In the midst of his cataloging of the accusations against the President, Bryant bluntly questioned the perception of the Clinton legal team. He was perplexed how they could come into the Committee room "and talk about how the president can give an incomplete answer and yet still comply with the oath he takes to tell the whole truth—incomplete answer, whole truth—and give a misleading answer, yet tell nothing but the truth. And I'm still waiting for an answer how you can square those concepts." He added, "But if anybody can do it, I'm sure this president can."[31]

In his district, Bryant related, an overwhelming number of people were supporting impeachment, yet this would still be the toughest vote facing him as a Congressman. "There are no winners, and there are no losers today," he wanted the members to know. "America has truly suffered, but the facts remain that our president has placed himself before the law and the nation. In conclusion, I would join the more than 100 newspapers and numerous other Americans to call upon the president to do the right thing and the honorable thing: to resign from the office of the presidency."[32] The passage of three months had led Bryant from a reluctance to appeal for resignation to a clarion call for the President to resign.

During the floor debate in the full House, Bryant felt he had to answer the accusation that the Republicans were engaged in "organized partisan persecution," as charged by Democratic Congressman Major Owens of New York. Owens also said that no prosecutor in America would press forward with a case of perjury as was presented in the articles of impeachment.[33] Perjury, stressed Bryant, was very important in this case: "This president did not have a lapse of judgment. On many occasions, through a pattern and practice, he gave false testimony, in the grand jury, the deposition, in answering written interrogatories and to this very Congress." For someone with President Clinton's background, there could be no excuse:

> This president is a lawyer. He is a former law professor at the University of Arkansas. He is the former attorney general for the State of Arkansas, and he very well knows how important people telling the truth is in our court proceedings . . . And yet he continues to parse his words. And his own lawyers . . . say, yes, he misled, he evaded questions. He gave incomplete answers. That is their defense.[34]

If he is misleading the nation in this matter, Bryant wanted to know, is he also misleading the nation over matters of public policy? In effect, Bryant was repeating the age-old axiom as expressed by Jesus in the New Testament: "Whoever can be trusted with very little can also be trusted with much, and whoever is dishonest with very little will also be dishonest with much."[35] Enough Republicans agreed with that axiom to vote for the impeachment.

Trying in the Senate

Bryant sought the House Manager position. He had been so involved in the process on the House side that it seemed only natural to continue in the Senate. At first, when the impeachment process was just beginning, he was rather ignorant about the role of a House Manager; in fact, he was not even acquainted with the term. "As I studied more," he recalled later, "I realized the House actually sends people over there to prosecute the case, and they're called House Managers. And I said, well, if it ever gets to that point, I'd like to do that." He contacted Henry Hyde to let Hyde know of his interest, realizing, though, that "it was going to be a real effort in not only time, but, just up here in Washington how difficult things can be."[36]

He knew for sure that the Senate would be next to impossible to convince: "I probably always felt we had no chance." He continued,

Honestly, it's a political process, and those were difficult times. The House Managers, the House itself, were both being portrayed as just out of control, dominated by people out to get the President and hardcore-right people—to the political right—trying to get the President. Of course, the President's entire communications machine and organization was out there and even preceded us, destroying Kenneth Starr. Kenneth Starr could not respond ethically because, as a Special Prosecutor, he couldn't get out and defend himself. In that process, he was pretty well attacked and destroyed by the whole network. Then they came after us, and even allegations were made by some people that they were trying to investigate us individually. And then you had the guy who was the magazine guy, Larry Flynt, offering rewards for people who could find something in our backgrounds. So the polls were not good, and we weren't sure (people up here watch those polls a lot) of the Senate in terms of how they were. They didn't seem to be just really sitting there with open arms saying, "Bring that thing over here; we want to try this. It appears to be meritorious." It was like, do they really want to do this, and is there any other way to avoid this from a purely political standpoint?[37]

All the House Managers knew, based on the full House vote, that the Senate vote would, in all probability, mirror that same party line. Bryant specifically remembers one Democratic Senator who referred to the Managers' case as "a pile of dung." Bryant hoped that one or two would break ranks, particularly Robert Byrd of West Virginia, who said that they had proved their case and that there were grounds for impeachment. But when it came to a vote, Byrd did not stray from the rest of the Democrats. "I don't know what you do, you know, when you prove it," Bryant lamented. He actually saw the Democratic vote as a type of jury nullification, in which a jury acknowledges the facts of a case but decides against conviction because the members simply do not like the law. "It was almost a jury nullification there," Bryant explained, "at least, in that instance, where you say, I think he did the acts, I believe those acts are impeachable offenses, but I can't vote to kick him out, to remove the President."[38]

The Senate "trial," according to Bryant, was not like any other trial in which he had ever participated. The case was prejudged, Senators appeared on television nightly to offer their critique of the Managers' presentations, commentators were doing the same, and the public generally felt that they were extremists, with daily polls helping to foment the "extremist" perception. Knowing that the verdict in the trial probably was settled before the first word had been spoken might have been a source of discouragement for most people. Yet, Bryant's quest for justice was not hindered. "You'd think you'd just kind of give up," he said later. "It had the reverse effect on me and, I think, the rest of us. That just strengthened our resolve to go out there and do the best we could to present the strongest case in the best terms that we could."[39]

His opportunity came on January 14. After a short introduction by Henry Hyde and an overview by James Sensenbrenner, Bryant was the first Manager to present the facts of the case. His opening comments on that day revealed his rationale for being part of the Manager team. He began with a clear statement that, given a choice, he would rather not be in the well of the Senate that day:

> Permit me to say that none of us present today in these hallowed chambers relishes the task before us. But, we did not choose to be involved in that reckless misconduct, nor did we make those reasoned and calculated decisions to cover up that

misconduct which underlie this proceeding. The collision at the intersection of the President, Ms. Jones and Ms. Lewinsky was not enough to bring us together. No. Had truth been a witness at this collision and prevailed, we would not be here. But when it was not present, even under an oath to tell the truth, the whole truth and nothing but the truth in a judicial matter, the impact of our Constitution must be felt. Hence, we are together today—to do our respective duties.[40]

Truth had been the victim; President Clinton had been its abuser.

Some might object that the Managers were raising a standard of perfection in political leadership that no one can attain. Untrue, Bryant protested. He was quite aware that no one in the world today could claim perfect conduct, but, in political life, one must react properly when confronted with one's failures. Without using the name "Bill Clinton," Bryant proceeded to detail exactly what Clinton had done in his political life and how he had not responded properly to his personal failures:

A person campaigning for a political office admits wrongdoing in his past and says he will not do that again. Most people accept that commitment. He is elected. Thereafter, he repeats the wrongdoing and is confronted again. What does he do? He takes steps to cover up this wrongdoing by using his workers and friends. He lies under oath in a lawsuit which is very important to the person he is alleged to have harmed. He then takes a political poll as to whether he should tell the truth under oath. The poll indicated the voters would not forgive him for lying under oath. So he then denies the truth under oath in a federal grand jury. If this person is the President of the United States, the House of Representatives would consider articles of impeachment. It did, and voted to impeach this President.[41]

Bryant decried the slogan, "We are not electing Saints, we are electing a President." Rather, he told the Senators, "let it be said that we are electing people who are imperfect and who have made mistakes in life, but who are willing to so respect this country and the Office of the President that he or she will now lay aside their own personal shortcomings and have the inner strength to discipline themselves sufficiently that they do not break the law which they themselves are sworn to uphold."[42]

The key issue for Bryant was that the President is the nation's chief law enforcement officer; if he does not obey the laws, how can anyone respect those laws? He appoints the Attorney General, U.S. attorneys, and federal judges, who, in turn, enforce "all federal civil and criminal law in federal courthouses" throughout the country. The U.S. attorneys prosecute over 50,000 cases each year. "Through these appointments and his administration's policies," Bryant continued, "the President establishes the climate of this country for law and order. Each and every one of these 50,000 cases handled by his U.S. Attorneys is dependent upon the parties and witnesses telling the truth under oath. Equally important in these proceedings is that justice not be obstructed by tampering with witnesses and hiding evidence."[43] President Clinton seemed to fail every requirement for being the nation's chief law enforcement officer.

The Senate's aversion to live witnesses led to three videotaped depositions by the House Managers. Monica Lewinsky, Vernon Jordan, and Sidney Blumenthal were the subjects deposed; Bryant was given the responsibility for deposing Lewinsky. Yet some within the Managers' ranks were not sure about the choice. While Bryant was a respected member of the team and had good relationships with all involved, there was some concern about whether he would be tough enough on her. At least four Managers—Graham, Rogan, Barr, and McCollum— asked Hyde to consider one of them to be the questioner. Hyde, though, hoped that "Tennessee gentility . . . might extract more from the young woman."[44]

After the fact, Bryant's handling of that deposition did receive criticism from those who believed that he had been too easy on her. One analyst of the Lewinsky deposition believes she apparently learned well from the master, repeatedly foiling Bryant "not with lies but with Clintonesque verbal tricks."[45] Bryant was stung by the criticism: "Most of these comments are from people who have never given a deposition. Probably most of them can't even spell deposition. The hardest thing is to read these reviews without wanting to commit acts of violence."[46]

He defends his approach. "She was not going to change," he says in retrospect. Therefore, he had two goals in the deposition: first, to get the basic facts; second, to finish the deposition without having Lewinsky cry or get upset. Anticipating what might erroneously be said about his treatment of Lewinsky as a witness, Bryant mused, "I could envision this whole issue of thirteen angry white men who want to win too badly. I said, all she's got to do is get in there and break down." The critics, he thought, would portray him wrongly, as if "here I am trying to beat her down, get her to change her testimony. She's not going to change her testimony! I've never in my years and years of taking depositions gotten somebody to admit, even in a courtroom, 'Yeah, I lied. I told you something there in that deposition, but, yeah, I lied.'"[47]

Even the attempt to get the deposition had been criticized by the President's defenders. "When we met with her, we were just ripped apart for trying to meet with her privately to talk to her," Bryant said. "The Senators said we were trying to get in there and strongarm her and make her testify a certain way. Of course, my fifteen to twenty years of experience at that point [said] you don't ever take a deposition or use a witness . . . without talking to that witness."[48] Bryant felt Lewinsky had disliked him least of the three Managers who had met with her, so he volunteered to take her deposition:

A week later, I think it was a Sunday, I took her deposition. Of course, she had her lawyers there, plus the White House lawyers. She was well prepared, as she should have been. Her lawyers did a superb job preparing her for her deposition. She had a different attitude. It was a closed attitude that day. It was "I'm not going to talk. . . ." She wasn't volunteering information. She told us what we had to have, but she was not going to do anything where she could create some answers she had not pinned down already. She would try to shade it and help the President . . .

I'm more low-key and laid back. I'm very pleased with the way it turned out. Maybe somebody could have gone in there and attacked her, gone after her throat, but, I guarantee you, we would have been vilified, even more so. Up here, if you go against, in this instance, the President, they're going to get you one way or the other. You're either too soft or too hard. You're going to be criticized either way. I don't like being criticized for my job as an attorney. It's right up there with my character being attacked. Right behind my character is my professional ability. I didn't like that. It's like an echo chamber up here. Once somebody jumps on it, it just resounds and goes back and forth. I'm sorry I didn't make those people happy, but I think we did the right thing.[49]

The bottom line for Bryant in discussing the relationship between President Clinton and Moncia Lewinsky was that "he took advantage of her . . . I know she maybe initiated it, but he was the real adult in that situation. But he didn't behave that way."[50]

Edited versions of the depositions were shown during the Senate trial; then the President's lawyers had their opportunity to respond. As part of his rebuttal to the lawyers' arguments, Bryant simply said,

I guess if you . . . accept each and every argument of these extremely fine defense counsel that the president wasn't behind any of this, then I guess you just have to reach the conclusion that the president was the luckiest man in the world, that people would commit crimes by filing false affidavits, by hiding evidence, by going out and possibly trashing the witnesses and giving false testimony in grand jury proceedings . . . But I suggest to you that the facts of this case are really not in contest.[51]

In his closing remarks, the Congressman took a page from the Democrats by introducing poll numbers. One that had just been released showed that over 80 percent of Americans believed that President Clinton was guilty of something. Since that was the case, why did they need to talk about facts any longer? "I use that tongue in cheek because that seems to beg the question that we are also going to talk about today, and that is whether the President ought to be removed for his conduct," Bryant explained. "And one of the arguments I have heard put forward since we have been here is the fact that the polls support this President."[52] The Senate, though, commented Bryant, was not convened to follow a poll, but to determine the facts in this case.

He rebutted the opposing counsels' stated belief that the Managers "want to win too much." He was willing to take an oath to the contrary. Furthermore, this entire impeachment process, in his view, had been very different from that of President Andrew Johnson's. Bryant felt that the media was continually altering the atmosphere: "It is almost as if we are performing, we are in a play, and every day we get a review. We have been good, bad or indifferent." Neither the television nor the polls should be deciding the outcome, he argued. The people of the country, and the Senators themselves, if they focused on the polls and the media, were "going to see the trees and not the forest here and miss the big picture."[53]

In addition, Bryant expressed his concern about Congress's legacy: "We have heard this issue about, 'Well, back in my hometown, 80 percent of the people who get divorces lie about this issue.' Certainly we don't want that to be the legacy of this Congress, that we legitimate lying in divorce cases; nor would we want to have the legitimacy of this Congress that we did not support the sexual harassment laws . . . And if we send a message out on the proportionality theory that it is just about sex and you can lie about it, it will be the wrong thing to do."[54]

Neither should anyone defending the President use the economy as a reason for letting him escape the consequences of his actions, Bryant argued. He insisted that the prosperity of the country, or lack thereof, was not the issue: "Just as if the economy were bad, you wouldn't want to be able to go in there and impeach the President because it is bad, you don't want to not impeach him simply because the economy is good."

In an attempt to appeal to the Senators' respect for justice, Bryant concluded by reminding them that their vote would set the standard for future generations:

> I simply ask you, as you consider these facts and do impartial justice, that you set a standard that, if you believe the President indeed did commit either perjury or obstruction of justice or both of those, that you set that standard high for the President, for the next President, for the next generations; you set that standard high for our courts that have to deal with perjury and obstruction every day, with people who are less than the President but yet who are watching, watching very closely what we do up here. But set that standard high for the President. Don't lower our expectation in what we expect of the President. And I think if you do that, if you look high, if you set the standard high, that the right thing will be done.[55]

A Retrospective

So, in Bryant's view, how did the Senate perform? Did it set a high standard? Looking back, he is incredulous that any Senator could have hidden behind the statement that the President's actions were not impeachable offenses. Some of those very same Senators had pushed Senator Bob Packwood out of the Senate for doing much less than what President Clinton had done. Partisanship was the problem, though not on the part of the House Managers, but on the Democratic side. "I ask myself this question a lot: if this were a Republican President, would I do that [vote for impeachment]? I genuinely feel like I would have done the same thing for a Republican President. I'm not so sure objectivity was present in the House or the Senate," Bryant lamented.[56]

Yet Bryant still tries to see the positive side. He believes that, in the end, the Constitution prevailed. He does not agree with the rules the

Managers labored under in the Senate, but he is glad for a system that forced each Senator to go on record with a vote. "We lost the actual removal," he admitted. "But the President was impeached; we made our stand. We followed the Constitution, and the Constitution worked in the end. Although the result was not what I would have preferred, it worked in the end."[57]

He sometimes wonders, reflecting on all the criticism and vilification the Managers received, whether it might have been better to "have just stayed out of it and spent the Christmas holidays with my family." Nevertheless, the bottom line is that he doesn't regret doing it:

> I tell people today, I'm glad we did it. I'm glad it's over. I think it was a sorry chapter in this country's history in terms of what the President did. I don't have any regrets. . . . Nobody calls anymore. . . . I'm not wanting to make a name. I don't want to be known only because I impeached the President. . . . I'm not going to make a reputation out of this. I still feel that way. I hope I can do more than just [having] been one of the House Managers. I hope I can do other things more positive than that. Although we weren't drafted, it was kind of like being in World War II or something, where duty calls and you have to go out there and do it. I feel like I did it.[58]

When asked about whether the country will learn any lessons from this experience, Bryant again tries to be optimistic. The President won in the short term, he says, and most of the people in the vast political "middle" probably will continue to attribute the entire episode merely to politics-as-usual. Although he knows that it will not happen for some time, Bryant hopes that eventually the people will see that the House Managers did their duty in an honorable fashion:

> But I think, as the events continue to unfold, as this Administration ends and people get out of the Administration and start writing their own books, I think even I am going to

be surprised at the depths this White House had gone to. And not only just in this impeachment issue, but in other issues that are important. Issues of integrity and honesty, maybe even morality. How they've denigrated the White House itself. . . . I think as the American people are exposed to this information that will be coming out over the next years, they will see all of this and just be greatly disappointed in this Administration.[59]

One potential problem Bryant does see in the American people is the tendency to care more about economic prosperity than truth:

I hope, as a country, we're not at that point where all we care about is the prosperity, and anything goes as long as we've got money in our wallets. There was a sense during this time that that was the case—the peace and prosperity doctrine that we talk about a lot. That what somebody does on their personal level in their private life doesn't matter. I hope we never get to that point in the country. I do think that is certainly in sight now. There are other issues there in terms of a moral and spiritual awakening, a revival in this country that I think is going to be necessary at some point. But that's longer term.[60]

Chapter Four Endnotes

[1] Congressman Ed Bryant, interview by author, tape recording, Washington, DC, 29 March 2000.

[2] Ibid.

[3] Ibid.

[4] Penny Bender, "Conservative Christian Lawmakers Say Religion Has Role in Political Mission," *USA Today*, 16 December 1996.

[5] Biographical material is drawn from the following sources: Congressman Ed Bryant, TN 7th District, Biography; available at http://www.house.gov/bryant/biograph.htm; House Managers PAC; available at http://www.housemanagers2000.org/bios/bryant.htm; both accessed 22 August 2000.

[6] Bryant interview.

[7] Ibid.

[8] Tim Tanton, "Voting for Pat Robertson Is Striking a Blow for Traditional Values," *Gannett News Service*, 3 March 1988.

[9] Bryant interview.

[10] House Managers PAC.

[11] "Ford Hospitalized After Ruling," *Associated Press News Service*, 23 February 1993; Bryant interview.

[12] Bryant interview.

[13] Kriste Goad, "Rising Star of Ford Jr. Shines Bright in DC," *The (Memphis, TN) Commercial Appeal*, 9 November 1998.

[14] Penny Bender, "Rep. Bryant Runs One of the Thriftiest Offices on Capitol Hill," *Gannett News Service*, 10 July 1996.

[15] "Three of Tennessee's Eleven Members in Congress Vote for Pay Raise," *The Associated Press Political Service*, 2 October 1997.

[16] Ellen Margulies, "Bryant, Hilleary Angry About Lawmakers," *Gannett News Service*, 14 October 1997.

[17] Penny Bender, "Bryant Only Tennessee Lawmaker to Announce Support for Gingrich," *Gannett News Service*, 31 December 1996.

[18] Penny Bender, "Tennessee House Members Say Gingrich Should Pay Fine," *Gannett News Service*, 21 January 1997.

[19] Joe Stephens, "Two Seek Scrutiny of Judges' Conflicts," *The Kansas City Star*, 25 April 1998, A1.

[20] Penny Bender, "Bryant: Justice Be Served," *The Jackson (TN) Sun*, 13 September 1998.

[21] Ibid.

[22] Ibid.

[23] Statement of Congressman Ed Bryant, House Judiciary Committee, 5 October 1998; available at http://www.house.gov/judiciary/bryant.htm; accessed 28 April 1999.

[24] Ibid.

[25] James W. Brosnan, "Bryant Refocuses on Perjury Question," *The (Memphis, TN) Commercial Appeal*, 9 November 1998, A1.

[26] Remarks of Congressman Ed Bryant to the Constitution Subcommittee, Hearing on the History of Impeachment, 9 November 1998; available at http://www.house.gov/judiciary/22410.htm; accessed 16 April 1999.

[27] Ibid.

[28] The Impeachment Hearings: Opening Statements: Ed Bryant, 10 December 1998; available at http://www.washingtonpost.com/wp-srv/politics/special/clinton/stories/bryanttext121098.htm; accessed 1 April 1999.

[29] Ibid.

[30] Ibid.

[31] Ibid.

[32] Ibid.

[33] McLoughlin, *The Impeachment and Trial of President Clinton*, 181-82.

[34] Ibid., 182.

35 Luke 16:10 NIV.

36 Bryant interview.

37 Ibid.

38 Ibid.

39 Ibid.

40 Opening Statement of Hon. Ed Bryant, Senate Impeachment Trial of President Clinton, 14 January 1999; available at http://www.house.gov/judiciary/brysenate.htm; accessed 16 April 1999.

41 Ibid.

42 Ibid.

43 Ibid.

44 Baker, *The Breach*, 368.

45 William Saletan, "Monica Saves Bill: How the House Prosecutors' Star Witness Outsmarted Them," *Slate*, 9 February 1999; available at http://slate.msn.com/framegame/99-02-09/framegame.asp; accessed 22 August 2000.

46 Paul Schwartzman, "The Trial That Wasn't: The House Managers Prayed, But Didn't Have a Prayer," *New York Daily News*, 14 February 1999, 29.

47 Bryant interview.

48 Ibid.

49 Ibid.

50 Ibid.

51 McLoughlin, *The Impeachment and Trial of President Clinton*, 396.

52 Closing Argument of Hon. Ed Bryant, Senate Impeachment Trial of President Clinton, 8 February 1999; available at http://www.house.gov/judiciary/brya0208.htm; accessed 9 February 2000.

53 Ibid.

54 Ibid.

[55] Ibid.

[56] Bryant interview.

[57] Ibid.

[58] Ibid.

[59] Ibid.

[60] Ibid.

CHAPTER FIVE

Steve Buyer: Combating the Double Standard

The House of Representatives had just voted to impeach President Clinton. Congressman Steve Buyer of Indiana was returning home for the Christmas holiday with a new title: House Manager. When he arrived at the Indianapolis airport, more press accosted him than on any previous trip back to his district. "It was a peculiar walk," he remembers. "It was the same walk I had done a hundred times down the corridor of the airport. Yet now people were yelling out either applause or cheers or cussing at me . . . The reaction from people was stunning."

He got to the escalator, where a woman confronted him. "Why did you impeach my President?" she demanded. How does one respond in such a situation? Buyer looked at her and replied, "Ma'am, I didn't impeach our President." Perhaps the response confused her. Buyer relates, "Like a third-grade child, she said, 'Did, too!' I've got two kids; I knew how to handle her. I said, 'Ma'am, all we did was follow the facts, follow the law, and the President impeached himself.'"[1]

This incident illustrates how Buyer's life changed once he accepted the responsibility to help present the case against the President. He no longer could be simply one of 435 congressmen; now he was on the front lines politically and would receive some unique battle scars.

From the Heartland to the Beltway

Except for college and stints in the military, Steve Buyer has lived in Indiana all of his life. Born in Rensselaer in 1958, he now resides in Monticello with his family. He earned his BA in business administration from The Citadel in South Carolina, graduating in 1980 as a Distinguished Military Graduate. Returning to his Hoosier roots, he obtained a law degree from Valparaiso University School of Law in 1984. Buyer then served for three years in the Army in the Judge Advocate General's Corps. He was assigned as a Special Assistant to the U.S. Attorney in Virginia and stationed at Ft. Eustis. Upon leaving active service, he returned to Indiana to serve as Deputy to the Indiana Attorney General and as counsel to the Indiana Commodity and Warehouse Licensing Agency.

Buyer opened a private law practice specializing in family law in 1988, but only two years later, with a notice of three days, he was called once again into active service for Operation Desert Shield/Desert Storm in the Persian Gulf. He had only three days to shift all of his clients to other attorneys. Once in the Gulf, he was an Operational Law Judge Advocate, providing legal advice to forward-deployed combat service support units within the combat zone, as well as to the Commander of the 22nd Support Command. He then worked with the Western Enemy Prisoner of War Camp, interrogating Iraqi war prisoners and again providing legal advice, this time on international law and the Geneva Convention's treatment of prisoners of war, detained civilians, and refugees. His service during the Persian Gulf operation earned him the Bronze Star.[2]

Prior to his Gulf War experience, Buyer was active in local Republican politics. He even toyed with running for Congress in 1988 but abandoned the idea in light of the strain that it would have put on his family and private practice. But the Gulf War changed all of that. First, he realized that his family could survive with him gone for an extended period of time. Second, while on duty in the Gulf, he had written eleven installments of a "Gulf War Diary" for a local newspaper, which gave him greater name recognition in his district. Third, when he returned and began speaking to veterans' groups and Republican gatherings, people in his audiences began to urge him to run for Congress.[3]

Winning the seat was not going to be easy. Although the largely rural district typically voted Republican, a Democrat had taken advantage of a split in Republican ranks in 1986 and, with the power of incumbency, had won reelection twice. A poll in late September showed Buyer losing 34 percent to 20 percent with 49 percent still undecided.[4] A good portion of that large undecided vote came in for him, putting the seat back into the Republican column. Two years before the Contract with America and the Republican takeover of both Houses of Congress, Steve Buyer joined the Republican minority in the House of Representatives.

In the House

Buyer is a conservative, but his name does not come to mind readily when commentators, both liberal and conservative, talk about the conservative wing of the Republican Party. He has not been in the forefront of the abortion debate in the manner of Henry Hyde, for instance. Yet he is conservative, believing that the Founders of America "established a government that had its basis and bedrock principles in a religious origin." He thinks it is "very clear that the Founders of our country were not only principled men and women, but they were faith-based," and he finds it strange that the Supreme Court has pushed the nation away from its origins. "It's not freedom *from* religion," he notes, "it's freedom *of* religion." Religion, he says, should play a central role in American life and government: "Even our criminal code is based in the teachings of the Bible. It's pretty important."[5]

Since coming to Congress, Buyer has focused on responsible fiscal practices and military issues. He supported a balanced budget amendment and promoted efforts to cut back federal spending. He also took a leading role in passage of the Telecommunications Reform Act of 1995, which helped deregulate that industry. Buyer has attracted enough attention to appear on a number of news programs such as *Meet the Press*, *McLaughlin's One on One*, and *Nightline*. Most of those appearances were the result of his high-profile stances on national security and defense issues.[6]

Due to his background in the military, Buyer received positions on the House Committee on National Security and the House Committee on Veterans' Affairs. With the National Security Committee, he also serves on two key subcommittees, Military Installations and Facilities and Military Personnel, chairing the latter.[7] Maintaining his commission in the Army Reserve with the rank of major, Buyer earned a reputation as a watchdog over the health of the military, both in its readiness for combat and for the members of the military themselves. He knows that many military personnel who fought in the Persian Gulf contracted undiagnosed illnesses, and he has become their advocate.[8] This is a more personal issue for him because he also suffered from symptoms of such illnesses from his time in the Gulf.

An early critic of the use of American troops in the Balkans, Buyer took a fact-finding trip to Bosnia-Herzegovina in late 1995. He returned unconvinced that the U.S. should send troops into the area. "Having gone over there, I saw nothing that has changed my mind," he commented. "If anything, it only solidifies my opposition." He became one of the key critics of the Clinton Administration's policy, helping to pass a House resolution advising the President to avoid committing troops to the area. Once the troops were committed, his goal was to ensure that "they have a direct U.S. chain of command in the international implementation force" and "to narrow the parameters of the mission and continue pushing for an exit strategy that will minimize loss of life."[9]

Two years later, Buyer was one of eight Members of Congress to accompany the President and Bob Dole during a Christmas visit to the troops in Sarajevo and Tuzla. He did so at the request of Speaker Gingrich. Buyer supported the extension of the troops' presence that President Clinton wanted, but he pushed Congress to attach strings to the extension: if the parties involved in Bosnia did not begin to make dramatic strides toward cooperation, Buyer wanted the U.S. troops to leave. "If they do not want to succeed as a multiethnic society, then we need to get out now," he said.

Working with the Administration on this did not mean that he was now an ally of the President. "I don't like his policy. I don't like what he's done, but as a constructive critic I'm going to try to change the dynamic so we can push these people in Bosnia to either start moving on the civil implementations of the peace accord, or figure out what they want to do with their own destiny," Buyer explained.[10] Buyer's willingness to labor within the process proves that he is not an ideological prisoner, but someone who tries to work with the opposition to achieve his ultimate goals.

Another issue with which Buyer had to grapple was the accusations of sexual harassment in the military. He led a congressional task force that investigated the allegations. When he commented that only a "few bad apples" were involved in harassment at the Army Ordnance Center and School at Aberdeen, Maryland, he faced the ire of the National Organization for Women (NOW). One of NOW's vice presidents, retired Air Force lieutenant colonel Karen Johnson, called for Buyer's resignation from the task force because she questioned his impartiality, due primarily to his ongoing military status. "When a person is still in the military, as Representative Buyer is, his or her first loyalty is to the military," she declared. "To establish integrity in the process, a reporting and investigative system outside the military chain of command must be created. Representative Buyer is not an outsider."[11]

Buyer did not see it that way. He continued on the task force and pointed to some structural deficiencies that contributed to the problem. He was especially troubled by what he considered to be a widespread breakdown of the chain of command that not only allowed the abuse, but also kept women from reporting it. Funding cutbacks, he felt, had contributed to the problem because Aberdeen had 50 percent fewer drill sergeants under the Clinton Administration. The result, according to Buyer, was "fewer instructors with much more power than before. They are not as easily restrained by peers and superiors, thus creating more opportunities for criminal behavior." Another reason why females were not coming forward with their complaints might have been reductions in the number of chaplains, he suggested.[12] Buyer was not ignoring or dismissing the allegations; he was instead trying to find the root causes.

In the midst of the unfolding Clinton-Lewinsky scandal, the Congressman successfully amended the Defense Authorization Bill to require "exemplary conduct" by civilians who are part of the military chain of command. There are only two such people: the President and the Secretary of Defense. The implication was lost on no one. On the House floor, Buyer told his colleagues that he thought it was time to end the double standard. The President was not being called to account for his actions, while military personnel conducting themselves in a similar manner could face a court-martial. "I hope this language sends a loud and clear message to the administration," Buyer continued. "They are being watched. From the 18-year-old recruit to the admiral that has served for 30 years, they all look to the commander in chief to set the tone and serve as an example of high moral and ethical behavior."[13]

Buyer's disagreements with the President on policy and his abhorrence of the President's personal conduct as commander in chief might mean that the Congressman had come to the point of hatred for Clinton. At least that was the accusation leveled at him and the other House Managers. Buyer claims that there is no truth to the charge:

> This thing about the House Managers doing this because, well, look at them—they're these white Protestant . . . middle-aged men who are whacked-out right-wing extremists bent on vengeance because they hate Bill Clinton. That's the most bizarre rhetoric, but we faced that. I don't hate anyone.
>
> When I was a prosecutor before I came to Congress, or even as a defense lawyer, I hated some of the things that the people I prosecuted and the clients I defended did, but that didn't necessarily mean I hated them. We are all human and we all make mistakes and we all err. It's not for me to make that judgment. We will all face God at one point. That's not up to me. But if we're going to have the rule of law for order in our society, there has to be accountability for the consequences of one's actions. That's what this was about.[14]

For Buyer, then, the impeachment was not about hatred, but about holding the president accountable for his actions.

Impeaching the President

As the Judiciary Committee pondered the feasibility of moving ahead with an impeachment inquiry, Buyer made the following statement, which ended with an important question:

> The Office of the President of the United States is one in which is reposed a special trust with the American people. Due to his position and the powers of his office, any President is entitled to the benefit of the doubt. The President takes an oath to see that the laws are faithfully executed. If the President, as the chief law enforcement officer of the land, violates this special trust by using the powers of his high office to impede, delay, conceal evidence in, or obstruct lawsuits and investigations of wrongdoing, could that not be subversive to constitutional government, doing great prejudice to the cause of law and justice; thus, bringing injury to the people of the United States?[15]

And as a military man, the vantage point from which the Congressman saw this issue caused him to raise even more troubling questions: "Should we ask the members of our Armed Forces to accept a code of conduct that is higher for the troops than for the Commander-in-Chief? Should we accept a double standard? One for the President as Commander-in-Chief and one for the military?" Even consensual relationships between superiors and subordinates in the military are "prejudicial to good order and discipline."[16] Why would this not be the case with the civilian leader of the military? Buyer pressed for the inquiry to proceed.

Buyer had been a member of the Judiciary Committee since the Republican Revolution of 1994. After serving with Henry Hyde on the

Republican Policy Committee during his first term, he was so impressed with Hyde that he wanted to work alongside him on the Judiciary Committee. "It was a real treat to serve with Henry Hyde," he recalled. "Some people may look back in history and say, gosh, I wonder what it would have been like to have served in Congress with some of the great orators of our nation—Clay, Calhoun. I say I know what it's like because I've served with Henry Hyde." In particular, Buyer witnessed how Hyde approached problem solving and was inspired by his dedication to promoting "the greater good." [17] He hoped that the impeachment process would be one avenue toward that greater good.

By the end of the Judiciary Committee hearings on articles of impeachment, Buyer began to question the Democrats' commitment to the greater good. As he began his statement on December 10, he said he wondered, after listening to some of his colleagues on the other side, if he and they came "from the same world." What would be the consequences, he asked, if the Committee left a perjurer in the White House? It would "drive a stake in the heart of the rule of law," he answered. Buyer found the defense that the President's lawyers offered to be astounding:

> The president's lawyers give us a fantasy defense. The president's defenders would have us believe that the president's misconduct was only private and therefore not impeachable. If the president's verbal engineering prevails, then an evasive, incomplete, misleading and even maddening statement is not a lie. No one is ever really alone in the cosmos. "Is" is not a state of being. A person performing a sex act is having sexual relations, but the person receiving the sexual favor is not having sex. And a cover story is not a concocted rendition of an event with the willful intent to mislead others by lies, but instead a cover story is a simple, harmless revision of a historical event.
>
> This is neither believable, reasonable, rational nor acceptable. The president's defense is completely misguided in its interpretations, parsing and hair-splitting of words. [18]

Such verbal contortions would, according to Buyer, undermine trust, all social interactions, commerce, and "the rule of law and government itself." No future President would have to worry about perjury if twisting the English language became commonplace, he argued. The President would face no consequences, yet everyone else committing the same offense could go to jail. Again, Buyer's military perspective came to the forefront as he talked about the double standard that would be established:

> Conduct that would strip an admiral or general of his position, land a sergeant in prison or deprive an administrative nominee of a Cabinet post, is condoned for the president. Our soldiers, sailors, airmen and Marines will be bound by the high ethical code, which they should be. But our president as commander-in-chief, who has the power to send them into harm's way, can conform his conduct to a lower standard. I disagree.[19]

President Clinton's trust with the American people had been broken. He should no longer be given "the benefit of the doubt as to his actions and his judgments." Buyer, by this statement, called into question the President's use of military force, in particular. How could one trust that the use of force was a necessity for national security rather than merely a perceived necessity for the President's personal political survival? "He is now second-guessed by everyone in coffee shops all across this country," Buyer said.[20] The Congressman felt he had a duty to forestall this scenario:

> I will defend the Constitution and serve as a protector of our national heritage and help define our nation's character. I will not cave in and permit our nation to be ruled by polls, emotion, or a distortion of words by verbicide.
>
> An ancient Greek philosopher stated, "A man's character is his fate." I am saddened and disappointed that the character of President Clinton brings us to an impeachment vote for only

the third time in over 200 years. We are debating articles of impeachment today, not because of any partisan spite or overzealous prosecutor, but because of the truth about the president's own actions.[21]

Two days later, the Congressman had one more opportunity to speak before the vote. He wanted to share some of his internal struggle over the impeachment, to let his colleagues, both Republican and Democrat, know that the decision to move forward with articles of impeachment was not easy for him. "You see, I didn't sleep very well last night," he began. "So what I did about 2 a.m. this morning is I went out and took a jog. Now some may say that may not be a smart thing to do in Washington at 2 a.m., but I took a jog down the Mall." His first stop was the Korean Memorial because his father had fought in that war. Then he spent some time at the Vietnam Memorial, which reminded him of a Vietnam veteran who had taught Buyer at The Citadel. This instructor had written on the blackboard the following statement, which he demanded that the students memorize: "Those who serve their country on a distant battlefield see life in a dimension that the protected may never know." Buyer said that he had not truly understood that sentence until his own service in the Gulf War, when a close friend died. "I understand the painful tears, and I understand the horrors of war," he commented.[22] The rest of his statement is worth quoting in full:

> As I jogged back, I stopped at the Washington Monument. The Mall is beautiful at night. And then I thought about the World War II veterans—Mr. Hyde and others—a unique generation. They were truly crusaders. They fought for no bounty of their own. They left freedom in their footsteps. And then I thought about something I'd read in military history. After D-Day, they were policing up the battlefield and lying upon the battlefield was an American soldier who was dead. No one was around to hear his last words, so he wrote them on a pad. Can you imagine the frustration knowing you're about to die and

there's no one around to say your last words? I don't know what you would write, but this soldier wrote, "Tell them, when you go home, I gave this day for their tomorrow."

You see, part of my conscience is driven by my military service. I'm an individual that not only is principled, but also steeped in virtues, and I use those to guide myself through the chaos. And then I think about people all across America, about our—America's values and American character, and I wanted to put it in plain-spoken words.

So when I think about America's character and common-sense virtues, I think about honesty. What is it? Tell the truth. Be sincere. Don't deceive, mislead, or be devious, or use trickery. Don't betray a trust. Don't withhold information in relationships of trust. Don't cheat or lie to the detriment of others, nor tolerate such practice. On issues of integrity, exhibit the best in yourself. Choose the harder right over the easier wrong. Walk your talk. Show courage, commitment, and self-discipline.

On issues of promise-keeping, honor your oath and keep your word.

On issues of loyalty, stand by, support, and protect your family, your friends, your community, and your country. Don't spread rumors, lies, or distortions to harm others. You don't violate the law and ethical principles to win personal gain. And you don't ask a friend to do something wrong.

On issues of respect, you be courteous and polite. You judge all people on their merits. You be tolerant and appreciative and accepting of individual differences. You don't abuse, demean, or mistrust anyone. You don't use, manipulate, exploit, or take advantage of others. You respect the right of individuals.

On the issues of acting responsibly and being accountable, the issue is to think before you act, meaning consider the possible consequences on all people from your actions. You pursue excellence. You be reliable. Be accountable. Exercise self-control. You don't blame others for your mistakes. You set a good example for those to look up to you.

On the issue of fairness, treat all people fairly. Don't take unfair advantage of others. Don't take more than your fair share. Don't be selfish, mean, cruel, or insensitive to others.

You see, citizens all across America play by the rules, obey the laws, pull their own weight. Many do their fair share, and they do so while respecting authority.

I have been disheartened by the facts in this case. It is sad to have the occupant of the White House, an office that I respect so much, riddled with these allegations. And now I have findings of criminal misconduct and unethical behavior. We cannot expect to restore the office of the presidency by leaving a perjurious president in office.[23]

Buyer's statement was the last real argument for the articles of impeachment. He hoped that the personal appeal would help sway votes, yet, a few minutes later, not one Democrat on the Committee voted for an article of impeachment. The personal appeal to honor, integrity, and accountability made no impact.

What conclusions did Buyer reach about those Democratic colleagues? He expresses sadness when he thinks back to the impeachment hearings. He recognizes that the Judiciary Committee probably is the most divided in the House. The most liberal Democrats serve on it because of a litmus test on abortion. "You have to be 100 percent pro-choice. . . . Republicans are pro-life and they're conservative. So, by political ideology, you have this huge split," Buyer observed. During the impeachment, however, the split became even more obvious:

It's unfortunate, as we moved then into the impeachment, the division that we already had was only highlighted. I look back about my service on the Judiciary Committee during impeachment. I feel that some of my Democrat colleagues dishonored themselves during the impeachment inquiry because they did not go and spend the time and be a good student in the Ford Building to even understand the evidence. That was not relevant to them. What was relevant to them was to protect the presidency at all costs. That was their plan, that was their design, and the facts didn't matter.[24]

In other words, Buyer contends that on the Democratic side, partisanship triumphed over principle.

The more Buyer looked at the impeachment situation before him, the more it reminded him of the Richard Nixon impeachment. Where Nixon had attempted to defy the Supreme Court in turning over White House tapes, Clinton had attempted to defy the judicial system in the Paula Jones case. When the Supreme Court ruled that the case could go forward while Clinton still was in office, he tried, as Nixon did, to circumvent the Court. Both set themselves above the law. According to Buyer, President Clinton also believed that the entire episode was nothing more than politics: "In his heart, I do believe he felt that it was politically motivated against him. . . . Bill Clinton is very good at always justifying his actions upon the guilt of others. . . . He never accepts personal responsibility for anything he's ever done."

Getting the President to accept personal responsibility was going to be an enormous task. First, there was the pressure from the press and the public. Second, the Senate did not welcome the challenge. Regarding the pressure, Buyer acknowledged,

> Well, we all felt pressure. The pressure was real. But I think the greater pressure was to do the right thing, not the pressure of to stop it or, gee, this was only about sex. There was such a disinformation campaign. I was so bothered that the media who prides itself in a free society as the fourth branch of government on the accountability function had gone to sleep or had chosen really to become blind, deaf, and mute. Then

took on the advocacy role of disinformation. The media would also think that, well, I asked the tough question and I accept the answer that they gave and, therefore, I've met my responsibility. So they would print the answer—even though they knew it was a lie—and never go beyond it, never pierce the veil to seek the truth. So we're sitting there with all the evidence and that was really distasteful and very sad to see. . . . They were pawns, and they were being used by a political party here that was seeking . . . its own survival.[25]

Buyer was less critical of the public because he knew they did not have all the facts and that "they were victims of the disinformation and the propaganda that was being put out."[26] That did not make some of Buyer's encounters any more pleasant, as evidenced by the story at the beginning of this chapter where the woman accosted him at the airport. But he was able to see the general public in a different light than the press and to hold the latter to a higher accountability.

The Senate was the other obstacle. Buyer refers to what occurred in the Senate as the "so-called impeachment trial." It was not a trial, he argues. The Managers were not allowed to go beyond what was presented in the House impeachment hearings, which were analogous to a grand jury. "I think any prosecutor in America would be stunned that, after they conducted the grand jury, that they were then to take the probable cause level of threshold that they achieved in the grand jury and that's what they were required to present to the judge," Buyer argued. They could offer no live witnesses: "We were restrained and restricted only to the report that came out of the impeachment inquiry. That was the most bizarre thing of trial advocacy we had ever seen. So we knew that as soon as they crafted these rules of the proceedings, they were crafted for us to lose, not to succeed."[27]

Buyer, upon reflection, realizes now that he had been naïve about the process. He had always believed that if he could control the substance of the argument, he could win. After his experience in the Senate, he sadly concluded that those who control the procedure are the winners. "If you

give me the power to control the procedure and the process, I can manipulate it to have the outcome I want," he learned. "You can . . . squeeze the
substance out in the process. That's exactly what happened in the Senate.
So we never got to even come close to presenting our case."[28]

The realization that the rules restricted the evidence and that the
verdict probably was sealed prior to the first spoken word did dishearten
Buyer:

> I was very disappointed. Those of us who made a competent
> judgment to uphold the rule of law and to follow the
> Constitution, not for the moment, but for the ages of our coun-
> try, were then being vilified as if we were the ones who were
> doing something wrong. Yet we were never given the opportu-
> nity to present the full case. It's one of those things where if
> people could know and see the facts, they would not have
> made some of the comments they would have made at the
> water cooler or at the Rotary, or at the grocery store, or on the
> sidewalk.[29]

Yet Buyer, in step with the other Managers, pressed forward with the
evidence, despite the odds.

In the Senate

Manager Buyer's task before the Senate was to convince the Members
that the President's offenses attacked the judicial system directly, and that
they were public, not private, acts. In the midst of presenting his case, he
took aim at the President's defense strategy. If you do not have a case on
the facts—because no one truly disputed the facts—what do you do? In
Buyer's words, "you argue procedure, you attack the prosecutor, you
attempt to confuse those who sit in judgment on the laws so you don't
follow precedent." Then you play the academic card: "You go out and
obtain, from your political allies and friends in the academic world,
signatures on a letter saying that the offenses as alleged in the articles of

impeachment do not rise to the level of an impeachable offense."[30]

That is what you do if you do not have a case, argued Buyer, but the Managers had a case. They did not need to go to academicians and formulate their own letter in response that would have stated that the offenses certainly were impeachable. All that would have achieved was an academic war: "They have a letter of 400 signatures. We get a letter of 400 signatures. They add 500 to it; now they have 900. We go out and get 1,000. We chose not to do that. Do you know why? Because the House managers have the precedents of the Senate on our side."[31]

As to the presumably private nature of the President's actions, Buyer responded:

> Acts that are not crimes when committed outside the judicial realm become crimes when they enter that judicial realm. Lying to one's spouse about an extramarital affair is not a crime; it is a private matter. But telling that same lie under oath before a Federal judge, as a defendant in a civil rights sexual harassment lawsuit, is a crime against the state and is therefore a public matter.
>
> Hiding gifts given to conceal the affair is not a crime; it is a private matter. But when those gifts are part of a court-ordered subpoena in a sexual harassment lawsuit, the act of hiding the gifts becomes a crime against the state called obstruction of justice and is, therefore, a public matter. Our law has consistently recognized that perjury subverts the judicial process. It strikes at our nation's most fundamental value, the rule of law.[32]

This case dealt directly with the evidence-gathering process in a federal civil rights harassment lawsuit. If the President's lawyers were successful in making everyone believe this is merely a case about an illicit affair, Buyer maintained, then civil rights laws would be undermined. Which laws would fall next? The rights of the disabled? Voting rights? "Who will tell the hundreds of Federal judges across the nation that the evidence gathering process in these cases is now unimportant?" he wanted to know.[33]

Returning to his military theme and his concern for a double standard, Buyer then offered a hypothetical situation about a military officer nominated by the President for promotion to major. What if, he asked, an investigation into that officer revealed allegations of misconduct that mirrored the allegations against the President? Buyer points out that the officer would, of course, be held accountable for his actions:

> After a very careful review of the Uniformed Code of Military Justice, this captain . . . could be charged with article 105, false swearing, and face up to 3 years; he could be charged in article 107, false official statement, facing up to 5 years; he could be charged with article 131, perjury—probably several times—and face up to 5 years; he could be charged with article 133, conduct unbecoming an officer; he could be charged with article 134, prevent seizure of property, and face up to 1 year imprisonment; he could be charged with article 134, soliciting another to commit an offense, with a penalty of up to 5 years; he could be charged with article 134, subornation of perjury, and face confinement up to 5 years; he could be charged with article 134 again, obstructing justice, and face 5 years. I could probably come up with about four others, but I won't get into the salacious details.
>
> You see, needless to say, the Senate would insist on this hypothetical officer's removal from the promotion list. You would do that. The Service would certainly relieve him of his duties.[34]

The principle of equal justice under law, Buyer continued, has been so integral to the American system of justice that it is carved on the front of the Supreme Court building. "But 'Equal Justice Under Law' amounts to much more than a stone carving," he stressed. It is a living principle that allows Americans of any class to bring the government to their side when

they are wronged. The President of the United States violated this principle. He concluded,

> I will leave you with the words of the First President of the
> Senate, and the Second President of our Nation, John Adams.
> He said: "Facts are stubborn things; and whatever may be our
> wishes, our inclinations, or the dictates of our passions, they
> cannot alter the state of facts and evidence."
>
> I believe John Adams was right. Facts and evidence. Facts are
> stubborn things. You can color the facts. You can misrepresent
> the facts. You can hide the facts. But the truthful facts are stub-
> born; they won't go away. Like the telltale heart, they keep
> pounding, and they keep coming, and they won't go away.[35]

Buyer had one more chance to keep pounding the facts—in his final
argument on February 8. From the outset of this appeal, he pointed to
the facts. He "complimented" one of the President's lawyers, David
Kendall, "for doing your best to defend your client in the face of overwhelming facts and compelling evidence."[36] The comment apparently
hit its target as it elicited laughter from the Senators assembled. Then he
focused once again on those facts, reminding Senators that the facts were
to be the basis for their decision.

Buyer also reminded them that they were not to use the standard of
"beyond a reasonable doubt." While that would have been appropriate for
a criminal trial, it did not apply in an impeachment. They were to be
guided solely by their consciences, not by "beyond a reasonable doubt."
And he chided some of them for saying publicly that the offenses did rise
to the level of high crimes and misdemeanors, yet also publicly stating
that they would not vote for removal from office. "That desire [not to
remove from office] . . . does not square with the law, the Constitution,
and the Senate's precedents for removing Federal judges for similar
offenses . . . You cannot vindicate the rule of law by stating high crimes
and misdemeanors have occurred, but leave the President in office
subject to future prosecution after his term is expired. Without respect

for the law, the foundation of our Constitution is not secure. Without respect for the law, our freedom is at risk," he contended.[37]

One hundred eighty-two Americans were in federal prisons for perjury; another 144 were serving time for obstruction of justice and witness tampering. What, Buyer asked, can you say to those prisoners if the President gets away with his actions? Neither was it enough for the President to say he is sorry, Buyer argued, nor that his victims forgive him:

> Our prisons hold many who are truly contrite, they are sorry, they feel pain for their criminal offenses, and some whose victims have even forgiven them, others who were very popular citizens and had many friends and apologized profusely, but they were still held accountable under the law.
>
> Just like the President is acclaimed to be doing a good job, many in prison today were doing a good job in their chosen professions. None of our laws provides for good job performance, contrition, forgiveness, or popularity polls as a remedy for criminal conduct.[38]

Yet in the Senate's final judgment, minimal contrition, job performance, and popularity polls were sufficient for acquittal.

Afterthoughts

From the moment the full House voted for articles of impeachment, Steve Buyer expected to be one of the Managers. It was clear to him that Henry Hyde was going to harness all the prosecutorial experience he could muster because the case was huge. "Not for a moment did I say, gee, if asked I will decline to be a prosecutor. That never entered my mind," Buyer recounts now. He saw it in the same light as when he received the phone call for Desert Storm and was told, "Steve, it's your turn." So when he was asked to be a House Manager, he knew it was part of his duty: "When you're called upon to perform a duty, the insult would be to decline because not often does a country ever turn to you and ask. So there was never any hesitation."[39]

What about afterwards? Buyer is emphatic that he does not regret having been a Manager. He is "hopeful that history will be kind because my heart was pure and my effort was pure. I sleep very well at night." Yet he also admits to some disillusionment:

> You know, I left the Judiciary Committee a week after the trial. I did. Life is about choices. I was so bothered that the United States Senate, even Robert Byrd, who prides himself on being "the constitutional scholar," self-professed, that is, would say that what the President did was impeachable, but he would not vote to impeach. That was bizarre. You had Members that just decided that, based purely out of partisanship, they were going to defend the presidency. What happened was they weakened the country because they upset the balance of power [so] that they strengthened the presidency. . . . Instead of the proper checks and balances, a future President now can be more egregious in his breaches of the law and get away with it because he will force partisanship to defend himself. . . . These individuals chose partisanship over principle and weakened the country. I chose not to serve with individuals who dishonored themselves. I left the Committee.[40]

The entire Clinton episode, says Buyer, impacted the country negatively. An incident in his own Indiana district seemed to summarize for him the extent of that negative impact. A judge told him the story of a divorce case in his courtroom. The father had testified that the second child in the marriage was not his, but the wife denied the accusation. The judge then ordered blood tests to determine who was telling the truth, and the results revealed that the second child indeed was not the husband's. This then became an issue of perjury, and the wife was put back on the stand. As Buyer recounts, "He reads the transcript back to the wife. As the judge reads the transcript, he asked her a question: Did you sleep around on your husband? Did you sleep with any other man? And she said no. She said, well, judge, I was truthful, I was literally truthful to your question. I never slept with another man. I had sex in the back seat of a car, but I never slept with another man."[41] That approach, noted the judge, was the effect of Bill Clinton on his courtroom.

For Buyer, the lesson we can all learn from this is that one's character is important:

> But, perhaps, in the end, the greatest lesson is that your character is your fate. Bill Clinton had a particular character throughout his life, and it caught up with him. Perhaps the best lesson that we can take and ask of our teachers and parents as we pass an experience on to the next generation [is] to use this as an example of what not to do. Your character is everything. What I saw through all this [is] you can take an individual, you can strip them of their wealth, you can strip them of their clothing and place them in shackles and pillory on the public square. I can do anything to that person, but I can never, never take away their character as to who they are. Bill Clinton's became his fate.[42]

Chapter Five Endnotes

[1] Congressman Steve Buyer, interview by author, tape recording, Washington, DC, 11 April 2000.

[2] Biographical information taken from the following sources: House Managers PAC, available at http://www.housemanagers2000.com/bios/buyer.htm; Buyer Biography, available at http://www.house.gov/buyer/Biographical/buyerregularbio.htm; and Buyer Military History, available at http://www.house.gov/buyer/Biographical/buyermil.htm; all accessed 5 September 2000.

[3] John Manners, "One Family's Finances: Aiming for High Office," *Money*, 1 November 1992, 110.

[4] Ibid.

[5] Buyer interview.

[6] House Managers PAC.

[7] Buyer Military History.

[8] House Managers PAC.

[9] George Stuteville, "After Bosnian Trip, Buyer Says Opposition to Troop Plan Firmer," *The Indianapolis Star*, 5 December 1995, B04.

[10] Larry MacIntyre, "Editorial: Reluctant Buyer Aids Bosnia Plan," *The Indianapolis Star*, 7 January 1998, A10.

[11] National Organization for Women, Press Release, "NOW Calls for Resignation of U.S. Rep. Steve Buyer from Task Force Investigating Military Sexual Harassment," 19 December 1996.

[12] George Stuteville, "House Task Force Leader Is Urged to Take Seriously Harassment in Military," *The Indianapolis Star*, 13 December 1996, B01.

[13] Larry MacIntyre, "Editorial: Exemplary Conduct Required," *The Indianapolis Star*, 6 May 1998, A22.

[14] Buyer interview.

[15] Statement of Congressman Steve Buyer, House Judiciary Committee, 5 October 1998; available at http://www.house.gov/judiciary/buyer.htm; accessed 28 April 1999.

[16] Ibid.

[17] Buyer interview.

[18] The Impeachment Hearings: Opening Statements: Steve Buyer, 10 December 1998; available at http://www.washingtonpost.com/wp-srv/politics/special/clinton/stories/buyertext121098.htm; accessed 1 April 1999.

[19] Ibid.

[20] Ibid.

[21] Ibid.

[22] Statement of Congressman Steve Buyer, Judiciary Committee, 12 December 1998; available at http://www.washingtonpost.com/wp-srv/politics/special/clinton/stories/articleiv121298.htm; accessed 19 September 2000. Some slight corrections were made in accordance with the final edited transcript of the statement. None of the corrections change the meaning of the text.

[23] Ibid.

[24] Buyer interview.

[25] Ibid.

[26] Ibid.

[27] Ibid.

[28] Ibid.

[29] Ibid.

[30] Opening Statement of Hon. Stephen E. Buyer, Senate Impeachment Trial of President Clinton, 16 January 1999.

[31] Ibid.

[32] Ibid.

[33] Ibid.

[34] Ibid.

[35] Ibid.

36 Closing Argument of Hon. Stephen E. Buyer, Senate Impeachment Trial of President Clinton, 8 February 1999; available at http://www.house.gov/judiciary/buye0208.htm; accessed 9 February 2000.

37 Ibid.

38 Ibid.

39 Buyer interview.

40 Ibid.

41 Ibid.

42 Ibid.

CHAPTER SIX

Charles Canady: The Integrity of the Constitutional System

"It's a shame when politicians do things for themselves and ignore the will of the people." That was not exactly what Congressman Charles Canady expected to hear when he and his wife dined at the Olive Garden restaurant in Lakeland, Florida, on December 21, 1998. The speaker was not another customer; she was a waitress. Olive Garden trains its employees to generate warmth toward their customers, but this was more heat than warmth.

When Canady overheard her comment, he spoke to a manager, who brought the waitress to his table. Canady then requested that she speak to him directly if she had something to say about his service as a Congressman. "I think you are a Democratic turncoat or traitor who stabbed my president in the back," she said. Later reflecting on the incident, Canady recalled, "She was hostile and belligerent, and it was very bizarre. We're sitting there, and all of a sudden—boom!"

The waitress then claimed that Olive Garden had fired her, a claim the company disputed. "Number one, we never fire anyone on the spot. That is a standard operating procedure for the company," explained a company vice president. "Her opinions weren't the issue. It was her attitude toward and her berating of a customer that was at issue." It was an attitude that Canady experienced more than once throughout the impeachment ordeal, and in more venues than a public restaurant.[1]

From Democrat to Republican

Charles Canady, Jr., in 1954, was born into a Democratic household, albeit a conservative Democratic household, in Lakeland, Florida. That was at a time, he says, when it was possible to be both a Democrat and a conservative. It was a political household. Charles Canady, Sr., served as chief of staff to Florida Senator Lawton Chiles.[2] The senior Canady, commenting on his son, notes, "Since a very young age, he's been around the political process. A lot of his interests evolved from being around politicians."[3]

The other major factor in his early life was the religious emphasis in his home, in the form of Presbyterianism. He has been a regular church-goer from his earliest remembrances.[4] Yet churchgoing is not simply a ritual for him. "My religious beliefs shape my view of the whole world," he remarked. He uses his religious beliefs to fulfill his duty as a Congressman as well:

> That obviously has an impact day to day in the way I go about doing my job as a Congressman. It's a worldview question. Believing in a Creator and the other things that I believe based on my religious conviction has, in some cases, a very subtle impact, in other cases a direct impact on the way I make decisions.[5]

Canady believes that all public policy issues have a moral element. For him, answers to policy questions come from "the Christian tradition and the answers that are found there." Further, his Christian beliefs integrated early with his political interests:

> My Christian background certainly had an influence in heightening my concern about certain issues which moved me toward running for office. When I first ran for office for the state legislature, I was concerned about religious liberty and potential threats to religious liberty in this country. That's one of the things that motivated me to run for office. There are

other issues that I was concerned about. I was concerned about the life issue. My concern with religious liberty and the life issue obviously are rooted in my own religious convictions. On the issue of religious liberty, of course, my goal is to protect religious liberty for everyone, not just people with convictions similar to mine.[6]

The religious views that Canady developed provided him with a moral compass that led to strong antiabortion views. "For as long as I can remember," his father commented, "he was vehemently opposed to abortion. But he wasn't a crusader." Canady himself says that no one event or incident transformed him into an activist; rather, he mused, "It's all just a part of my overall philosophy."[7]

Canady studied political science at Haverford College, earning his BA in 1976. He followed that with a law degree from Yale in 1979. At Yale, he was a hardworking and conscientious student who continued to link politics and his religious beliefs. Classmates remember Canady as prominent in political discussions. Even some who later did not agree with the impeachment respected his involvement. As one former classmate remarked, "I'm glad that he is bringing to this whole controversy a reasoned, disciplined way to think of what impeachment is about. You have to admire a person who's willing to live according to principles, regardless of whether or not you agree with those principles."[8]

Although his father thought that the younger Canady would end up with a high-profile position in Washington, DC, or New York, Charles, Jr., chose instead to return to Lakeland, where he set up a law practice specializing in civil appellate work. As a Democrat, he lost his first race for the state legislature in 1982, then won in 1984. Winning reelection in 1986, he became one of the Democratic leaders, serving as majority whip. He also won the chairmanship of the appropriations subcommittee on criminal justice. From all outward appearances, Canady was a rising star in the Party; however, he began to feel more and more uncomfortable with the disparity between his personal views and those of the Democratic Party as a whole. As he remembers,

I had always been a conservative. The longer I served as a Democrat in public office, the more difficult it became for me to reconcile my conservative political philosophy with my party affiliation. What put me over the limit was running on the same ticket with Dukakis. Friends of mine who were not particularly political, but who know my convictions, asked me how I could run on the same ticket with Dukakis, and I didn't have a good answer for them. I said something, but I don't think it convinced them and it didn't convince me either. That started me on a process of evaluating what party I really wanted to be affiliated with.[9]

In 1989, Canady switched to the Republicans. The Florida House Speaker at the time, Democrat Jon Mills, knew that Canady was unhappy in the Democratic Party. When he switched, Mills understood: "I believe he is philosophically representing his constituency and his beliefs. I think that is a matter of principle, and I don't fault him for it."[10]

Adherence to his principles cost Canady his position in the majority party. He went from majority whip and chairman of an important subcommittee to just another member of the minority, in the process confounding colleagues who placed position and partisanship above principle. His switch moved him out of a "suite of offices with a view" and placed him "in a windowless, basement office" instead.[11] Yet he did not regret his decision: "I did it because I felt that my political philosophy was more in line with the Republican Party than the Democratic Party. It was based on a desire to be in a place where I'd be more philosophically comfortable."[12]

As a new Republican, Canady lost his bid for a state Senate seat in 1990, but two years later succeeded in his run for the national House, representing Florida's Twelfth District. One of his pledges when he ran was that he would not serve more than four terms, a pledge he kept when those terms ended in 2000. Again, for him it was a matter of principle. "First and foremost for me," he said later, "it's a matter of keeping the commitment that I made. There's a lot of cynicism about politics in this country. Some of it is quite justified, but I think sometimes it's not justified. I certainly wouldn't want to do anything in my public service that would unnecessarily add to that cynicism. . . . I know some of my constituents urged me to stay. I think most of my constituents, even those who would like for me to stay, understand that a commitment like that is important to honor."[13]

Leadership came quickly to the new Congressman. In his first term, he received a slot on the Judiciary Committee and also on the Committee's Subcommittee on the Constitution, both positions that he sought. When the Republicans took the majority in 1994, Canady then became chairman of the Constitution Subcommittee. "I . . . sought that out," he explained, "because there were some issues there, the life issue preeminently, that I thought we might have an opportunity [to act upon]. . . . I did not dream that two years later I would become the chairman of that subcommittee because I did not expect that we would be in the majority on the Republican side."[14] At the time, Henry Hyde, who appointed Canady to the chairmanship, said, "I felt he was the most competent with a conservative agenda. He is a man of great principle and integrity. He knows the law."[15]

Some of the most controversial issues passed through Canady's subcommittee. He promoted bills that advanced the social conservative wish list. One was a ban on partial–birth abortions, which was passed by Congress but vetoed by President Clinton. He also conducted hearings on a religious liberty amendment to the Constitution, a flag desecration amendment, the Defense of Marriage Act, which became law, and a bill that would do away with gender or racial quotas in federal government hiring practices. His concern with the affirmative action quota system was that it divided Americans into groups rather than treating them as individuals. "I believe that this is a system which reinforces prejudice," he explained. "We need to transcend the system and move on toward a truly color-blind system."[16]

Chairing the Constitution Subcommittee and dealing with controversial social issues was not an easy task. Canady's views made him a target for those who disagreed with him philosophically. Some ideological opponents castigated him: "All I know," charged Kate Michelman, president of the National Abortion and Reproductive Rights Action League, "is, he's one of those politicians who embraces the radical right's views on social issues and is becoming kind of a leading star in their drive to turn back the clock on personal and religious liberties." Reacting to criticism from the ideological Left, Canady notes, "We have fundamental differences. I didn't come here to please them."[17]

Yet even in disagreement, Canady earned a reputation for politeness. Democrat Congressman Barney Frank, nearly always at odds with Canady, nevertheless considered him to be a fair and decent guy. In addition, a spokesman for the liberal lobbying group, People for the American Way, acknowledged that he always allowed both sides of an issue to testify in his hearings.[18]

In 1997, Congressman Canady made a plea for the right of judges to display the Ten Commandments in their courtrooms. On the House floor, he pressed the case for the Commandments being "the foundation for the legal order in the United States and throughout western civilization." He remarked that people seemed to be confused regarding what is required by the First Amendment. It did not, he argued, "require us to drive every such document or symbol from the public square." For further proof, he noted,

> The Ten Commandments, held by Moses the Lawgiver, are found in the chamber of the U.S. Supreme Court. Moses is one of the 23 marble relief portraits of the lawgivers displayed over the gallery doors of this Chamber.
>
> Mr. Speaker, if you will look back at the back of the Chamber, you will see Moses displayed prominently looking down over this Chamber. There are several other religious symbols and items on the Capitol grounds which time does not permit me to name. In addition, we begin our daily business in this Chamber, as we did today, with prayer, either by a chaplain paid for by the House or by an invited member of the clergy . . .

Throughout this debate, I have been struck by the fact that inscribed over the Speaker are the words "In God we trust." All of the arguments that are being made that the Ten Commandments should not be displayed in a courtroom are equally applicable to the display of the motto "In God we trust" here in this Chamber.

Does "In God we trust" here mean that we are denying people religious freedom? Does it mean that the people who come into the Chamber to watch our proceedings are somehow discriminated against if they do not believe in God? Does it mean that we are threatening the Constitution? Does it mean we are undermining the Constitution or undermining religious freedom? No. It does not.

And I would like to ask any of the Members who are opposed to this resolution to state whether they wish to have these words effaced from the wall here. If they do, then maybe they would be consistent. But if they are not willing to say that, then I think they should not oppose this resolution because displaying the Ten Commandments in a courtroom does nothing more to establish a particular religion or religion in general in this country than the display of these words on the walls of this Chamber.[19]

This somewhat lengthy quote reveals Canady's respect for the roots of American law and their obvious religious connotations. Again, it is clear that, for him, politics and religion could not be separated in such an artificial fashion.

Canady's concern for constitutionality led him to oppose one particular conservative initiative. Republican Congressman Steve Largent of Oklahoma sent a bill, the Parental Rights and Responsibilities Act, to Canady's Constitution Subcommittee that Canady did not act upon because he considered it an opening for further judicial activism. Although he shared the proposed act's goals, he did not want a law that entrusts parental rights to the federal judiciary. He feared it would give the judiciary control of another aspect of people's lives. "There is uncertainty here and enormous potential for spawning litigation over a wide range of issues," he warned. "With this legislation as it is currently drafted, the uncertainties are greater than is usually the case, and are of such a magnitude that any legislator ought to pause and say, 'What are we doing? What will happen as a consequence of this?'"[20] Canady was not simply a foot soldier in the conservative army; he thought carefully about the constitutional issues involved with every piece of legislation. This overriding concern for constitutionality made him a natural for the role of House Manager.

Impeachment in the House

Accusations that the Republicans were "out to get" the President bother Congressman Canady. The accusations usually center on personal hatred of the man or on a partisan attack to remove him from office for political gain. Canady denies both motives. The pressure was the opposite within Republican ranks, he claims. Many Republicans thought it would be a mistake to impeach President Clinton because it would actually give a boost to Al Gore as the nation rallied around a new leader. Canady agreed, but that analysis did not lead him to join the ranks of the concerned. Instead, he stayed true to what he believed: "I thought it would have been wrong for us to fail to act because we might cause ourselves some political disadvantage in the next election. The issue for me was protecting the integrity of the system of justice, the integrity of the office of the Presidency, and ultimately, the integrity of our constitutional structure."[21]

What about hatred of Bill Clinton? When asked about his feelings toward Clinton, Canady points to the facts of the case, not personal feelings. Personal feelings were irrelevant. His primary concern, he said, was getting at the truth. He wanted people to judge the case based on the facts: "I think if people honestly look at the facts, they would conclude that the President committed perjury in a civil deposition, committed perjury before a grand jury, and engaged in other acts involving the obstruction of justice." The issue again was constitutional integrity:

> All the rhetoric flying around the controversy does not alter the fundamental facts related to his conduct. Any honest appraisal of the facts will lead to a conclusion that the man is guilty of those felonies. Then the question becomes what are the implications when a president who has the constitutional duty to take care that the laws be faithfully executed, steps outside that role as the preeminent defender of the rule of law and, himself, becomes an outlaw. I think that is not acceptable. For those who believe it's acceptable, I will have to say I simply disagree.[22]

When the Judiciary Committee began its hearings on whether there should be an official inquiry, Canady, in his first statement on the Committee, bemoaned the "sad train of events that has brought us to this day." But he believed the issues were significant and needed to be dealt with "expeditiously." He did not want these issues to linger for months, but neither did he want the Committee to treat them as inconsequential and brush them aside.[23]

Three days later, in the same Committee hearings, he voted to open an inquiry. He urged the Committee to follow the model for impeachment set by the Rodino Report in the Richard Nixon inquiry. He referred to that report to answer charges that the current accusations did not rise to the level of high crimes and misdemeanors. "The very report cited by the President's lawyers, which was prepared by the impeachment inquiry staff in the Nixon case, recognizes that conduct of the President which 'undermines the integrity of office' is impeachable. The unavoidable consequence of perjury and obstruction of justice by a President," Canady continued, "would be to erode respect for the office of the President. Such acts inevitably subvert the respect for the law which is essential to the well-being of our constitutional system. If perjury and obstruction of justice do not undermine the integrity of office, what offenses would?"[24] The question was rhetorical.

Canady ran unopposed in the November 1998 congressional elections and knew he would be returning regardless of the overall outcome. Yet he would have joined in the Party's suffering if the Republicans had lost their majority. That would have altered the entire course of events. No impeachment proceedings would have occurred under the Democrats. Canady himself no longer would have been chairman of the Constitution Subcommittee. Through the potential uncertainties, Canady remained on course. "I went through this whole process trying to figure out what the right thing to do was under the Constitution, trying to put the political concerns to the side," he insisted. "Obviously, politics is part of any elective body, but I really felt we had an issue here where it was a mistake to focus on the politics and who would be politically bene-fited or disadvantaged by whatever we did."[25]

The Constitution Subcommittee opened its hearings on the back-ground and history of impeachment on November 9. Canady, as chair-man, made the initial comments and explained the framework within which the subcommittee would operate. He reminded the subcommittee members that in no previous impeachment inquiry had the House adopted a fixed definition of high crimes and misdemeanors or concocted a "catalog of offenses that are impeachable." Instead, each accu-sation of misconduct always had been treated on a case-by-case basis. This reminder was to forestall Democratic efforts to list impeachable offenses before looking at the specifics of the Clinton case.

Canady did declare that the power of impeachment did not give the House "unfettered discretion" in determining impeachable offenses. It had to follow the Constitution and constitutional precedents:

> Contrary to the assertion of Gerald Ford that "an impeach-able offense is whatever a majority of the House of Representatives considers it to be at a given moment in our history," the power of the House to impeach is not an arbitrary power. Impeachment must not be a raw exercise of political power in which the House impeaches whoever it wishes for any reason it deems sufficient. Instead, it is the solemn duty of

all the members of the House in any impeachment case to exercise their judgment faithfully within the confines established by the Constitution. When an impeachment is at issue, all partisan considerations must be put aside, and members must be guided first and last by their oath to support the Constitution.[26]

Thus, his opening remarks revealed the need to abide by the Constitution and the rule of law, and not to act arbitrarily. Someone operating purely out of partisanship would not have wanted to draw attention to the "confines established by the Constitution" and would have accepted Ford's comments eagerly as advantageous for the current situation. Canady refused to endorse Ford's views, thereby putting himself at odds with a former President from his own Party. The final sentence eschews partisanship and calls upon each member to be principled according to the Constitution.

Canady concluded his opening remarks with another clarion call to fidelity to constitutional precedent:

> If the President is guilty of the offenses charged against him, he must be called to account under the Constitution for the commission of "high crimes and misdemeanors." He must be called to account for putting his selfish, personal interests ahead of his oath of office and his constitutional duty. He must be called to account for undermining the integrity of the high office entrusted to him by the people of the United States. He must be called to account for setting a dangerous example of lawlessness and corruption. He must be called to account for subverting the respect for law, which is the foundation of our Constitution.[27]

When the matter moved into the full Judiciary Committee and the vote for articles of impeachment was imminent, Canady took the opportunity to stress again the need for constitutionality. "Do we move on under the Constitution," he asked, "or do we move on by turning aside from the Constitution? Do we move on in faithfulness to our own oath to support and defend the Constitution, or do we go outside the Constitution because it seems more convenient and expedient?" The focus of his statement was that although impeachment is not convenient, it is constitutional:

> A constitution is often a most inconvenient thing. A constitution limits us when we would not be limited. It compels us to act when we would not act. But our Constitution, as all of us in this room acknowledge, is the heart and soul of the American experiment. It is the glory of the political world. And we are here today because the Constitution requires that we be here. We are here because the Constitution grants the House of Representatives the sole power of impeachment. We are here because the impeachment power is the sole constitutional means granted to Congress to deal with the misconduct of the chief executive of the United States.[28]

He noted that in other countries, these types of problems would be "quietly swept under the rug," and that while there might be some advantages to that—such as less "embarrassment, indignity and discomfort"— the cost would be too high: less respect for the rule of law and an eroded Constitution. The typical approach of practical politics, Canady continued, would be more to everyone's liking, but he could not endorse the "typical" approach:

> I don't think there's much doubt in this room that the practical political thing to do in this matter would be to ignore the facts and drop these proceedings. All our lives would be more comfortable if we had never started this impeachment inquiry. All our lives would be more comfortable if we simply ignored the facts, folded our tents and went home. That would be the politically practical thing to do.

But there are moments when constitutional duty collides with practical politics.

We on this committee, through no choice of our own, have come to such a moment. We cannot ignore the facts. The oath that we have taken to protect and defend the Constitution requires that we acknowledge the facts before us and exercise the momentous power entrusted to us under the Constitution. It is our duty to act against the misconduct of President William Jefferson Clinton within the framework established by the Constitution.[29]

In the full House debate prior to the vote that impeached the President, California Democratic Congresswoman Zoe Lofgren critiqued the Republicans for saying "that the president's dishonesty about sex has destroyed our constitutional form of government." She insisted that the people did not agree with that assessment: "They think that it is you who threaten our country by this cynical and political distortion of impeach-ment. As is generally the case, the American people have it right." Canady could not let this comment pass without a rejoinder. "The question is not whether the president has destroyed our system of government," he instructed. "We know that has not happened . . . The question is whether by his conduct he has undermined the integrity of the law; whether by his conduct he has undermined the integrity of the high office that has been entrusted to him."[30] His concerns remained consistent: the rule of law and the integrity of the presidency.

The Senate Battle

Henry Hyde wanted Canady's expertise on the Manager team. Even before the articles of impeachment had been voted on in the Judiciary Committee, he approached Canady about his availability. It was not an opportune time for the Congressman. His wife was about to have a baby—their first. The child was born on January 9th, right in the middle of preparations for the Senate trial. Canady was able to be present at the birth, but missed much of his child's first month and a half of life. So there was a personal cost. Yet he was committed, in his view, to the defense of the integrity of the constitutional system. He had to remain faithful to that commitment.

It is never easy to enter into a situation where you believe the deck already is stacked against you. That was how Canady saw the upcoming Senate trial. He thought it quite unlikely that President Clinton would be removed from office, but he kept in the back of his mind the thought that "you never know what's going to happen once the process starts in some inherently unstable kind of situation." Public opinion, though, was strong against removal, and he realized that would influence the Senators, even though the facts, not public opinion, were supposed to be the determinant. If only "some courageous Democrats in the Senate" had been willing to go against the partisan tide, Canady estimated, they might have helped shift public opinion:

> You see, public opinion is not just a one-way influence of whether you've got the mass of the people out there and it flows up to the Senate and the Senate simply reflects that. I think the Senate could have helped shape and influence public opinion. It would have taken some prominent Democrats to change it—to change the dynamic. You've gotten in what was a partisan division, in fact, and absent something that broke that dynamic, I think public opinion was going to, at least, while the trial was going on, was going to stay where it was. But nothing like that happened. I didn't really even think that anything like that would. It's always possible that some-one's conscience would take control, but that doesn't happen.[31]

Canady had some of the same complaints as the other Managers over the Senate procedures for the trial, particularly the ban on live witnesses, and he expressed his thoughts to Majority Leader Lott. Quite pointedly, he said, "You know, Senator, if this is the way you're going to operate in the Senate, maybe we'll just appear on the floor of the Senate and say we won't participate in this kangaroo court or this travesty."[32] Yet, in retrospect, Canady says he does not believe any structural changes would have produced a different result. Due to the partisan nature of the trial, he concluded that procedural changes would not have made any real difference at all.

Still, his fervor was unaffected. He felt he was on a mission to highlight the President's damaging actions—damaging to the Constitution, to the rule of law, and to the integrity of the presidential office. He did not consider these actions to be merely private. "Perjury is very much a public act," he recounted later. "When someone takes an oath in a proceeding in a lawsuit to tell the truth, and then they lie while under oath, that is a public offense. It's a crime. When someone goes before a grand jury and takes an oath and then lies, that's a public offense. When someone engages in conduct designed to obstruct justice, it's not a private matter; it's a public matter."[33]

Neither did Canady accept another variant of the argument, the distinction some were making between *official* misconduct and *private* misconduct. Any time a president violates the law, Canady believed, he is breaching his official duties because he is the chief executive of the nation:

> What do you do if the President commits murder? Are we going to allow a murderer? Let's say he murders someone just in a drunken brawl. . . . I mean, yeah, it's private conduct. He doesn't send the FBI to murder someone, but he gets in a drunken brawl with someone and murders that person in the course of this. Under this distinction that some have purported to apply, because it's not official misconduct, the President would be allowed to remain in office. I suggest that's absurd.[34]

In his opening statement to the Senate, Canady tried to stress the absurdity of allowing this particular President to remain in office, but without using the word "absurd." He referred to the first impeachment trial conducted by the Senate, which occurred in 1799. At that trial, an argument made in defense of the Senator who was facing charges was that impeachment could be used only with respect to official offenses. One of the House Managers at that time, Robert Goodloe Harper of South Carolina, had responded by asking, "Suppose a Judge of the United States to commit a theft or perjury; would the learned counsel say that he should not be impeached for it? If so, he must remain in office with all his infamy." Since one of the charges against President Clinton was perjury, the exact issue raised by the earlier Manager, Canady raised the question again:

> The argument of the President's lawyers that no criminal act by the President subjects him to removal from office unless the crime involves the abuse of his power is an argument entailing consequences which—upon a moment's reflection—this body should be unwilling to accept.
>
> Would a President guilty of murder be immune from the constitutional process of impeachment and removal so long as his crime involved no misuse of official power? Would a President guilty of sexual assault or child molesting remain secure in office because his crime did not involve an abuse of office?[35]

He hoped his examples would make the absurdity of the claim painfully obvious.

The President's lawyers even said that tax fraud, if committed by a President, would not be sufficient to remove him from office. They attempted to show that this was the conclusion drawn by the Rodino-led Judiciary Committee during the Nixon inquiry. Not so, said Canady. The only reason tax fraud was rejected as an article of impeachment against President Nixon was because there was insufficient evidence for that particular charge; it had nothing to do with the nature of the crime not being allowed as grounds for impeachment. In fact, in the subsequent impeachment of Judge Harry Claiborne, the Senate had removed him from office for filing false income tax returns. The irony is that then-Senator Al Gore had supported this action, stating, "It is incumbent upon the Senate to fulfill its constitutional responsibility and strip this man of his title. An individual who has knowingly falsified tax returns has no business receiving a salary from the tax dollars of honest citizens."[36] With that quote, Canady revealed the difference between the Vice President's views in 1986 and his "new perspective" in the presidential impeachment. He did not have to say that partisanship had trumped principle—it was self-evident.

Canady then turned to another argument used by the defense: while a President may be removed for "*misusing* governmental power," he cannot be removed for "*corruptly interfering* with the proper exercise of governmental power." Such an argument, contended Canady, "exalts form over substance." He continued,

> It unduly focuses on the manner in which wrongdoing is carried out and neglects to consider the *actual impact* of that wrongdoing on our system of government. Whether the President misuses the power vested in him as President or wrongfully interferes with the proper exercise of the power vested in other parts of the government, the result is the same: the due functioning of our system of government is in some respect hindered or defeated.
>
> There is no principled basis for contending that a President who *interferes with the proper exercise* of governmental power—as he clearly does when he commits perjury and obstruction of justice—is constitutionally less blameworthy than a President who misuses the power of his office. A President who lies to a federal grand jury in order to impede the investigation of crimes is no less culpable than a President who wrongfully orders a prosecutor to suspend an investigation of crimes that have been committed. The purpose and effect of the personal perjury and of the wrongful official command are the same: the laws of the United States are not properly enforced.[37]

The removal power, Canady continued, should not be viewed in negative terms. It is not employed merely to stop the government from crumbling. It is not "brought into play only when the immediate destruction of our institutions is threatened." Instead, it should be seen "as a positive grant of authority," giving the Senate the ability "to preserve, protect and strengthen" the constitutional system. "It is a power that has the positive purpose of maintaining the health and well-being of our system of government," Canady explained. And it should not be withheld simply because of the popularity of a certain President. Canady was direct: "Such a view finds no support in the Constitution."[38]

A popular President who commits impeachable offenses is actually more dangerous than an unpopular one, the Manager stressed. Canady then reminded his hearers that the Senate, in particular, was set up to act for the long-term good of the nation rather than follow public opinion or allow short-term political considerations to determine its course. He lauded the Senate that voted against Andrew Johnson's removal. President Johnson was an unpopular President, but that did not determine the result: "Those who refused to use presidential popularity as their guide are hailed as great statesmen and heroes. Those Senators who then stood against the tide of public sentiment, today are acknowledged as champions of constitutional government." He concluded, "A popular President guilty of high crimes and misdemeanors should no more remain in office than an unpopular President innocent of wrongdoing should be removed from office. Under the standards of the Constitution, popularity is not a sufficient guide."[39]

Responding to the argument that the question of the President's guilt or innocence should be left to the courts after he leaves office, Canady tried to convince the Senate that it should take its constitutional responsibility seriously:

> In the case before it now, the Senate must decide if William Jefferson Clinton as President will be "subjected to the same rules of conduct that are commands to the citizens." It is no answer that he *may one day* after leaving office *perhaps* be

called to account in a criminal court proceeding somewhere. Justice *delayed* is justice *denied*. Because he has taken and violated the oath as President, William Jefferson Clinton is answerable for his crimes to the Senate *here* and *now*.

Will he as President be vindicated by the Senate in the face of crimes for which other citizens are adjudicated felons and sent to prison? Or will this Senate acting in accordance with the provisions of the Constitution bring him as President into submission to the commands of the law? Will the Senate give force to the constitutional provision for impeachment and removal which Justice Story said "compels the chief magistrate, as well as the humblest citizen, to bend to the majesty of the laws"? . . .

By his conduct President William Jefferson Clinton has set an example the Senate cannot ignore. By his example he has set a dangerous and subversive standard of conduct. His calculated and stubbornly persistent misconduct while serving as President of the United States . . . has set a pernicious example of lawlessness—an example which by its very nature subverts respect for the law. His perverse example has the inevitable effect of undermining the integrity of both the office of President and the administration of justice.[40]

On February 8, in his closing argument, Canady, while reiterating points he already had made, strove to emphasize the culpability of the President. The President's lawyers had said that mitigating factors should be considered. Commenting on the greatest mitigating factor, they said, "We have all heard this 1,000 times. It goes like this: The offenses are not sufficiently serious because it is all about sex." Therefore, said the President's defense, he "was simply trying to avoid personal embarrassment in committing these crimes."[41]

Canady freely acknowledged that people naturally lie to avoid personal embarrassment. People always try to extricate themselves from embarrassing situations. Then he pointed again to President Nixon: his actions also could be excused under that rationale. He simply wanted to avoid embarrassing revelations. But, asked Canady, "Did that reduce his culpability? Did that lessen the seriousness of his misconduct? The answer is obvious. It did not. The desire to avoid embarrassment is not a mitigating factor." Neither could the defense use the argument that this is all about sex without making sexual harassment laws meaningless: "Any defendant guilty of sexual harassment would obviously have an incentive to lie about any sexual misconduct that may have occurred. But no one—no one—has the license to lie under oath about sex in a sexual harassment case or a divorce case or any other case."[42]

As Canady neared the end of his final comments, he hoped to underscore the premeditated nature of President Clinton's actions. "The conduct of the President was calculated and sustained," he argued. Canady stresses his point further:

> His subtle and determined purpose was corrupt. It was corrupt from start to finish. He knew exactly what he was doing. He knew that it was in violation of the criminal law. He knew that people could go to prison for doing such things. He knew that it was contrary to his oath of office. He knew that it was incompatible with his constitutional duty as President. And he most certainly knew that it was a very serious matter. I am sure he believed he could get away with it, but I am equally sure that he knew just how serious it would be if the truth were known and understood.[43]

When the prosecutors went down to the White House to get President Clinton's grand jury testimony, Canady noted, "he lied to a Federal grand jury. He sat there in the White House, and he put on his most sincere face. He swore to God to tell the truth, and then he lied. He planned to lie, and he executed his plan because he believed it was in his personal and political interests to lie. Never mind the oath of office. Never mind the constitutional duty. Never mind that he solemnly swore to God to tell the truth." Canady concluded his plea with an appeal to the Founders:

Those who established our Constitution would have understood the seriousness of the misconduct of William Jefferson Clinton. They would have understood that it was the President who has shown contempt for the Constitution, not the managers from the House of Representatives. They would have understood the seriousness of the example of lawlessness he has set. They would have understood the seriousness of the contempt for the law the President's conduct has caused. They would have understood the seriousness of the damage the President has done to the integrity of his high office. Those wise statesmen who established our form of government would have understood the seriousness of the harm President Clinton has done to the cause of justice and constitutional government. They would have understood that a President who does such things should not remain in office with his crimes.[44]

The Founders of 1787 would have understood; the Senate of 1999 did not.

After the Trial

Canady is convinced that there would have been no impeachment trial if President Clinton had confessed fully and cooperated with the investigation. The Judiciary Committee would not have brought forward articles of impeachment. "I don't think there would even have been serious consideration of articles of impeachment if the President had simply, having been caught, fessed up," he deduced afterward. Yet Canady has no regrets about his involvement. His only regret is for the country: "I regret that the whole episode occurred. I think it would have, obviously, been preferable for the country and for all concerned if the President had never committed those offenses and we had never been put in the position of having to consider impeaching him."[45]

He also was disturbed by the treatment of people such as Henry Hyde.

The impeachment process took a heavy toll: "When your motives are attacked, that's very difficult, but particularly for someone like Mr. Hyde to be portrayed as a hater. That's got to be very difficult because that is just the antithesis of Henry Hyde. . . . It is so contrary to his character. Henry Hyde is a person who really wants to work with everyone, respects everyone, shows everyone respect and courtesy. He is the most unhateful person that I know. It's just not his nature. . . . Of course, he bore the brunt of all this in a way that none of the other Managers did. He was the leader, and he took more of the criticism and the attacks and dredging up his past history in a way that others did not endure."[46]

Canady hopes that the people of the country will understand that the Presidency should be held to a standard of integrity. The House did its part in trying to establish that standard, and fifty members of the Senate agreed with the standard that was set. Canady hopes that President Clinton's behavior and the consequences of his behavior serve as a caution to future presidents:

> I would hope that future presidents would understand that they cannot obstruct justice and commit perjury while they are in the office of the President. That's inconsistent with the office, and there will be consequences.
>
> Some people will say, well, he escaped consequences. But he did not escape all consequences. He did escape the consequence of being removed from office. But he has been impeached, and he is impeached forever. That will always be a mark on the Presidency of William Jefferson Clinton; there is no escaping it. I think that will serve as a warning to future presidents who would consider engaging in such misconduct.[47]

Chapter 6 Endnotes

[1] The Olive Garden episode appeared in the following: Carolee Westcott, "Waitress Says Giving Congressman Her Two Cents Cost Her the Job," *The Washington Post*, 27 December 1998; "Olive Garden Says Waitress Who Berated Congressman Still Has Job," *The Associated Press*, 29 December 1998.

[2] Ellen Debenport, "He's Politely Party Line," *St. Petersburg Times*, 4 July 1995, 1A.

[3] Edwin Chen, "A Leading Player in the Move to the Right," *Los Angeles Times*, 8 August 1995, E1.

[4] Ibid.

[5] Congressman Charles Canady, interview by author, tape recording, Washington, DC, 28 March 2000.

[6] Ibid.

[7] Chen, "Leading Player."

[8] Perry Bacon, "Yalie in Spotlight as Impeachment Manager," *Yale Daily News*, 26 January 1999.

[9] Canady interview.

[10] Debenport, "Politely Party Line."

[11] Chen, "Leading Player."

[12] Canady interview.

[13] Ibid.

[14] Ibid.

[15] Debenport, "Politely Party Line."

[16] Ibid.

[17] Chen, "Leading Player."

[18] Debenport, "Politely Party Line."

[19] Charles Canady, Comments Regarding the Ten Commandments, *Congressional Record*, 4 March 1997.

[20] Jessica Gavora, "Courts Cast a Pall over Parental-Rights Bill," *Policy Review* 82 (March-April 1997): 12.

[21] Canady interview.

[22] Ibid.

[23] Statement of Congressman Charles Canady, House Judiciary Committee, 5 October 1998; available at http://www.house.gov/judiciary/canady.htm; accessed 28 April 1999.

[24] Statement of Congressman Charles T. Canady, House Judiciary Committee, 8 October 1998; available at http://www.house.gov/judiciary/canadyfl.htm; accessed 28 April 1999.

[25] Canady interview.

[26] Statement of Chairman Charles T. Canady, Subcommittee on the Constitution, Hearings on the Background and History of Impeachment, 9 November 1998; available at http://www.house.gov/judiciary/22406.htm; accessed 16 April 1999.

[27] Ibid.

[28] The Impeachment Hearings: Opening Statements: Charles Canady, 10 December 1998; available at http://www.washingtonpost.com/wp-srv/politics/special/clinton/stories/canadytext121098.htm; accessed 1 April 1999.

[29] Ibid.

[30] McLaughlin, *The Impeachment and Trial of President Clinton*, 180-81.

[31] Canady interview.

[32] Schippers, *Sellout*, 10-11.

[33] Canady interview.

[34] Ibid.

[35] Opening Statement of Hon. Charles Canady, Senate Impeachment Trial of President Clinton, 16 January 1999; available at http://www.house.gov/judiciary/canady0116.htm; accessed 12 April 1999.

[36] Ibid.

[37] Ibid.

[38] Ibid.

[39] Ibid.

[40] Ibid.

[41] Closing Argument of Hon. Charles Canady, Senate Impeachment Trial of President Clinton, 8 February 1999; available at http://www.house.gov/judiciary/cana0208.htm; accessed 9 February 2000.

[42] Ibid.

[43] Ibid.

[44] Ibid.

[45] Canady interview.

[46] Ibid.

[47] Ibid.

CHAPTER SEVEN

Chris Cannon:
Justice Denied

The House had voted articles of impeachment. The House Managers, planning their strategy in the tension-filled interregnum between the House vote and the Senate trial, felt the heat from those who did not want a genuine removal effort. One evening, Chris Cannon of Utah received back-to-back phone calls from two Senators. One of the calls, Cannon remembers, was terse and direct: "You're going to do the following. We're going to have a 24-hour period. You're going to make a presentation. There's not going to be any trial. You're not going to have any witnesses. And that's what you're going to do." Cannon's response was just as direct: "No, Senator. I don't think that's what we're going to do." This did not please the Senator, who ended the call with what sounded like a threat: "Well, you're going to do that or you're going to have a problem."

The other call was not as direct at first, and it certainly was not terse because it continued for forty-five minutes:

> Of course it started out, I hope you'll do this. Then it was, you're going to do this. Then it was, I'll beat the hell out of you if you don't do this. And then it was profanity and vulgarity, and it kept going, and I realized this guy was going to talk to me until I capitulate. And so I said, "You know, Senator, my staff has been with me while I've been talking on the phone

for the last forty-five minutes. They are working their hearts out. They haven't had dinner. I thought this would be a two-minute Senatorial conversation and it's been forty-five minutes. I've got to go." And it was "Chris, don't you hang up; don't you leave." I said, "Senator, I've got to go." So I hung up. Now, that was pressure that we clearly felt. As it turns out, they went to have dinner, and I had to go to a meeting without dinner—and I was low on sugar and feeling very cranky—to a meeting of the House Managers. I walked in and the thirteen Members were there and I said, "Henry, you just need to understand about two phone calls I got." I explained those phone calls. Henry looked up and said has anybody else had those phone calls? Three guys nodded their heads.[1]

The pressure was on to "take a dive," but Chris Cannon rejected that advice. By the time the Senate portion of the impeachment ended, Congressman Cannon knew he could not say that the House Managers had won—President Clinton remained *President* Clinton. Yet he felt a certain satisfaction. "I think we won the trial," he insisted, "because the masterful people who made the presentations—and that was not my main burden—did a great job of convincing people that we have a liar and a perjurer and an obstructer of justice for President."[2] All that was lacking was a conviction.

The Road to Manager

Chris Cannon is quintessential Utah. Born in Salt Lake City in 1950, he received both his bachelor of science degree and law degree from Brigham Young University. A lifelong Mormon, Cannon now appreciates the mixture of religious and academic instruction he received from his university education. At the time, he was not interested in the religion classes, but later he recognized their significance. Mormons, he believes, share "common themes" with the Methodists, Baptists, and other

Christian denominations—themes that were not common in Europe, such as independence and self-reliance. "And Mormonism is certainly in that tradition of praying like everything depended on God, working like everything depended on yourself," he adds.[3]

Cannon sees no separation between religious beliefs and politics. "Nowhere," he says, "do you have that problem of the divine and the true come more into juxtaposition with reality than in politics, where we don't have the opportunity very often to have a pure bill that is right, correct, and divine." He believes firmly that the Constitution established by the Founders was divinely inspired even though it came into being only "after a lot of intense and painful and aggressive and, in some cases, harsh debate." Convinced that God had His hand in the establishment of the nation, Cannon points to religious belief as his guide for how he approaches everything in life: "It also gives me some guidance, I think, in how we make decisions in the short term to get toward the ultimate goal."[4]

Upon graduation, Chris Cannon worked as a lawyer. His first foray into the realm of government service came in 1983, when President Reagan appointed him Associate Solicitor in the Department of the Interior. Nearly one hundred attorneys served under him, working primarily on surface coal mining issues. This experience led naturally to a seat on the Resources Committee when he entered Congress later. While at Interior, he served also as a consultant for the Commerce Department on matters related to productivity, technology, and innovation.[5]

Cannon's congressional service began in 1996 when he defeated a three-term Democratic incumbent, a rare feat in that election year when Republicans lost some of their majority in the House. His service on the Resources Committee, mentioned above, also placed him on two of its subcommittees: Energy and Mineral Resources and National Parks and Public Lands. On the Science Committee, where he served under the chairmanship of fellow Manager James Sensenbrenner, Cannon received assignments to the Space and Aeronautics and the Technology subcommittees. His other committee appointment, of course, was Judiciary, which drew him into the impeachment process.[6]

Direct involvement began with the hearings on whether to hold an official inquiry. In his statement at those hearings, the Congressman drove straight to the point of the President's character and the effect it might have on average citizens. He told of a town hall meeting he had held a few days before, in which one of his constituents, a woman with two sons in the military, shared her concerns about her sons' commander-in-chief. "Ms. Updike shed tears while she spoke of her sons, not because she isn't willing for them to risk all in the defense of the freedoms embodied in the Constitution and our American way of life," Cannon explained. "She, along with all 600 or so people in the audience who gave her a standing ovation, is concerned that the sacrifices her sons may have to make may be in support of decisions that have more to do with the President's will to retain power than our national interest."[7]

The President's conduct, noted Cannon, was the reason for this hearing. It was his conduct that deserved condemnation. "For instance," he recounted, "the President of the United States was apparently engaged with Ms. Lewinsky while he was on the phone trying to convince Sonny Callaghan, the Chairman of the Foreign Operations Subcommittee of the Appropriations Committee, to support his plans for Bosnia."[8] This was not the proper conduct for the commander-in-chief.

The President's treatment of the women in his life raised legitimate questions. Why, Cannon asked, did a number of women who previously had given affidavits saying that they had not had sexual relations with this President now acknowledge that they did indeed have such a relationship? "Are they lying now? Or were they pressured to lie earlier? Their reluctance and apparent shame suggest the latter. What force may have been brought against them to influence their earlier decisions? Was that force derived from the power of high ranking public office?" Cannon asked. If so, President Clinton had used his powerful office in a criminal manner. And in the Paula Jones case, Cannon continued, "he apparently lied under oath. Can we allow those who disagree with claims against them to lie in court?"[9]

The Democrats on the Committee, Cannon complained, were demanding "ad nauseum" that the Committee first come up with a clear standard for impeachable offenses, but the rule of law—a concept he believed they misunderstood—did not require that clarity. Ambiguity was part of the President's defense, Cannon noted, as Clinton's attorneys seemed to be quite adept at parsing words and terms. Likewise, the Founding Fathers chose not to give a precise list of impeachable offenses. One thing they did make perfectly clear, though, was that no one, not even the President, could place himself above the law. Cannon addressed the fact that the members of the Committee would later be judged by future generations:

> After the arguments, we must set aside the partisan drive and vote for truth as we see it. Our duty is to assure that the President is not above the law as set out in the Constitution.
>
> We as a committee are sitting to judge, but at the same time we will also be judged.
>
> Historians with the aid of hindsight are often harsh. But our children will be our harshest of critics. Our children and their children's children. They must know that we know the difference between right and wrong.
>
> If we proceed unjustly, our colleagues will reject our determinations.
>
> If we urge drastic action, our rationale must be clear.
>
> If we judge rightly, we will be honored.[10]

On December 11, as the Judiciary Committee was preparing to vote on articles of impeachment to send to the full House, Cannon, in his opening statement prior to the votes, claimed that the Committee was "at a defining moment in our history." What standard would the Committee set for future presidents? Drawing from one of the Founders, co-author of the *Federalist Papers* and first Chief Justice of the Supreme Court, John Jay, Cannon commented that he agreed with Jay, "who said, 'When oaths cease to be sacred, our dearest and most valuable rights become insecure.'"[11] President Clinton had defiled his oath of office, according to Cannon. Continuing with his history lesson, he then played a video of President John F. Kennedy, President Clinton's boyhood hero, in which Kennedy warned that presidents must "strictly uphold the law or 'we would begin to unwind this most extraordinary constitutional system.'"[12] Agreeing with President Kennedy, Cannon said,

> Now, our system can take a lot of abuse. It is resilient. It can handle strong, spirited debate. It can even handle violent conflicts like the Civil War. But attempts to make a sacred oath flexible is like introducing solvent into [a] system that is glued together; the whole system comes apart.[13]

President Clinton, through his oathbreaking, insisted Cannon, was introducing a solvent that would destroy America's political structure.

In a not-too-subtle indictment of the Democratic members of the Committee, Cannon exclaimed, "There are some, who call themselves American and who understand these principles, who cover them over with facile arguments because they want to preserve their power." The facts of the case, he concluded, were compelling enough that the Democrats on the Committee had to admit the President had lied under oath.[14] That was good enough for Cannon. He voted for the articles of impeachment.

As a family man with eight children, Cannon was not seeking extra work. He felt that he needed to be home with the family. But he also felt an obligation to be part of the House Manager team. He took as his confidant David Schippers, the Judiciary Committee's Chief Investigative Counsel, who urged him to volunteer. Schippers wanted to be sure that there were fighters on the team, and he believed that Cannon was one who could be counted on to stay faithful to the cause in the looming combat. "I don't think of myself as a brawler or a fighter or anything like that," Cannon reflected later, "but, you know, when you're talking about right and wrong, when you're talking about these *big* principles, you just can't roll. You've got to be willing to stand up and take a blast and return a blast. So that was the reason, after talking to Schippers, I decided that I would ask Henry, who chose. Henry, I think, had talked to Schippers and invited me to be a Manager."[15]

The pressures on the Managers mounted as the Senate trial approached. For Cannon, it was not as bad as for some of the others because he came from a district that overwhelmingly supported his efforts. He commiserated with Henry Hyde and the attacks on him: "I thought it was a great tragedy." But as the attacks came, Cannon saw them in a somewhat different light:

> I believe that that was done, by the way, not to hurt Republicans as much as *to terrify Democrats.* In other words, it was not a partisan "we're gonna get Republicans." It was stated as "Republicans are bad and they're trying to get the President and everybody does this and everybody lies about it," but it had a huge effect on Democrats who might have voted against the President and for impeachment. Clearly, there were a lot of Democrats who had things in the closet they didn't want to have come out.[16]

The pressure was on the Democrats from their own leadership as well, Cannon argues. The seats that the Republicans won in 1994, he says, were seats formerly held by senior moderate Democrats. After their removal from the House, the Party leadership fell to more "hard-line socialists who have the ability to threaten their rank and file and keep them from voting their conscience and voting against impeachment both in the House and the Senate." That is precisely what happened in the Clinton impeachment. House Republicans had counted on some of those Democratic votes to ensure a bipartisan impeachment: "We thought that we would have Democratic votes in committee for impeachment. A half an hour before the vote on the floor, the whip count was that there would be thirty to fifty Democrats voting with us. We got five! That happened because the Democratic hierarchy was willing to exert enormous pressure on Democratic representatives."[17]

Cannon developed a deep respect for the Manager team itself. He was impressed with the "remarkably coherent presentation" the Managers made, despite only minor attempts to coordinate what everyone would be saying. "There was this, I thought, incredible complementarity of what was said. So I think we succeeded at that," Cannon said. Regardless of personal motivations at the beginning, Cannon felt that "everyone subordinated their own personal interests at one time or another in the process to achieve a better outcome." He particularly respected Bob Barr, who laid aside his desire to be one of the four principal prosecutors: "He decided that, to advance the overall object, he would carry his baggage on the TV rather than the presentation on the floor, which I thought was noble." There was a great deal of selflessness. "There [were] only two or three selfish acts in the whole process," Cannon remembers. "Those made the process much more difficult. The guys who did that, if I might use a religious term, I think repented sorely of having made mistakes. It was a remarkably coherent team when it all came together. It was just remarkably coherent."[18]

Cannon denies hating Bill Clinton, but he admits that he has had strong feelings toward him because of the consequences of his actions for the country:

> I will tell you that I have a great deal of animosity for the man. I think he has been enormously destructive to the institutions that have made America great. . . . So, personally, I have a lot of animosity. I can't stand watching him because he lies all the time. He will say anything to any group that he wants to appeal to. So while I have some residual personal animosity, it's not a personal thing. I don't even know the guy. I've never shaken his hand. I don't want to shake his hand. I don't want to meet him. I don't think about him except to the degree that we need to make adjustments to what he's doing from a policy point of view. Anybody can call anybody else a name; they can say you're a racist, you're a bigot, you're a nasty person, you're a

mean-spirited person, you hate him, and you're only acting out of anger. That's not the case.

I believe in America. I believe in the responsibilities of a President to embody the best in America, and he is a very bad man who should not be in office. So being accused is painful, but it's just not true. . . . I don't think [it] is true or reflective of any of the attitudes by any of the Managers.[19]

Cannon had "personal animosity" toward President Clinton, but it was not "a personal thing." That may sound contradictory to some, but in Cannon's mind, he could separate his personal animosity from the decision he had to make for the good of the country. A "very bad man" should not continue in office.

The Senate Show Trial

"There's not much precedent," commented Cannon during the tense period between the impeachment vote and the start of the Senate trial. "I think we're all trying to figure it out as we go."[20] The Congressman was referring to the rules for conducting the trial. The negotiations between the Managers and the Senate Republicans, who held the majority, were intense; the results were not to Cannon's liking. By the time the trial was half finished, Cannon, frustrated by the straitjacket he felt the Managers' had been made to wear, made his views known publicly: "The rules are awkward and are another difficulty created by the Senate for our presentation. The Senate is conveying the idea they are a superior body. I'm offended that senators hold themselves wiser or better than those of us from the House."[21]

Were these sentiments simply sour grapes over a flawed presentation or justifiable complaints? After Cannon had received those two senatorial phone calls mentioned at the beginning of this chapter and reported them to the other Managers, their discussion of the subject was disrupted by the arrival of Majority Leader Trent Lott and Senator Rick Santorum, who had come to go over the ground rules for the trial. A forty-minute debate ensued, and the Senators laid out the process as they saw it, a process that severely limited the presentation of the case and the calling of witnesses. "The Senate strategy at that point seemed focused on trying to get us to make a very long opening argument, after which everybody would be exhausted by the so-called trial before a real trial even began," Cannon complained.[22] The Managers voted on the Senate proposal and rejected it unanimously. The discussion continued. Lott argued that the Managers were putting the Senate in a box. "Someone—it could have been Barr or Chabot or Lindsey Graham—said *no*, you're putting *us* in a box, pointing out that we recognized what they're doing," Cannon recalled. "Then we had this long internal debate about what the role of the House was as opposed to the Senate. Are they equal bodies or were we going to subordinate ourselves by going forward and making a presentation in a context where we knew we couldn't win?"[23]

Cannon considered resigning from the team, believing the Senate's attitude was inappropriate and demeaning:

> We [the Managers] were solidly for a Senate trial. We were always in agreement on that. But we were thoroughly and evenly divided between those people who did not want to create a precedent of the House being subordinate to the Senate in an impeachment proceeding, and those who believed we should move ahead no matter what. Half believed that if we were presented with rules that would prevent us from prosecuting our case, we should withdraw. The other half believed we should present whatever case we could as best we could, given whatever rules the Senate would give us.[24]

It was his respect for Henry Hyde that kept him from resigning. To resign, he thought, might have been interpreted as a vote of no confidence in the Chairman, or it would have sent a false message that the Managers did not have a case. The other option was to "make a case under bad circumstances and acquit ourselves well." As meetings with Senators continued, Cannon felt that the Managers finally made some headway: "It became clear that they were moving away from the fear of juveniles presenting a case that was salacious in the Senate to a bunch of seasoned prosecutors who were politically savvy, and who were committed to presenting a persuasive case."[25]

Cannon's task on January 15 was to provide an overview of the law of obstruction of justice and to show legal precedent for applying it to President Clinton. "Wherever law ends, tyranny begins," intoned Cannon at the beginning of his presentation, quoting John Locke. His presentation would not be simple, he warned his listeners, because he had to walk them "through case history and statutory elements." There were seven separate instances, he explained, in which President Clinton sought to obstruct justice. Seeking to do so was sufficient, Cannon argued: "Federal court rulings clarify that it is not necessary for a defendant to succeed in obstructing justice."[26] All that was necessary was to show that the defendant acted with the intent to obstruct, something that Cannon felt was self-evident in this case.

Manager Cannon pointed to the President's attempts to impede the administration of justice and to tamper with the testimony of witnesses. He then addressed the assertion that none of this had any bearing because these acts occurred in the context of a civil trial. "There is simply *no merit* to this view," he countered. "There is no question that the obstruction and witness tampering statutes can be violated by acts that occur in civil proceedings. And, case law is consistent in upholding that any attempt to influence, obstruct or impede the due administration of justice in a civil proceeding violates section 1503."[27] He concluded,

> President Clinton corruptly endeavored to persuade witnesses to lie. In some cases, he succeeded. In every case, he violated the law.
>
> President Clinton engaged in misleading conduct in order to influence the testimony of witnesses in judicial proceedings. He succeeded. In each case, he violated the law.
>
> President Clinton acted with an improper purpose to

persuade a person to withhold objects from a judicial proceeding in which that person was required to produce them. He succeeded and in so doing violated the law.

President Clinton made misleading statements for the purpose of deterring a litigant from further discovery that would lead to facts which the judge ordered relevant in a Federal civil rights case. In so doing, he obstructed the due administration of justice in that case and violated the law.

Whether attempting to persuade a person to testify falsely or to ignore court orders to produce objects; whether suggesting to an innocent person a false story in hopes that he or she will repeat it in a judicial proceeding; or testifying falsely in the hopes of blocking another party's pursuit of the truth—

All these acts obstruct justice;

All these acts are Federal felony crimes;

All these acts were committed by William Jefferson Clinton.[28]

After all the Managers made their presentations, the Senate rules again intervened, in Cannon's estimation, to prevent justice. He expressed his disappointment:

> Then we go into the other side's presentation and what did they do? Cheryl Mills gets up there—and she's given great credit for her statements—but if what she said had been testimony instead of argument, she would have gone to jail. President Clinton would have had to commute her sentence. She only told half the truth! So what was our chance of rebuttal after that under the rules the Senate had set up? In effect: None. In a real trial we would have gone back and taken her fallacious arguments point by point and showed what the truth was. But under the procedure set by the Senate, we had to sit and take questions from Senators for 8 hours—one of the greatest soporifics in American history. Nobody could have stayed awake through that.[29]

In the period after the House vote on impeachment and the opening of the Senate trial, Cannon had told a reporter, "This is not like the House. This is weighing the evidence, and I think we ought to have witnesses. We ought to be able to get the evidence out, and the president ought to be able to cross-examine because these are very serious allegations. . . . If I were a senator and judging this, I would want to know what those people were thinking, and I'd like to see cross-examination."[30] Obviously, the Senate had disagreed with his perspective.

This theme—denial of justice through the rules of the proceeding—dominated Cannon's closing argument on February 8. He wanted the Senators to realize just how "unique" this trial had been and that a real possibility existed that the result would not bring the needed closure. "America is deeply divided," he warned, and an impeachment trial, as designed by the Founding Fathers, was intended "to salve those wounds." He continued, "Traditionally, after an airing of the facts and a vote by the Senate, either a President is removed or he is vindicated. In this case, it seems, neither of those results may be realized." The fact that the President committed perjury and obstruction of justice was clear, Cannon asserted. It also was becoming equally clear that the Senate probably would not remove him from office. If that did happen to be the result, he feared that the public would not consider it legitimate. "How well you do the work of divining that outcome will affect the way we as a nation deal with the divisions among us. To proceed in a manner that will be trusted and viewed as legitimate by the American people, you must deal with the differences between this proceeding and prior impeachment trials," he noted.[31]

One of the primary differences between the Clinton impeachment and the preceding thirteen impeachment trials was Senate resolution 16, which, according to Cannon, prevented the Managers from making their case as they saw fit. The resolution called for a twenty-four-hour presentation that the public saw only as "the yammering of lawyers." Further, Cannon argued,

Time was equally divided rather than sequenced as it is in a trial where opening statements are made and then evidence is put on through witnesses. In a trial, each side typically takes the time necessary to establish its case or undermine the witness through cross examination. After the moving party has made its case, the responding party makes its case. Time is dictated only by what each side feels it needs. Each witness is subject to whatever cross examination is appropriate. The case develops tested piece by tested piece, and ultimately one side prevails.

Here, the Managers had to cut very important portions of our limited case. We had a limited number of witnesses, limited to video taped appearances, limited to fit an arbitrary three hour rule. That time was lessened because we had to reserve time for rebuttal.[32]

These rules, said Cannon, did not give the Senate the opportunity to assess the credibility of each witness. Inadequate time for rebuttal by the Managers limited their ability to make the case. The questioning period by the Senate merely "had the unfortunate side effect of focusing the public on the partisanship of the Senate." Clearly, Cannon was not pleased with the "uniqueness" of this trial. The issue was grave, he stressed, and the Senate's responsibility was great. "So I am here today to ask you to set aside some natural inclinations for the good of the country. I would implore you, Senators, both Republican and Democrat, to set aside partisanship, politics, polls, and personalities and exchange them for loftier inclinations—those of 'procedure,' 'policy,' and 'precedents.' These are the only guidelines this body should have," he stressed.[33] In Congressman Cannon's estimation, those were not the guidelines the Senate followed, and partisanship won the day.

The Triumph of Partisanship

Partisanship dominated on both sides of the Senate aisle, Cannon concluded. The Democratic version was obvious: not one Senator voted for removal. They all chose to protect one of their own, regardless of the wrongdoing or the damage to the rule of law and the Constitution. Yet the Republicans displayed their own brand of partisanship. It became clear to Cannon that the Senate Republican leadership was less concerned about what really had occurred and what was impeachable than it was about how to inflict the greatest political damage on Democrats. The Republican leadership figured "it's better to have a weakened President Clinton and a tainted Al Gore than it is to have an incumbent Al Gore." If the Managers had been truly partisan, as so many of the critics declared, Cannon says, "we would have jumped on the bandwagon with Trent Lott, who did, I think, the very clever partisan thing. I'm a great respecter of Trent Lott, but he did the partisan thing, and it made some sense then and probably makes sense now, that is, to help the party long-term to just impeach the guy, make a credible case that he's a nasty, awful person, let that sink in, and win the next election. That was the partisan thing to do." Instead, the Managers stood "for the Constitution when it was very unpopular."[34]

As a result, with the Republicans' acquiescence, no real pressure was put on the Democrats to consider removal seriously. Cannon reflects, "It was very clear before we made our presentation to the Senate that it was a foregone conclusion within the Senate. There was no way on earth in those circumstances we could ever get even all of our Republicans to vote because they had already committed." The Senators, believes Cannon, violated the oath they took to judge impartially: "They operated in a way that was inconsistent with all the legal precedent of the United States by having a trial that didn't have a trial." There were enough Senators, both Republican and Democrat, "who had already made a conclusion about what they wanted the political outcome to be that their oath didn't stand in the way."[35] Justice was denied.

Can anything be salvaged from this trial that was not a trial? Cannon believes that Americans are now more energized in their desire to get rid of the kakistocracy: "You've got the aristocracy, which is the rule of the elite; gerontocracy is the rule of the aged; theocracy is the rule of God; kakistocracy is the rule of the lowest level of society. People want to get rid of that and replace it with someone of honor and integrity." He also is encouraged that the episode made people think more about the Constitution:

> All of a sudden the Constitution has meaning to people. And you cannot open up a dark place, something that has been hidden by schoolteachers and civics leaders—oh yeah, there's something out there called the Constitution, but you don't know how it works. You open that Constitution up and people start thinking about what does impeachment mean. . . . Going through the process leads you to a lot of other ideas, and those ideas become foundational. . . .
>
> The hope is that we will elect people who believe in the foundational principles of American government, and then we'll move the other way to more freedom, to less regulation, to less control, to a broader market environment, an environment where individuals' rights are viewed as coming from God and delegated to government instead of the other way around. Where religion goes back to its proper role instead of this perverse role that's been crafted by court decisions over the last forty years. That's my hope.[36]

Chapter Seven Endnotes

[1] Congressman Chris Cannon, interview by author, tape recording, Washington, DC, 28 March 2000.

[2] Ibid.

[3] Ibid.

[4] Ibid.

[5] Cannon Biography; available at http://www.house.gov/cannon/bio.html; accessed 9 October 2000.

[6] Ibid.

[7] Statement of Congressman Chris Cannon, House Judiciary Committee, 8 October 1998; available at http://www.house.gov/judiciary/cannonfl.htm; accessed 28 April 1999.

[8] Ibid.

[9] Ibid.

[10] Ibid.

[11] The Impeachment Hearings: Opening Statements: Chris Cannon, 11 December 1998; available at http://www.washingtonpost.com/wp-srv/politics/special/clinton/stories/cannontext121198.htm; accessed 1 April 1999.

[12] Francis X. Clines, "Panel Votes to Impeach," *The San Diego Union-Tribune*, 12 December 1998, A-1.

[13] The Impeachment Hearings: Opening Statements: Chris Cannon, 11 December 1998.

[14] Ibid.

[15] Cannon interview.

[16] Ibid.

[17] Ibid.

[18] Ibid.

[19] Ibid.

[20] Frank Bruni, "13 Impeachment 'Managers' Must Learn the Ropes as They Go," *The Orange County Register*, 27 December 1998, a09.

[21] Eric Schmitt, "House Managers Chafe in Culture Clash with Senate," *The Orange County Register*, 30 January 1999, a06.

[22] Transcript of *Human Events* interview with Chris Cannon provided by Congressman Cannon's office; transcript date 22 June 1999.

[23] Cannon interview.

[24] *Human Events* transcript.

[25] Ibid.

[26] Opening Statement of Hon. Chris Cannon, Senate Impeachment Trial, 15 January 1999.

[27] Ibid.

[28] Ibid.

[29] *Human Events* transcript.

[30] Ruth Marcus, "Trial's Managers Chart an Uncertain Course," *The Washington Post*, 22 December 1998, A16.

[31] Closing Argument of Hon. Chris Cannon, Senate Impeachment Trial of President Clinton, 8 February 1999; available at http://www.house.gov/judiciary/can0208.htm; accessed 9 February 2000.

[32] Ibid.

[33] Ibid.

[34] Cannon interview.

[35] Ibid.

[36] Ibid

CHAPTER EIGHT

Steve Chabot:
Doing His Duty

"We weren't out to get this President. It wasn't our motivation or the goal of anybody to just get this President," explained Congressman Steve Chabot of Ohio. Sitting behind his desk in his office in the Cannon House Office Building, he was reaching back mentally, trying to recall exactly how he felt going through the impeachment experience. "We were determined to make sure the Senate had all the facts and then to let the Senate make the decision that they felt was appropriate," he remembered. But he wanted to make a very clear distinction:

> There really wasn't a lot of hatred or animosity toward the President, which probably a lot of people wouldn't understand. . . .
> I believe that many of the Democrats on the [Judiciary] Committee decided that their best strategy for defending the President was to make this appear to be as partisan as possible. Henry Hyde, to his credit, really did bend over backwards to be fair, although you wouldn't get that from what our Democratic colleagues on the Committee were saying.[1]

When asked whether he thought the Democrats on the Committee really believed the Republicans hated the President and were out to get him or whether they simply were using that approach as a political ploy, Chabot refused to judge their motives. "I don't know what they thought," he began. "I can't really look into their minds or hearts and know how they felt about it." Actions, though, were another matter: "I do know what they said in the Committee and what they said in press conferences and what I saw on television when they were talking. They were clearly trying to portray us as doing this for purely partisan reasons, and that really was not the case."[2]

The partisanship accusation made no sense to Chabot. Why would he or any other Republican seek to undermine their own Party by pursuing a popular President? "We were taking a hit in the polls," the Congressman recalled. "Two-thirds of the country, if the polls are to be believed, were saying that they wanted this President to stay in office. Republicans were going down substantially in the public opinion polls. Our popularity was plunging." Removal of President Clinton would have made way for President Gore—hardly an improvement because that would have positioned the new President as the incumbent, who could not only finish the remainder of the Clinton presidency, but also run twice more himself. Chabot was made aware of the potential political benefits of the situation:

> I had a lot of folks—Republicans—that I would talk to that said things along the line of, you know, the best thing is if Clinton stays in office. That's gonna hurt the Democrats in the next election and Republicans have a lot better chance of taking back the presidency. That may well have been the case, and it may be the case this year, but I don't think that was our responsibility—to just do what was politically expedient. We should do what was proper for us to uphold the Constitution.[3]

Upholding the Constitution was Steve Chabot's primary concern, even if that ran counter to his political success. And he was not one of those House Managers who came from a "safe" district.

From Ohio to Impeachment

Chabot represents Ohio's First District, which includes most of Cincinnati. Born in Cincinnati in 1953, he is no stranger to the area.[4] Chabot was raised in a Catholic family and has remained a devout Catholic, placing both of his children in Catholic schools. The nation was founded by religious people, he notes, "who had a firm belief in God ... and didn't shrink from saying that in their public dialogue." He considers religion to be an important part of America's moral foundation, and he does not believe that Congressmen have to hide their beliefs. "I try to make sure that it [religion] plays a role in my duties and responsibilities as a legislator—as a lawmaker," he adds.[5]

Chabot's only significant time spent away from his hometown was while he was an undergraduate at the College of William and Mary. But then he returned to Cincinnati to attend the Salmon P. Chase College of Law, earning his law degree in the evening program while teaching in a downtown elementary school during the day. Upon completion of the degree, he opened his own law practice.[6] It did not take long for him to gain a reputation as a highly conscientious attorney. Hamilton County prosecutor and later Ohio Treasurer Joseph T. Deters remembers that Chabot "took lots and lots of time with his clients. He was one of those guys who was a plodder. Not the most expensive lawyer in Cincinnati, but very thorough and tenacious."[7]

Chabot's political career began in 1985 when he won an election for a City Council seat. He remained in that seat until 1990, when he was appointed to the Hamilton County Board of Commissioners. He subsequently won two elections to that same Board, stepping down only because he had won election to Congress as part of the Contract-with-America Republican Revolution of 1994.[8] His election was a surprise, given that the three previous Members of Congress from the district had been Democrats, yet he held onto the seat through two subsequent elections, both bitterly contested. In 1996, he won 54 percent of the vote and gained 53 percent in 1998, in the heat of the impeachment battle.[9] The Democrats considered him vulnerable in both elections, yet he was able to emerge victorious.

Although soft-spoken and not one to grab the limelight, Steve Chabot has been one of the most ardent conservatives elected to the House. He has fought every effort to dilute the original Contract with America, even to the point where he challenged Speaker Gingrich and the rest of the Republican House leadership. When Gingrich talked about postponing tax cuts, Chabot immediately wrote a strong letter of protest, urging the Speaker to keep his promises. "I was obviously disappointed in the speaker's comments," he said at the time. "I strongly disagreed with him." And when the GOP leadership proposed a congressional committee funding bill, Chabot joined with Democrats in opposing it because it increased funding for some committees. His mission in Congress, as he saw it, was to cut spending and to reform programs, not to do business as usual. "I came here (in 1995) very serious about balancing the budget and giving the American people tax relief. I feel just as strongly now as I did before I came to Congress," Chabot commented in 1997.[10]

His efforts to hold the line on spending and to shrink the federal government have earned Chabot praise from watchdog groups such as Citizens Against Government Waste, the Concord Coalition, the National Taxpayers Union, and Americans for Tax Reform. Citizens Against Government Waste named the Congressman one of the top four House members in voting against unnecessary government spending. Part of his leadership role in the House was as co-chairman of the Education Task Force, where he worked to develop legislation to return education funds to the states. His goal was to allow parents, teachers, and local communities to take control of education policy.[11]

Yet, as conservative as he is, Chabot has shown in his congressional career that he is able to labor with the other side when he sees points of agreement. He has worked on certain issues with such staunchly liberal Congressmen as Charles Schumer, Joseph Kennedy, and Major Owens, all with impeccable liberal voting credentials. Schumer called him "open and honest." According to Pat Cooksey, head of the True Blue Patriots of Cincinnati, Chabot works with his political opponents without compromising his principles: "He may work with liberals, but he doesn't compromise with liberals . . . He sticks to his guns on the conservative agenda. He's good on balanced budget amendment, and capital gains tax, and the Contract with America." Her perspective has been echoed by Grover Norquist of Americans for Tax Reform, who commented, "On each of the issues, he's not conceding on principles."[12]

Even though he has been at odds with his own leadership at times, Chabot has gained their respect. One of the leaders, John Boehner of Ohio, praised him: "Everybody knows where Steve's coming from. He's a conservative who sticks to his principles more than most. They're not co-opting him. He's working to build a coalition to move some issues he feels strongly about." Bob Barr, his fellow Manager, stated more than a year before the impeachment proceedings began, "He gets along very, very well with people, both personally and in the public discussions. I don't think if you ask people about me they'll say the same thing."[13] And then there is Chabot on Chabot:

> I really do try to put politics aside. I looked at what Democrats were out there that had been active in the past on the same issues. That's how we found Mr. Schumer. We have pretty significant philosophical differences on a number of issues, which is putting it mildly. [But] we both feel very strongly that these government rip-offs should be ripped out wherever they're at. It's about policy, and it's generally on a pretty narrow issue.[14]

The Judiciary Committee was a natural choice for the Congressman. He did not consider the possibility of being involved in an impeachment when he took his seat on the Committee. Rather, he was drawn to it because it dealt with issues that he considered important, particularly abortion. While other politicians skirt the abortion issue, Chabot faces it directly. "Some people kind of shrink from that in public life," he notes, "[and] don't want to take a stand. I'm strongly pro-life, and that issue comes up in that Committee quite often. I feel very strongly about that, so I am able to take a stand both in the Committee and when it comes to the floor on issues like that. Like the death penalty and other issues which are important to me."[15]

As the impeachment drama unfolded, Chabot remained optimistic that the parties could work together in a nonpartisan manner, perhaps because he had done so with individual Democrats. At the time, he said, "I think members, hopefully on both sides, will rise to the occasion. This is one instance when we really ought to put partisan politics aside and do what is in the best interests of the country." For his own part, Chabot pledged to set aside "his personal qualms" about President Clinton and stated that he had not yet reached any conclusions.[16] But he discovered that his evenhanded approach was not reciprocated. He was disappointed that the Democrats seemed to be crying "partisan" throughout the proceedings. "We really weren't," he insists. "We were faced with a situation where some of us felt that a President had abused his office and had committed perjury and obstruction of justice and really disgraced the office. So we were going to do what we thought was right for the country and uphold the Constitution despite any possible political consequences."[17]

When the Judiciary Committee opened hearings in October 1998 to determine whether to launch an official inquiry, Chabot believed that harm already had been done to the country no matter how the House proceeded. In his comments at that hearing, he deplored the necessity that had been placed upon the House:

> Like most of my colleagues and, I suspect, most of the American people, I would prefer that the President's actions had not forced this hearing today. Regardless of how this committee, and this Congress, chooses to dispose of this serious matter, the nation will have paid a dear price. The office of the Presidency has been demeaned. The standards of public morality and decency have been diminished. And the American people have been forced to endure a painful process that could have been avoided.[18]

There are those, he noted, who would like to stop the proceedings immediately, relying on the argument that nothing can be an impeachable offense that does not result in "injury to the state." They contend further that perjury relating to sexual matters in a civil lawsuit could not be considered an impeachable offense. "That argument is wrong," he concluded. "It is a misstatement of the historic record." Chabot then gave some evidence to the effect that perjury always had been a consideration for impeachment and finished his statement:

> Strong evidence exists that the President may have committed perjury, and the historic record demonstrates that perjury can be an impeachable offense. Based on the facts, and the law, this committee has a constitutional duty to proceed to a formal inquiry. It is my sincere hope that we can work together, in a bipartisan fashion, to complete this task as expeditiously as possible and do what's in the best interest of the country.[19]

By the end of the inquiry in early December, any doubts that Chabot had entertained concerning President Clinton's complicity in perjury and obstruction of justice had vanished. He was troubled, he commented just prior to the Committee votes on articles of impeachment, by what the President had done to the country. Chabot's own children had been taught "that honesty and integrity do matter." The President's actions had undermined that parental instruction. Meanwhile, in courthouses throughout the nation, every day Americans had to swear to tell the whole truth under penalty of perjury. "Yet in this case the President of the United States, the chief law enforcement officer of this land, has made an utter mockery of that fundamental precept," he lamented. "That is a travesty. No person stands above the law. All Americans, no matter how rich, how powerful, how well connected, should be held accountable for their actions."[20]

Chabot then provided some insight into his own presidential voting history. Although he had voted for Richard Nixon in 1972, he switched in 1976 to vote for the Democrat, Jimmy Carter. Why? "That decision stemmed from my profound disappointment over Watergate and a strong conviction that President Nixon should not have received a pardon, that he should not have gotten away with his actions," he said.[21] Chabot now felt the same about Bill Clinton.

Continuing with his Watergate comparison, Chabot then quoted former Congresswoman Elizabeth Holtzman, who was on the Judiciary Committee for the impeachment of President Nixon. She said that she voted for impeachment because the cover-up was continuing even while the inquiry was seeking answers. The parallel, to Chabot, seemed obvious:

> We find ourselves facing a similarly unfortunate situation. To this day, President Clinton continues to deny and distort. He continues to dispute the undeniable facts before our committee and before the American people. The president refuses even to admit what several prominent Democratic members in this committee have publicly concluded to be true. President Clinton lied under oath. Several Democratic members of this committee have acknowledged that.[22]

The only constitutional option available for dealing with an offending President was impeachment, Chabot concluded.

He had tried to keep an open mind, he told his colleagues, "giving the president every opportunity to refute the facts that have been laid before our committee, but now all the evidence is in and a decision is at hand." This was not an easy decision for him, confessed Chabot, and he declared that he had done his share of soul searching. He had "listened carefully to the views" of his constituents and had "reviewed the evidence in excruciating detail. And much of it," he assured them, "wasn't particularly pleasant." Above all, though, he had been guided by the Constitution:

> The argument has been made by the president's defenders that voting for articles of impeachment would set a terrible

precedent. I respectfully disagree. To the contrary, burying our heads in the sand and refusing to acknowledge the gravity of the president's crimes would set a far more dangerous precedent. Giving the president a pass, or a censure, would set a dangerous precedent for future presidents, for those who testify in our courts and for our children, whom we try to raise with respect for the truth and a sense of what's right and what's wrong.

. . . When we cast our votes, we are not voting as Republicans or Democrats, we are voting as Americans. Our allegiance does not lie with any one president but with our country. Our charge is not handed down from any one political party but from the Constitution. Every member of this body is duty-bound to put politics aside, follow our conscience, and uphold our oath of office.

William Jefferson Clinton has disgraced the sacred office of the president. I've come to the conclusion that it is our duty to impeach.[23]

During a break in the hearings, Chabot commented to a reporter, "You can't help but feel the weight of history on your shoulders." When President Clinton tried to forestall the vote with another Rose Garden "apology," Chabot was not impressed. "I was disappointed with the president's speech," he said afterward. "He still has not admitted what everyone but the president seems to know—that he lied under oath."[24]

Chabot and the Senate

After the November 1998 elections, Chabot sensed somewhat of a divide between the Republicans who had served on the Judiciary Committee and the rank and file. The loss of five seats in the House had sobered some of his fellow Republicans. "There was, at that time, talk amongst some of my Republican colleagues that this needed to be put to rest as quickly as possible and move on because this was hurting Republicans politically. But, interestingly, the members of the House Judiciary Committee itself and the Managers, we heard our colleagues take that position, but we just felt we were really not going to consider the politics of this thing. We didn't think it was right for us to consider the politics of it. We really should do what we thought was right, and that's what we did," Chabot said. When asked to be a House Manager, Chabot certainly did consider the political consequences in his tough district but, ultimately, decided that serving was the right thing to do, regardless of what might happen to him politically. "I felt it was my duty," he stated simply.[25]

Responsibility for explaining the law of perjury to the Senate fell to Chabot. As he stood in the well of the Senate chamber, he admitted to the assembled Senators that he felt far removed from his small neighborhood law practice in Cincinnati. "But while this arena may be somewhat foreign to me, the law remains the same," he reminded them. He knew that his discussion of the law of perjury might not be as "captivating" as the discussion of the facts of the case that they had heard the day before, but he reminded them that it was essential to "thoroughly review the law" as they moved forward "in this historic process."[26]

Perjury, instructed Chabot, was "to knowingly and wilfully make a false statement about a material matter while under oath." Another more specific federal statute focused on false statements made before a federal court or a federal grand jury, of which the President was accused. The President had taken the oath; no one had challenged that fact. Was his intent to falsify? Could it conceivably be argued that President Clinton's "carefully calculated statements" were merely mistakes or accidents? Chabot pointed out that even Charles Ruff, one of the President's attorneys, had testified before the Judiciary Committee that the President "wilfully misled the court." The Congressman added, "In an extraordinary admission, the President's own attorney has acknowledged the care, the intention, the will, of the President to say precisely what he said."[27] So much for intent.

The falsity of President Clinton's statements had been exposed the day before in other Managers' presentations, so Chabot moved on to the issue of materiality. If a false statement had a natural tendency to influence an official proceeding, it was material, according to the Supreme Court. The false statements did not even have to succeed in influencing the proceeding; all that was necessary was that they *could have succeeded*. Chabot noted,

> The law regarding materiality of false statements before a grand jury is very straightforward: Because a grand jury's authority to investigate is broad, the realm of declarations regarded as material is broad. The President's false statements to the grand jury were material because the grand jury was investigating whether the President had obstructed justice and committed perjury in his civil deposition.[28]

Case closed, as far as Chabot was concerned.

Apologists for President Clinton were trying to distinguish between reprehensible actions and impeachable actions. Chabot understood the distinction, but he felt that it did not apply to perjury, which was both *reprehensible* and *impeachable*. Allowing perjury to go unchecked "strikes a terrible blow against the machinery of justice." The President's lying under oath was more than a simple act of perjury; it was an act "that chipped away at the very cornerstone of our judicial system." Chabot then invoked the authority of the nation's first Chief Justice, John Jay:

> On June 25, 1792, in a Charge to the Grand Jury of the Circuit Court for the District of Vermont, the Chief Justice said:
> "Independent of the abominable Insult which Perjury offers to the divine Being, there is no Crime more extensively pernicious to Society. It discolors and poisons the Streams of Justice, and by substituting Falsehood for Truth, saps the Foundations of personal and public Rights—Controversies of various kinds

exist at all Times, and in all Communities. To decide them, Courts of Justice are instituted—their Decisions must be regulated by Evidence, and the greater part of Evidence will always consist of the Testimony of witnesses. This Testimony is given under those solemn obligations which an appeal to the God of Truth impose; and if oaths should cease to be held sacred, our dearest and most valuable Rights would become insecure."[29]

The President was on trial before the Senate, therefore, because falsehood under oath would destroy the nation's most sacred rights.

The Senators had a "daunting task and an awesome responsibility" that could not be taken lightly. Chabot urged the Senators to weigh the impact of their decision not only on what they perceived to be good for the country at the present time (i.e., putting the matter behind us), but to consider the message they would be sending to future generations:

> It is my belief that if the actions of the President are ultimately disregarded or minimized, we will be sending a sorry message to the American people that the President of the United States is above the law. We will be sending a message to our children, to my children, that telling the truth doesn't really matter if you've got a good lawyer or are an exceptionally skilled liar. That would be tragic.
>
> Mr. Chief Justice, Senators, let us instead send a message to the American people and to the boys and girls who will be studying American history in the years to come that no person is above the law and that this great nation remains an entity governed by the rule of law. Let us do what is right. Let us do what is just.[30]

On February 8, Manager Chabot had one more chance to convince his audience. The country had survived the trial, Chabot began, despite the "dire warnings, scare tactics and heavy-handed threats by those who would circumvent the solemn constitutional process that we are all engaged in." The nation had not grounded to a halt while the deliberations had gone forth. "But, Senators, before you turn out the lights and head home, you must make one final decision," he reminded them. "It is a decision that should not be influenced by party affiliation or by politics or by personal ties. It is a decision that should be guided by our Constitution, by our laws, and by your own moral compass."[31]

He understood their situation because he had cast one of the hardest votes of his career just two months earlier. He had tried to be fair and to keep an open mind, and he had examined the evidence scrupulously. That House vote for impeachment was the most important vote in his tenure as a Congressman. "Now it is your turn to cast what could be the most important vote of your political careers. The question is, Will moral fortitude or political expediency rule the day?" he asked.[32]

The past weekend, Chabot divulged, he had returned to his alma mater, William and Mary. Walking around the campus had made him recollect not only his college days, but also why he had desired to seek public office—what had motivated him in the first place. He related how his disappointment over the actions of President Nixon and the immunity Nixon had received had led him to vote for Jimmy Carter in the subsequent election. The troubled spirit he experienced at that time had returned due to the actions of President Clinton and the possibility that he also would escape any real consequences:

> As I started to think about what to say to you today, I wasn't sure how to begin. How exactly do you wrap up in 10 minutes or less everything we have witnessed in the last year? We have seen Bill Clinton's finger-waving denial to the American people. We have seen the President lie before a Federal grand jury. We have seen the President obstruct justice. We have seen the President hold a public celebration immediately following the House impeachment vote . . .
>
> President Clinton, however, refuses to admit what all of us know is true. To this day, he continues to deny and distort; he

continues to dispute the undeniable facts that are before the Senate and before the American people. The President's attorneys have done their best to disguise the truth as well.[33]

Some of the President's most partisan defenders, Chabot warned, want the truth "ignored, distorted, or swept under the rug," but it would be wrong for the Senate to do so. Those same defenders had harshly criticized the Mangers and anyone "who would dare believe the President committed any crimes." While Chabot wanted as much as anyone for the page to be turned on this "unfortunate chapter" in America's history, he had one question first:

> How will this chapter end? Will the final chapter say that the U.S. Senate turned its back on perjury and obstruction of justice by a President of the United States, or will it say that the Senate took a principled stand and told the world that no person, not even the President, stands above the law; that all Americans, no matter how rich, how powerful, or how well connected, are accountable for their actions, even the President? . . . So how will this chapter end? The decision is yours.[34]

The decision was made, but to Chabot, it was a sad concluding chapter.

The Consequences?

One year after the Senate trial, Steve Chabot assessed his role in the proceeding: "I do not regret my role in this. I did what I thought was right at the time. Looking back on it, I would do it again because it was my duty." He also rejects all accusations that he and his fellow Republicans are to blame for putting the country through a traumatic episode. "The President's actions brought this about, nobody else, despite the fact that he and many of his allies have tried to point the finger in every other direction. But he is the reason the country had to go through this," Chabot insisted.[35]

He hopes the country has learned something positive through the experience—in particular, as he stated in his closing argument to the Senate, that no one is above the law, not even the President. He consoles himself with the fact that Bill Clinton was the first *elected* President to be impeached formally by the House and put on trial in the Senate. At least that will be "a major part of his legacy." So there have been consequences to President Clinton personally even though he was not removed from office. One could argue, Chabot reasons, that because Clinton was not removed from office, the country could learn the wrong message: "that if you can spin things enough and you're slick enough, maybe you can get away with anything." He tries, however, to maintain his optimism:

> I would hope that's not the lesson. I think if you really look at this, that won't be the message people will get. But, you know, I'm not going to be writing the history—you will. So we'll see what the conclusion is.[36]

Chapter Eight Endnotes

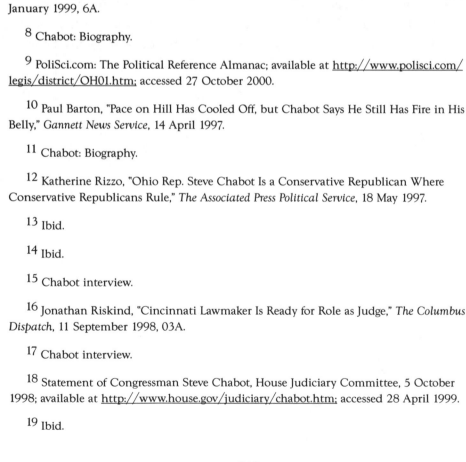

[1] Chabot interview.

[2] Ibid.

[3] Ibid.

[4] Congressman Steve Chabot: Biography; available at http://www.house.gov/chabot/BIONEW98.html; accessed 31 January 2000.

[5] Chabot interview.

[6] Chabot: Biography.

[7] Keith Epstein, "Chabot Has Reputation for Looking after Details," *The Plain Dealer*, 8 January 1999, 6A.

[8] Chabot: Biography.

[9] PoliSci.com: The Political Reference Almanac; available at http://www.polisci.com/legis/district/OH01.htm; accessed 27 October 2000.

[10] Paul Barton, "Pace on Hill Has Cooled Off, but Chabot Says He Still Has Fire in His Belly," *Gannett News Service*, 14 April 1997.

[11] Chabot: Biography.

[12] Katherine Rizzo, "Ohio Rep. Steve Chabot Is a Conservative Republican Where Conservative Republicans Rule," *The Associated Press Political Service*, 18 May 1997.

[13] Ibid.

[14] Ibid.

[15] Chabot interview.

[16] Jonathan Riskind, "Cincinnati Lawmaker Is Ready for Role as Judge," *The Columbus Dispatch*, 11 September 1998, 03A.

[17] Chabot interview.

[18] Statement of Congressman Steve Chabot, House Judiciary Committee, 5 October 1998; available at http://www.house.gov/judiciary/chabot.htm; accessed 28 April 1999.

[19] Ibid.

[20] The Impeachment Hearings: Opening Statements: Steve Chabot, 10 December 1998; available at http://www.washingtonpost.com/wp-srv/politics/special/clinton/stories/chabottext121098.htm; accessed 1 April 1999.

[21] Ibid.

[22] Ibid.

[23] Ibid.

[24] Paul Barton, "Chabot Feels 'Great Emotion' in Voting for Clinton Impeachment," *Gannett News Service*, 11 December 1998.

[25] Chabot interview.

[26] Opening Statement of Hon. Steve Chabot, Senate Impeachment Trial of President Clinton, 15 January 1999; available at http://www.house.gov/judiciary/chabotsenate.htm; accessed 16 April 1999.

[27] Ibid.

[28] Ibid.

[29] Ibid.

[30] Ibid.

[31] Closing Argument of Hon. Steve Chabot, Senate Impeachment Trial of President Clinton, 8 February 1999; available at http://www.house.gov/judiciary/chab0208.htm; accessed 9 February 2000.

[32] Ibid.

[33] Ibid.

[34] Ibid.

[35] Chabot interview.

[36] Ibid.

CHAPTER NINE

George Gekas:
Meeting the Challenges

"If I see you I am going to shoot you in the (expletive) head. . . . You make me sick. You need to be shot. You need to be executed." That was the gist of a message left on the voice mail of Representative George Gekas's district office in Harrisburg, Pennsylvania. The call came in at 4:00 a.m. on December 11, the day after Gekas had made his opening statement in the House Judiciary Committee hearings on the impeachment of President Clinton. The caller even left his name and number. Apparently, he had been drinking while watching impeachment coverage. He told FBI agents later that he really had no intention of harming Congressman Gekas, but the episode showcases the emotions engendered by the impeachment.[1]

George Gekas is not easily intimidated. Three years earlier, just outside his Harrisburg home, three teenagers attacked him to steal his car. Although they hit him on the head with a wrench, leaving a gash that took three stitches to close, Gekas chased after them as they sped away in the car.[2] And in Congress, some Capitol Hill insiders who do not agree with his forthright support for the death penalty have referred to him as "Dr. Death."[3] Clearly, George Gekas does not avoid challenges.

The Impeachment Challenge

Gekas never has strayed too far from Harrisburg, or for too long, ever since he was born in the city in 1930. He graduated from a Harrisburg high school and spent his college years in Carlisle, Pennsylvania, eventually earning a law degree from the J.D. Dickinson School of Law in 1958. His undergraduate degree and law degree sandwiched a stint in the military from 1953 to 1955, but once military service and college were behind him, Gekas settled down in Harrisburg. He opened a law practice in 1959 and then served as Assistant District Attorney for Dauphin County from 1960 to 1966. Politics beckoned, and he won a seat in the Pennsylvania House in 1966, laboring there until 1974, when he moved up to the State Senate.

The combination of his American and Greek heritages led him to public service. It was part of the "creed" of his upbringing, he explains. "The creed to which I refer is multi-edged. In learning about American history and learning about Classical Greek history, being of Greek descent and being exposed to the Greek Orthodox faith brought to me a special flavor of public service. It was expected of Athenians in the first great democracy, that everyone must, or should, participate in government and lend one's self to the improvement of the society," he said. His religious background provided the basis for his demeanor: "My exposure to church as a Greek Orthodox Christian played an unnoted role. That is, without my really recognizing it during my formative years, but looking back at it, I'd have to say that that helped a great deal to establish standards of behavior."[4]

As a state senator, Gekas focused on reestablishing the death penalty "after the Supreme Court had knocked it out nationwide." He also advocated tort reform. His position as Chairman of the Senate Judiciary Committee in the state gave him the experience he needed to move onto the same committee at the national level. "As a matter of fact," he remembers, "I prepared, at that time, a ten-point program of why I should be elected to Congress, most of which was based on the fact that I was Chairman of the Judiciary Committee. . . . So I ran on the strength that, if I am elected, I will seek a position on the Judiciary Committee and try to bring about the same progression of ideas that I had developed as a Member of the Pennsylvania legislature, both in the House and Senate."[5]

Gekas ran for Congress in 1982 and won—and has continued to win every two years since. He achieved his goal of being assigned to the Judiciary Committee, where eventually he became Chair of the Subcommittee on Commercial and Administrative Law. Underscoring his tough stance on the death penalty, he authored the law that allows judges to impose the penalty for drug-related murders. In 1993, when the killing of foreign tourists in Florida made national news, Gekas promoted the death penalty for anyone who murders a foreign tourist.[6] He has pushed for an "instant check" system for gun purchases, was a leader for the Regulatory Reform and Relief Act, and was an architect of the Biomaterials Access Assurance Act, which guarantees the public's access to biomedical devices and the right to sue for any defects in the devices.[7]

The term limits campaign came to the forefront when Republicans swept into the majority in 1994. Gekas, not being part of that new wave of Republican legislators, never caught the term limit fever. He recognized, though, that there was a lot of sentiment for it and tried to forge a compromise solution. While he acknowledged that term limits might reduce the number of career politicians who seemingly were interested only in the next election cycle, he also was concerned that valuable congressional experience would be lost, thus allowing nonelected bureaucrats to take an even more prominent role in making policy. "The benefit derived from the continued experience of legislators being cut off does not serve the interest of the country," he commented.[8] Any term limits legislation, he felt, should not apply to Members who had been elected prior to its passage. His solution was to establish a limit of twelve years, with a Member being forced to take the next two years off, but then being eligible to run again and serve for an additional twelve years.[9] This was one Contract with America provision, then, that he could not support wholeheartedly.

George Gekas's first involvement with any aspect of the Clinton scandals was in early 1994 when he and Representatives Chris Cox and Bob Livingston sent what one commentator called "political letter bombs" to the White House, the Security and Exchange Commission, and the Office of Governmental Ethics. The subject of the letters was Hillary Clinton's investments, particularly the $100,000 the First Lady invested in a fund called Valuepartners I, which practiced the art of "short-selling," which allows one to make money when the value of a stock falls. The congressional letters questioned the propriety of this venture: "The ability of president and Ms. Clinton to affect prices in the securities markets is unique. The questions already raised publicly concerning their investments, particularly the short sales, must be addressed."[10]

Did he co-author those letters because he disliked the First Family? Were those letters merely the opening salvo of an impeachment mentality driven by hatred for Bill Clinton? Gekas denied any such motivation. In fact, he admitted to an admiration for President Clinton's communicative skills and his ability to connect with people. Gekas described the relationship he had with Clinton:

> Never once did I try to inflict punishment on him because he was of a different party. That never entered into it as far as I was concerned. I never had ill feelings against him. The two conferences that I had with him resulted in a one-on-one conversation: one was on health care, the unlamentable Hillary foray into government, and one other issue. [These conversations] were as good as the ones I had with Ronald Reagan and George Bush.[11]

That is not to say that Gekas did not resent some of Clinton's actions as President. "I did think that he grossly manipulated public sentiment with respect to the government shutdown episodes. . . . I really felt that that was politically motivated and Clintonian motivated rather than a good look at the consequences," he explained.[12] The use of the phrase "Clintonian motivated" was, to Gekas, quite appropriate because he felt that the President, by his actions, had invented a unique approach to politics that quite clearly should be named after him. Gekas did not offer that insight as a compliment.

Some of his constituents wrote letters criticizing his participation as a House Manager, but Gekas is convinced that his television appearances on programs such as Geraldo and Larry King blunted those criticisms. "Even those who opposed my point of view or my conclusions were beginning to acknowledge that I was pursuing it out of a sense of duty and of honor, not of vindictiveness or animus against the President," he believes.[13]

Despite his disagreements with President Clinton, some of Gekas's public stances reveal a dedication to the office of the presidency, even though Bill Clinton occupied it. Gekas opposed, for instance, the 1997 Supreme Court decision that allowed Paula Jones to sue the President while he still was in office. Stating a position with which not all Republicans agreed, Gekas said, "I personally believe the president should be immune from these types of legal actions while he is still president. In plain reading of the Constitution I find no justification for, or an allowance for, an indictment during incumbency." And in the middle of the Senate trial, he responded to a report that Ken Starr might bring an indictment of President Clinton while he was still in office by promising hearings to look into who had leaked the information. No matter the source of the report, even if it was the Office of the Independent Counsel, Gekas stated that such a leak was deplorable.[14]

The setting up of independent counsels bothered Gekas, and after the impeachment trial ended, he held hearings to consider how best to proceed. He concluded that "we'd be better off without it if we could ensure to the best of our abilities that an internal Justice Department investigation of matters that involved conflicts of interest could carry the day with the minimum vulnerability for connivance with the Administration."[15] Gekas proposed that such investigations in the future be handled by the Justice Department's Office of Public Integrity. The head of that office should be elevated to the level of an assistant attorney general, subject to Senate confirmation, for a fixed term that would extend beyond the next election cycle.[16] As of this writing, none of his proposals have been adopted.

Congressman Gekas became part of the impeachment process by virtue of his seat on the Judiciary Committee, not because he sought involvement. When the Committee held its hearings to determine whether a full investigation should proceed, Gekas was not yet convinced that President Clinton should be impeached, but he was quite concerned that perjury might have been committed. He commented,

> In the courthouse, which is so familiar to all of us, in every seat of every county government in the United States, the entire structure is bolstered not by the concrete of its foundation, but by oath: An oath is taken by the judge to exercise his responsibilities; an oath taken by the jury to exercise its responsibilities; an oath taken by the sheriff, by the bailiff, by the clerk of the court; an oath to administer justice, or all of us lose the chance at justice.
>
> To allow then a witness at this courthouse . . . to revert the entire process, the rights of everyone concerned, by giving false testimony—by committing perjury—crushes down against that courthouse and it collapses because of that one fatal blow that could arise in any single case, whether it is a traffic ticket or murder in the first degree.
>
> So, I am not yet satisfied that there is guilt or innocence with respect to the perjury allegation, but by darn it is worth fuller inquiry by this body.[17]

When that fuller inquiry concluded two months later, he was convinced that the President indeed deserved to be impeached. In his opening statement in the Committee just prior to the debate and votes on specific articles of impeachment, Congressman Gekas lamented the passing of a certain moment of truth: "If the president had indulged in a moment of truth in that first deposition a long time ago, in January of 1998, one small moment of truth, we would not be debating this momentous issue here today. But the president chose otherwise, throwing us into this morass of trouble and distinct tumult that we've engaged in for months now. So that moment of truth went by, was ignored, and now we're in trouble."[18] And, Gekas explained, it was trouble of a very serious nature:

> I say that a thousand historians and a swarm of political opinion polls and a gaggle of media programs and talk shows—nothing—none of those things can change the vital facts in this case, and that is that falsehoods were uttered in a court proceeding under oath, both in the depositions and later in a criminal federal grand jury. . . .
> . . . Leaping out of that mass of documents in those boxes in the Ford Building, and in all the testimony that we've had here, is the recurring theme of perjury—perjury—falsehood under oath. We can't escape it.[19]

Neither should the Committee, he urged, try to escape the fact that perjury is on a par with bribery. Bribery, which may last no longer as an act than ten minutes, constitutes grounds for impeachment; and perjury is even more grave than bribery, particularly when one considers that President Clinton perjured himself not only in January, but again in August before the grand jury. Gekas explained,

> Perjury, which is viewed by scholars and these same historians who enter our premises and spout the holiness of their positions would agree, that perjury, even in our statutory law, in our common law perceptions, and in practical application of the statutes, is more serious than bribery.
> And when coupled with the reality that every act of perjury strikes at the heart of the judicial system, endangers our individual rights to receive justice at the hands of our fellow citizens in the court system, then you can see . . . that perjury, falsehood under oath, has the capacity to destroy a branch of

government, two branches of government, as a matter of fact all three branches of government. If it's uttered by the president of the United States, he is diminishing the presidency, the executive branch. If he does so in a court of law, he is trampling against the walls of security that the court system provides all of us. And he injures the legislative branch because he forces upon us the indignity, I say, of having to deal with misconduct of the president that might lead to impeachment.

When all is said and done, the moment of truth will recur, and it will recur as each one of us finally indicates to the chair and to the clerk the final vote in this issue. I cannot erase from my mind or from the atmosphere of the Capitol of the United States, or from the entire land, from the entire globe, the falsehoods uttered under oath.[20]

Gekas did vote for the first three articles of impeachment, but when it came to the fourth, he offered an amendment. Part of the proposed fourth article dealt with the abuse of Executive Privilege. Gekas did not want that to be part of what was to be sent to the full House. He was not happy with it because he wanted to preserve the mechanism of Executive Privilege for future presidents: "I thought it was a disservice to the President, whose motivations we cannot, it seems to me, criticize on the impulse he would have to invoke Executive Privilege. After all, Executive Privilege may, in the long run, be the only feature that the President has in which he can act to preserve the national security almost without question, and subject only to the political price that he's willing to pay later."[21]

His amendment picked up support first from some fellow Republicans, then perhaps grudgingly, from a couple Democrats. In the end, he gained enough support for its passage. He looks back on that act as evidence of his independent thinking:

It would seem that that action on my part would silence forever anyone who would say that I was a rubber stamp for anti-Clintons or a rubber stamp for Ken Starr or for Gingrich or for anybody. And here not only was I not a rubber stamp, but I was an opponent of the Chairman's position—Chairman Hyde's position—on this particular issue. But that was not noted by anyone—my little venture there—as being anything out of the context of rigid Republican antagonism toward the President. So that shows you, it would seem to show you, that I had no animus against Clinton, and, certainly, I had a love of the Presidency and its attributes in moving the way I did.[22]

Gekas is adamant that there was no orchestration of the Republicans on the Committee in their move toward impeachment. Minority Leader Gephardt had been accusing Speaker Gingrich of directing the members of the Committee. Gekas explained that Gephardt thought the impeachment "was a Republican conspiracy to bring the President down. Gingrich was telling Hyde what to do and Hyde was telling us what to do, etc." Gekas denied the accusation: "None of that ever existed, not for one minute." Then Gephardt changed his tactic. "Ironically," noted Gekas, "when the Judiciary Committee was about to vote on articles of impeachment, Gephardt stood up and said, 'Here go the [Republicans] without direction, without leadership, no one advising them on the real course that they should take.' Here was just the opposite of his first accusation of directed action. . . . So I was very successful in my own mind of shutting all of that out and pursuing the job at hand."[23]

When the time came to choose the Managers, Gekas's seniority all but assured him a spot. In addition, he had served as a Manager previously in the impeachment of federal judge Alcee Hastings. "I knew the ropes, as we would say in the vernacular. I had participated in all phases of the impeachment: the original inquiry by the Judiciary Committee, the drafting and passage of the articles of impeachment, the appointment as a Manager, and the addressing of the Senate in the trial—debating from the Senate floor of the trial in presenting the wind-up speech in one of the sessions against the judge whom we were impeaching," Gekas explained.[24] He was going back to the Senate.

The Removal Challenge

Manager Gekas claims not to have been influenced by the pressures of conducting a trial against a popular President. He considered critics of the impeachment process to be "voices of blind opposition," and he "never allowed them to dissuade" him from the pursuit of his duty. "This was true before the election and after the election. The reduced margin that we received as a result of those elections, I think, played a role in the media saying it's a repudiation. I didn't see it as a repudiation. I saw it as a fact of political life that was due to a lot of other rationales," he explained. When asked by a reporter whether there should be a shakeup in the leadership, Gekas turned the tables by responding, "yes, Gephardt's got to go, meaning that we had won—three terms in a row retained the majority. He, Gephardt, had lost three time in a row. If anyone should be removed for failure, it would be the leadership of the opposition."[25]

As the Managers met to plot their strategy, Hyde assigned Gekas to be chair of a working group comprised of Chabot, Cannon, and Barr, "to demonstrate the legality or the legal definitions or the effects of perjury and obstruction of justice." As he studied the history of the President's statements under oath, Gekas detected something that he thought everyone else was missing. The impeachment articles centered on President Clinton's statements in the January deposition in the Paula Jones case and the statements he made during the grand jury questioning in August. His problems actually began prior to those incidents, noted the Congressman. The attorneys for Paula Jones had sent interrogatories to the President in December of 1997. He lied in those as well, in advance of the later statements. Those lies strengthened the contention that there was a pattern of lying and that "he committed falsehoods under oath right at the start." Gekas was concerned that no one else considered this significant enough to pursue:

> My contention was to the Managers, to my colleagues on the
> Judiciary Committee, was like a voice in the distant wind; they
> didn't catch what I was trying to say. He had not only already

committed falsehoods under oath, but even, if you felt that the deposition on January 17th or the grand jury in August were important cycles, he had established a pattern of conduct in December. Even if you had doubts about the 17th or the August testimony that he gave, he had already colored it with falsehoods so that you had the right to conclude that this parsing he did here and the hedging he did there were all meaningless or irrelevant because he had established the pattern back then.

... When the whole thing was over a month later, Judge Wright finds the President in contempt of court because of the interrogatories of December of 1997, vindicating my position, in which she said practically the same things that I was saying all this time. I said, where were you when I needed you, Judge Wright? I'll never understand fully why she had to wait until the end of all of this to come forth with those conclusions. ... The point is that I'll always feel that my theories, my presentation, were not given full credit by my fellow Managers and the Chairman, not out of any feelings of unfriendliness or anything like that, but just because they didn't see it the way I did.[26]

After the first set of Managers offered the evidence against President Clinton, the Gekas group came forward. Gekas's job was to introduce the legal presentation, then summarize after Chabot, Cannon, and Barr had made their cases. Their responsibility, said Gekas, was "to apply the statutory laws, the laws of our Nation as they obtain to the facts that you now have well ingrained into your consciences." He apologized to the Senators that they would have to hear some overlap from earlier presentations, but he urged that they give the Managers their undivided attention because of the seriousness of the charges.[27]

It all started with Paula Jones, Gekas noted, a "fellow American" who "no matter how she may have been described by commentators and pundits and talking heads ... did have a bundle of rights at her command. Those rights went into the core of our system of justice to bring the President into the case as a defendant." If the President truly committed perjury and obstruction of justice, then Paula Jones's rights were paramount:

> We are not saying that the President—even though the weight of the evidence demonstrates it amply—should be convicted of the impeachment which has brought us to this floor just because he committed perjury or obstructed justice, but because as a result of his actions both in rendering false-hoods under oath ... or in obstructing justice, that because of his conduct, he attempted to, or succeeded in, or almost succeeded in—it doesn't matter which of these results finally emerges—and attempted to destroy the rights of a fellow American citizen. That is what the gravamen of all that has occurred up to now really is.[28]

Obstructing justice sought by another American citizen "is soul search-ing in its quality," Gekas insisted. "That goes beyond those who would say, 'He committed perjury about sex. So what?' That goes beyond saying that 'This is just about sex. So what? Everybody lies about sex.'" When Senators had gone on the record with a "so what," that was a disturbing development, according to Gekas. There was a victim here. Her rights had been violated. At that juncture, he launched into his concern about the December 1997 interrogatories: "I say to the ladies and gentlemen of the Senate that this was the first falsehood stated under oath which became a chain reaction of falsehoods under oath, even without the oath, all the way to the nuclear explosion of falsehoods that were uttered in the grand jury in August of 1998.[29]

The perjury was important, Gekas continued, because of its conse-quences. Nearly everyone acknowledged that perjury had been commit-ted. Some were saying that it was not significant enough. But, Gekas countered, "If someone, a member of your family, or someone who is a witness to these proceedings has a serious case in which one's self, one's property, one's family has been severely damaged, would you suffer without a whimper perjurious testimony given against you?" He hoped that the application would make the matter more personal.[30]

When fellow Managers Chabot, Cannon, and Barr completed their tasks, it was Gekas's turn again. He concentrated on duty—the duty of the Managers to make their case and the duty of the Senators to judge rightly. "The moment of truth is fast approaching," he warned. It would "swoop down" on the Senators in the near future when they would cast their vote. That would prove to be "an awesome moment in the history of this Chamber, in the personal history of your own careers in public service, and of your own life, as well, your personal life, your surroundings, your family, all that means anything and everything to you." President Clinton had turned away from his moment of truth—would the Senate do the same?[31]

He then made the Managers' motives his next subject. The referral from Ken Starr was not the final word for his colleagues, Gekas explained: "We did not, as some people began to accuse and to orate, adopt 100 percent of what the independent counsel said were the allegations and accept them as fact, and then move on and skip from September to this moment, not having used our intellect, our sympathies, our sense of right, our sense of wrong, our sense of fairness . . . our experience . . . and our own consciences. . . . Everyone should know that. But it is not recognized. We have been pilloried many times over the course of these proceedings on the notion that we simply adopted that referral and walked with it into the Senate Chamber." They had too much respect for the Presidency to do that:

> But here is the point. The managers and I and every Member of the Senate, every individual who is with us here today reveres the office of the Presidency. . . . The Presidency is America. The Presidency is the banner under which we all work and live and strive in this Nation. We revere the Presidency. Any innuendo . . . to attribute any kind of motivation on the part of these men of honor who have prepared this

case for you today on any whim on their part other than to do their constitutional duty should be rebuffed at every conversation, at every meeting, at every writing that will ultimately flow from the proceedings that we have embarked upon.[32]

Gekas went on to assert that the Managers' reverence for the Presidency would be on display the very next week when President Clinton would give his State of the Union Address. They would stand and applaud his entrance, he predicted. Yet even while according him that privilege, they would not set aside the impeachment proceedings: "We compartmentalize ourselves as Americans recognizing that he holds the most powerful, most respected, and most admired office on the face of the globe. That is part of our duty, as it is our duty to impart our knowledge and our work, our theories, and our analysis to the impeachment proceedings which are at hand."[33]

No Senator, Gekas asserted, should vote for conviction or acquittal based upon personal feelings toward Bill Clinton. Any vote based on distaste or hatred toward the man "should never be recognized or countenanced, and history will condemn any individual who does that." The same applied to the other side: "And if the votes at the last moment, at this moment of truth, are based on an admiration of President Clinton, of friendship with President Clinton, a deep tie to and with the President, on family and community and national matters, a vote of acquittal should not be based on that." As for the Managers, they simply were doing their job:

> We cannot account for the friendship or enmity that might exist with and for President Clinton. All we can do is to do the job that was thrust upon us, that was placed in our hands by a statute that this Congress created—that independent counsel statute. The Congress said that we had to listen to the referral, to accept the referral. The Congress said that we must look towards whatever recommendations might be contained in that. It was the Congress, our Congress—many of you who

voted for that statute—which mandated that we consider all of this. We did not simply walk around one day and seize upon a moment of deep thought and say let's impeach the President; let's find something upon which we can base a full 6 months' inquiry into the President's actions in front of a court.

This was a duty, much as it is your duty to stay here and listen to what I am saying.[34]

The Senators kept listening, and on February 8, they heard Gekas make his final appeal. The American people, he summarized, know that there is only one real issue, even with the confusion of "all the fury and the tumult and the shouting and the invective, the language, and just the plain shouting that has occurred across the Halls of Congress and every place else in the country." That issue is this: "Did the President utter falsehoods under oath?" And Gekas said he was going to call as a witness the American people themselves. Greg Craig, one of the President's lawyers, had been delighted "to quote a poll that showed that 75 percent of the people of our country felt that there was no need to present videotapes to the Senate in the trial—75 percent, he said with great gusto, of the American people." Gekas then presented the Senate with another poll:

Of course the polls of all types were quoted time and time again by the supporters of the President as showing why you should vote to acquit. The polls, the polls, the polls.

I now call the American people's poll on whether or not they believe that the President committed falsehoods under oath—80 percent of the American people—I call them to my side here at the podium to verify to you that the President committed falsehoods under oath.[35]

That was one poll that did not impress half of the Senators.

The Ultimate Challenge:
Preserving the Government

So was this entire impeachment process a partisan witch-hunt, as some have asserted? Gekas acknowledges that partisanship does play a role. Impeachment always includes partisanship, particularly at the beginning. He notes, "In the impeachments about which we know something in the 1860s and in the President's case and in the halfway impeachment of Richard Nixon, it began with the opposite party beginning the movement. So that, by itself, shows that, historically, we have a partisan impetus to begin the impeachment. But that does not mean that the impetus is based solely on politics. There's a difference."[36]

The difference in the Clinton impeachment, according to Gekas, was the Independent Counsel statute. The Republicans followed a procedure that had been produced by the Democrats. "In doing so, we were bound, at least I felt we were bound, to review the product of the Independent Counsel and the recommendations and to act on them as lawyers—as members of the Judiciary Committee—and as citizens as well," he explained. So when critics say it is all politics, Gekas responds, "They gleefully overlook the fact that we were pursuing a statutory and constitutional duty thrust upon us—slammed down on our laps. I counter that charge of politics by enunciating these pegs of the chronology of events."[37]

In retrospect, he has no regrets over his involvement. In fact, he says he is proud of the fact that he "participated in that historic event." His biggest concern is for the health of the governmental system itself:

> I suppose that the main feature of the impeachment proceedings which I would like to have remain in historic perspective is that there will always be those who will scoff at misconduct or even reward it in plausible ways. There are others who, even though no matter how insignificant the infraction might be in the eyes of some, consider that the rule

of law is more important than anything for our system of government.

My chief tenet in this whole thing was the preservation of the three branches of government to prevent an assault by one of them on the other—or any of the other two. I considered that what the President did with respect to the falsehoods under oath and the manipulation of the judicial process (Judge Wright's forum) and the Judiciary Committee later and the grand jury later—all of that was an attack on another branch of government. I cannot to this day tolerate that. I want the lesson to be that the three branches of government are not just a nice lesson to be learned in civics, but they are actually important, vitally important, to our society.[38]

Chapter Nine Endnotes

[1] Jeffrey Gold, "Judge: Suspect in Threat to Rep. Gekas Was Probably Drunk," *The Associated Press*, 22 May 1999.

[2] "Robbers Mug Congressman," *Scramento Bee*, 6 November 1995, A8.

[3] Chase Squires, "Congressman Wants Death Penalty for Tourist Killers," *States News Service*, 27 September 1993.

[4] Gekas interview.

[5] Ibid.

[6] Squires.

[7] Gekas Biography; available at http://www.house.gov/gekas/biography.htm; accessed 13 November 2000.

[8] Brett Lieberman, "Midstate Republicans Say They Back Term Limits," *States News Service*, 29 November 1994.

[9] Paul Gigot, "You Didn't Mean that Term-Limit Stuff, Did You?" *The Wall Street Journal Europe*, 13 March 1995.

[10] Tony Snow, "Troubling Questions of Money," *The Arizona Republic*, 1 February 1994.

[11] Gekas interview.

[12] Ibid.

[13] Ibid.

[14] A. B. Stoddard, "Gekas to Probe Indictment Leak," *The Hill*, 3 February 1999, 1.

[15] Gekas interview.

[16] Alexander Bolton and Amy Keller, "House Prosecutors in President's Trial Propose Independent Counsel Reform," *Roll Call*, 15 March 1999.

[17] Statement of Congressman George W. Gekas, House Judiciary Committee, 5 October 1998; available at http://www.house.gov/judiciary/gekas1.htm; accessed 28 April 1999.

[18] The Impeachment Hearings: Opening Statements: George Gekas, 10 December 1998; available at http://www.washingtonpost.com/wp-srv/politics/special/clinton/stories/gekastext121098.htm; accessed 1 April 1999.

[19] Ibid.

[20] Ibid.

[21] Gekas interview.

[22] Ibid.

[23] Ibid.

[24] Ibid.

[25] Ibid.

[26] Ibid. Susan Webber Wright was the federal judge in Arkansas presiding over the Paula Jones lawsuit. She decided, after the impeachment trial ended, to hold President Clinton in contempt of court for his answers in the Jones deposition.

[27] Opening Statement of Hon. George Gekas, Senate Impeachment Trial of President Clinton, 15 January 1999; available at http://www.washingtonpost.com/wp-srv/politics/special/clinton/stories/gekastext011599.htm; accessed 24 November 2000.

[28] Ibid.

[29] Ibid.

[30] Ibid.

[31] Summary Statement of Hon. George Gekas, Senate Impeachment Trial of President Clinton, 16 January 1999; available at http://www.washingtonpost.com/wp-srv/politics/special/clinton/stories/gekastext011699; accessed 24 November 2000.

[32] Ibid.

[33] Ibid.

[34] Ibid.

[35] Closing Argument of Hon. George Gekas, Senate Impeachment Trial of President Clinton, 8 February 1999; available at http://www.house.gov/judiciary/gek0208.htm; accessed 9 February 2000.

[36] Gekas interview.

[37] Ibid.

[38] Ibid.

CHAPTER TEN

Lindsey Graham:
The Quotable Manager

Is this Watergate or Peyton Place?[1]

Everybody is sick to death of this! Count me in that category?[2]

I've talked in 30-second sound bites for so long, I've never had this much time . . . I can't believe 10 minutes went by so quick.[3]

Mr. President, you have one more chance. Don't bite your lip; reconcile yourself with the law.[4]

When I hear stomachs growling, I know it will be time to wrap this up.[5]

If I had been on the Supreme Court, I don't know if I would have ruled that way. There's not much chance of that happening any time soon, if you're worried about that.[6]

Baptists love repentance. I am a Baptist. In my church, everybody gets saved about every other week.[7]

There are more Baptists in my district than there are people.[8]

I come from a district where I am the first Republican in 120 years. They told me they hung the other guy, so I know I am doing better.[9]

If you could bring the Founding Fathers back, as everybody has suggested, the first debate would be, could we call them as

a witness? There would be some people objecting to that. Live
or dead, it's been hard to get a witness.[10]

Where I come from, you call somebody at 2:30 in the morning, you are up to no good.[11]

South Carolinian Lindsey Graham has a way with words. Of all the
House Managers, he probably came closest to being a media darling
because the media thrives on pithy phrases. Beyond the words themselves
was the folksy style in which they were uttered. Graham's humorous
comments and the manner in which he delivered them received the
attention, but his goal was not to entertain; he believed in what he was
doing: "I think we did a good enough job, the thirteen of us, going
against some very good lawyers on the other side . . . There is a *solid* case
that this President perjured himself and did the things that were alleged
by the House."[12]

Family and Faith

Lindsey Graham was born in 1955 in Seneca, South Carolina, and
lives there today, a lifelong bachelor. Graham's parents ran a combination
restaurant/bar/liquor store/pool hall in the small town of Central.
Lindsey ran the pool hall. "I've heard every story and then some," he
remembers. "At 3 o'clock in the afternoon the first shift would get off
from the mill, and people would come in just full of cotton and dust,
and they'd drink beer till midnight. And I've heard 'Satin Sheets to Lie
On and Satin Pillows to Cry On' a thousand times."[13] Some children
with that type of upbringing would have followed in those mill workers'
steps, but Graham saw the bad side of drinking and became a teetotaler.

He entered the University of South Carolina in 1977, but before he
graduated, his life circumstances changed dramatically. Both of his
parents died, and he was left as the unofficial guardian of his thirteen-
year-old sister, Darlene. Graham jokes that she turned out great "in spite
of" him. "I was probably a nut. I never let her date. I smelled her clothes if

she smoked. I listened in on her phone calls. I was probably pressing too hard, just 'cause I felt such responsibility for her," he explained.[14] Darlene, now married and a mother herself, offers nothing but praise for her older brother: "He's been more like a father than a brother to me. He could have just pawned me off on my aunt and uncle, but he didn't."[15]

The deep responsibility he felt for his sister matured him in another way. "I guess it was during that time that my faith grew," he recalls. Now he has faith in God as the ultimate judge and jury: "It sort of relaxes me a little bit that, you know, you pursue justice and your political agenda as hard as you can, and you take losses in a very disappointing way because I'm a competitive person. But the big picture is that our time on this world is limited and I believe very much in an afterlife where justice prevails, including [for] me. I mean, I'll pay for my sins. I just hope that, in spite of my sins, I'm forgiven."[16]

The Road to House Manager

After completing his undergraduate degree, Graham remained at the University of South Carolina, obtaining a law degree in 1981. He then joined the Air Force and became a member of the Judge Advocate General staff. Europe was his duty station. Major General Bryan Hawley, chief trial judge for Europe during Graham's tenure, praised Graham's work: "One, he was very intelligent, and two, he understands people. He has more common sense than I do."[17] Graham even was featured in a 1984 60 Minutes segment that critiqued the Air Force's drug-testing procedures. At the time, he was defending an Air Force pilot who had been accused of marijuana use.

Having completed his Air Force stint, Graham returned home to set up shop as a lawyer. His first political victory occurred in 1992 when he was elected to a state House seat. A mere two years later, he was part of the "Republican Revolution" when the GOP took control of the full Congress for the first time since the 1952 elections. He won with 60 percent of the vote.

As a member of that 1994 freshman class, the group that ran on the Contract for America, one might have expected complete loyalty from Graham, but often he showed an independent streak. He was one of eleven Republican Congressmen, in March 1997, to go against the House Republican leadership "on a procedural measure that effectively blocked Congress's ability to fund its own activities."[18] This was a response to their exasperation with Speaker Newt Gingrich's increasing, and what they considered unilateral, compromises with the Clinton Administration. Four months later, he took part in an internal coup attempt, which the Speaker survived. At the time, Graham was quoted as saying that Gingrich should stop "playing footsie with the White House," stay faithful to Republican principles, or step aside to allow a truly committed conservative to lead.[19]

Then, in 1998, Graham personally scolded fellow Republican Bud Shuster on the House floor for sending up a highway bill out of the Transportation Committee that would make "a sham" out of the Party's stated goal for a balanced budget.[20] While these departures from orthodoxy did not endear him to certain Party leaders, his political star continued to rise.

Although Graham wanted from the first to be on the Judiciary Committee, that did not materialize until 1998, after the deaths of Congressmen Steve Schiff and Sonny Bono. Graham did not realize at the time that the Clinton scandals would escalate: "When I came on, this [impeachment] was something that we may have to deal with. But lo and behold, six months later we're in the middle of this thing."[21]

What were his personal feelings toward President Clinton? To be sure, Graham disagreed with the President's politics, but he felt an internal pressure to ensure that he was not simply taking an opportunity to score a political triumph. Neither did he wish to focus merely on a man's personal failings. He wanted to "make sure people understood that I understood it can't be about sinning. If you bring impeachment cases against people for human failings, you'll run good people out of politics. As much as I dislike the President's political agenda and him politically, I tried very hard to make sure that my vote and my analysis of the evidence wasn't driven by my desire to take advantage of his failings. If it's just about an affair, even though it's embarrassing and inappropriate, you can't use that type [of] human failing in a constitutional manner because you'll distort what impeachment is about historically and in the future. It will become a political tool."[22]

One of his deepest disappointments was how the White House attacked Independent Counsel Kenneth Starr, who, according to Graham, simply was doing his job. The unfairness of the treatment he received bothered Graham considerably. "Ken Starr is a good example of [the] sort of the world we live in," he observed. "If you get the right people who are talented and gifted in maybe a bad way, you can make the guy pursuing the evidence who has lived a life beyond question, somebody you would love to have as your neighbor . . . a guy like Ken Starr, in the eyes of the public, can be the bad guy." He continued,

> Can you only imagine what Ken Starr went through every day? He probably said, "What have I done?" You know, you wake up every day and you're the bad guy in the paper. Doing my job. Following the evidence trail, three-judge panel approved the investigation, the attorney general said, "Go look into this." Yet, over time, people see you as the villain and the President's being the victim . . .
>
> The Ken Starr experience was something I'll always remember—how a very nice, God-fearing man could become the bad guy to so many people.[23]

Graham also felt that hypocrisy dominated the entire episode. A Republican never would have been treated with such kid gloves by certain groups and the media:

> I'm convinced if this had been a Republican President accused of messing with the evidence and tampering with witnesses and giving false testimony when he was in a power-

ful position allegedly abusing a young lady, that the outrage would have been beyond belief. The National Organization of Women and other liberal groups would have been chained to the White House demanding an answer to the whining debauchery charge, "Did the President commit rape?" So, I think it was a good example of sort of a double standard here. You know, what Clarence Thomas went through and the scrutiny there. That's the political aspects of what we were dealing with. Sort of a media filter that was always going to seize on the opportunity to paint us and Ken Starr as being part of the problem.[24]

When the Judiciary Committee began discussing the possibility of impeachment, despite his concerns, Graham was unsure at first whether he could support impeachment articles. In a statement in the Judiciary Committee hearings on whether to open an impeachment inquiry, Graham clarified his position at the outset: "I have no clue what I am going to do yet. I can tell you that and look you in the eye and honestly mean it. I don't know if censure is appropriate, we should just drop it, or throw him out of office."[25] His now-famous "Watergate or Peyton Place" question followed, but then he focused on the issue of political expediency:

> Let me tell you, if I followed the polls, I know what I would do. In my district, people have no use for this president—none, zero, zip. Eighty-two percent of the people in one part of my district want to throw him out of office. If I followed the polls, I could sit up here and rant and rave and become governor at home. I don't want to be governor that way.
>
> I want to be a good congressman who thirty years from now, not just thirty days from now, people thought did the right thing. And the right thing is to take this seriously. . . .
>
> Nobody can tell me yet whether this is part of a criminal enterprise or a bunch of lies which build upon themselves

based on not wanting to embarrass your family. If that's what it is, about an extramarital affair with an intern, and that's it, I will not vote to impeach this president no matter if eighty-two percent of the people back home want me to because we will destroy this country.

If it is about a criminal enterprise where the operatives of the president at every turn confront witnesses against him in illegal ways, threaten people, extort them; if there is a secret police unit in this White House that goes after women or anybody else who gets in the way of this president, that is Richard Nixon times ten and I will vote to impeach him.[26]

Over the next two months, Graham became convinced that President Clinton had done a good deal more than just try to cover up personal embarrassment. Graham always was comparing the case before him with Watergate. Was it the same? Were the issues at stake as significant? He eventually saw a parallel. "It wasn't the classic abuse of power," he concluded, "using the IRS to get political enemies, breaking into people's offices and trying to get dirt on them. But it was just as *important* . . . It was just as abusive and potentially fatal to our system. Nixon abused his power for political gain. He was trying to use the office of the White House, and all of his operatives went too far in trying to get an upper hand on their political rivals because they didn't trust the American *electoral* system to get it right. Well, Clinton didn't trust the American *legal* system to get it right. So he went on a full-scale assault on the legal system, as Nixon did on the electoral system. He used his position as President, in my opinion, to start manufacturing stories against potential witnesses like Monica Lewinsky."[27]

The key for Graham was those manufactured stories.[28] They highlighted an inexcusable manipulation of the system for personal survival. He was particularly galled by the President's lies about Lewinsky to aide Sidney Blumenthal, knowing that Blumenthal would then make sure Clinton was vindicated in the press:

After he told that story to Mr. Blumenthal, White House sources were telling reporters all over this town that "she wears her dresses too tight, she's known as Elvira," they called her a stalker . . . the whole family was a little crazy, she had an abortion. All this stuff started leaking out to reporters throughout the town where interns would say, yes, she followed the President around; she really had a thing for the President. The whole purpose of these leaked stories was to set her up as being an unbelievable witness if she ever turned. I believe, and I know now, the President started that whole scenario. It went on for about two months. He sat on the sidelines, and he was willing to let it happen. He knew it was untrue. In fact, they did have a relationship. He was willing to let her become the predator and he be seen as the victim. He did it in a clever and sophisticated way.[29]

Graham considered the highlighting of the President's manipulation of his aides to be his biggest contribution to the entire impeachment inquiry discussion. "Once that became clear and better known," he opined, "a lot of the rhetoric on the Democratic side, about how this was a witch-hunt, *changed*. It was lowered, and it went to 'this is not a removable offense.'"[30]

By the time the vote came for articles of impeachment, Graham had become convinced the President should be removed from office. Before that vote, he got the opportunity to express his views one last time. In the Committee hearing and in front of all the media crushed into the room, Graham commented first on the issue of partisanship: "We are going to have a partisan vote, but that's okay. You have parties, you have political thought, you have political differences. That's a good thing, not a bad thing. A lot of people have fought and died so you could have those differences."[31]

He then gave what credit he could to the Democratic side when he noted that not one Democrat on the Committee had "ever suggested that the president's conduct was acceptable." He wanted the record to reflect that. He decided that it had come down to a difference between "a Republican conscience versus a Democratic conscience." For his part, he had "tried to take a tone here that the law has to win out over politics."[32] The President's unwillingness to set matters right made his vote for impeachment the only viable option:

> I have asked the president on numerous occasions to reconcile himself with the law. I never meant for him to have to humiliate himself. . . . I do not want to take money out of his pocket. I do not want to humiliate him in front of his family or daughter. I merely want him to have the character and the courage to come forward and admit to criminal wrongdoing, that he violated his oath, that he engaged witnesses in an improper way. I was willing to make sure, if I could in any fashion, that the whole affair would end then, that two years from now he need not have to face prosecution. I think the chances of that are almost zero.
>
> That's all I ever wanted from my president. I'm about to vote. I have yet to receive that. I don't know if I will ever get it. Bill Clinton's fate, ladies and gentlemen, is in Bill Clinton's hands. The biggest enemy of Bill Clinton, just like with all of us, is Bill Clinton. . . .
>
> God knows he's a polarizing figure. God only knows what's in his heart. I'm having to judge Bill Clinton based on the evidence.[33]

Should the President be impeached? "Very quickly," Graham concluded. Any President called upon to testify before a grand jury must tell the truth; any President who does not should lose his job. "I believe that about Bill Clinton, and I'll believe that about the next president. If it had been a Republican," he continued, "I would have still believed that, and I would hope that if a Republican person had done all this that some of us would've went [sic] over and told him, 'You need to leave office.'"[34]

Prior to his statement, Graham had exchanged caustic comments with one of the President's lawyers, Charles Ruff. Exasperated by the approach the President's lawyers had taken to defend their client, Graham's patience ran out. "If people in America follow Bill Clintonspeak, we're going to ruin the rule of law," he lectured Ruff, "and he's not worth that. No one person in America is worth trashing out the rule of law and creating a situation where you can't rely on your common sense. I can only believe your defense if I check my common sense at the door and I forget the way the world really works."[35] He felt he had tried to be open to any viable defense for the President, but he had never heard one.

Ultimately, he voted in favor of three of the four impeachment articles. "I voted against Article 2, his deposition testimony [in the Paula Jones case], which was the most obvious lie, because the judge dismissed the deposition. The lawsuit was dismissed. I thought an average person wouldn't be prosecuted with a case being dismissed, with a deposition deemed inadmissible, but the judge fined him $90,000, which I thought was an *appropriate* response," he explained (emphasis added).[36]

In the full House debate, Graham again emphasized that partisanship was not the reason for this critical crossroads in American government. Rather, America come to these crossroads because of "the conduct of one man who happened to be the president, who happened to be elected by the people and given the most solemn responsibility in the nation, to be the chief law enforcement officer of the land, and he failed miserably in that responsibility. . . . The day that William Jefferson Clinton failed to provide truthful testimony to the Congress . . . is the day that he chose to determine the course of impeachment."[37]

In between the Committee vote and the debate in the full House, actor Robert DeNiro made phone calls to undecided House Members, hoping his star power might impress the Members to vote against impeachment. Somehow, Graham got on DeNiro's list. He took the call good-naturedly, asking DeNiro to take him off the list "until [Clinton] admits to criminal wrongdoing; then you can call me back." DeNiro's spokesman denied any White House involvement, but Graham was unconvinced. "I don't know who's in charge down there [at the White House]," he commented, "but Bill Clinton is impeaching himself. They talk about the House [being] out of control? They're out of control."[38]

Unlike some of the other Republicans, Graham continued to consider the censure option. Yet he believed a full Senate trial was essential first; otherwise, conflicting claims never would be resolved. He felt that anything less would leave "chaos in its wake because you've got unresolved [legal] issues." If the Senate decided not to remove President Clinton from office, Graham was willing to live with that decision, as long as the Senate also concluded that the President had indeed violated the law. "Don't bastardize the process because we're tired of it," Graham offered. "If you acquit the president, so be it. But I would like for the House to have a chance to prove why we thought he committed a crime." Neither should it be a quick affair such as a one-day trial. "History should be able to look back and say this was not about partisan politics—this was based on the record. . . . The key thing to me," he continued, "is that the president is a lawbreaker. . . . But everyone who breaks the law doesn't get the death penalty."[39]

Graham did have a different view of the viability of censure than some of the other Managers. For others, censure could not be an option because the Constitution made no provision for it. Censure would be a penalty beyond the authority granted by that document. It also would be a bill of attainder, which was clearly unconstitutional. Yet as he moved forward toward the Senate trial, he agreed with every one of the other Managers that the President ought to be removed from office.

The Senate Trial

Graham's task on the Senate side was to show that previous Senate decisions on impeachment bolstered the Managers' argument that President Clinton should be dismissed from his position. He chose not to prepare a full text ahead of time; instead, he spoke from an outline only. "Reading to somebody for an hour would put ME to sleep," he told an interviewer prior to his presentation. He thought he would do a better job just talking to his audience rather than giving a smooth speech. He understood the potential pitfalls of his approach: "It sometimes doesn't come across as coherent or polished as you sitting there reading something," he admitted, then added, "but I think it's more interesting."[40]

Speaking before the Senate, particularly on such a weighty matter, did generate some nervousness in the Congressman. He knew he was speaking not to the Senate only, but to an unknown number of citizens across the country. Specifically, he was aware that all lawyers nationwide would be sitting in judgment on his words. "It's all so surreal," he acknowledged. "It's like a movie you're watching—but you're in it. And there's no intermission."[41]

Graham realized that his presentation—comparing the Clinton situation with other impeachments—was important: "We need to take a good shot on the issue that our case . . . when compared to other cases where people lost their jobs through impeachment, is better." He also added, "The David and Goliath thing is a good example here. I think I know a little bit how David felt."[42]

He also felt similar to David because of the rules enacted by the Senate for conducting the trial. Graham, like all the other Managers, wanted to bring in live witnesses, but the Senate said no. As Graham remembers, "When we wanted to bring witnesses, they [the Senators] were very resistant, and it was politically smelling up the place. The polls were against us. The Senate Republicans were getting no help from the Democrats, so they came up with this convoluted system that basically prevented you from calling witnesses, and all you do was sit there and argue among lawyers for two weeks."[43]

The Senate rules so upset some of the Managers that a few considered not participating in what they saw as a fiasco. Graham, although just as incensed, offered this insight: "Well, let's think of this politically. What happens if we go in there and take on the Republicans in the Senate by refusing to participate?" According to Chief Investigative Counsel David Schippers, that comment caused fuming Managers to reconsider. The trial would proceed.[44]

When asked if he thought the Senate verdict was a foregone conclusion, the Congressman characteristically answered point-blank:

> Yeah. The only thing that would have changed it is to create some drama. If you have a trial based on paper, you'll never get where you want to go as a prosecutor. So what we had to do was somehow get a live witness to create some interest in the trial. People wanted it over. I knew that if we couldn't call witnesses to fully explore the facts and show people how bad this actually was—and to get through the sound bites and actually have a witness testify without somebody telling you what the witnesses said and dramatically lay it out—if we could have done that, then I think you'd have had some public interest. The offenses and the gravity of the offenses would have jumped out at you more, [creating] a possibility of changing the political dynamic, which may have kicked loose some Democratic votes. As long as it became a paper case . . . political interest was low.[45]

But, foreordained conclusion or not, Graham pressed ahead with his contribution to the Managers' argument.

Although he was supposed to concentrate on past Senate impeachments, it took a while for Graham to get to that particular subject. He had a number of other statements he wanted to make first, beginning with some comments about seeing Japanese tourists in the Capitol, and comparing that with his father's service in World War II against the Japanese. His point was that America was incredibly resilient and that no matter what the Senate decided, the nation would survive. He also commented on the tedious process of listening to so many lawyers, and he said that people may be bored with it. But he did not think boredom was a problem; it spoke instead of how the country went about its business in spite of what was transpiring in the Senate chamber. "How many countries would love the chance to be bored when their government is in action? How many countries fear that the government won't work for them, that to get it right, you've got to pick up a gun?" he asked.[46]

Graham then talked about the rule of law and the extension of it to all Americans, drawing on his personal knowledge of civil rights issues for blacks in South Carolina. He then applied the rule of law to sexual harassment cases. That naturally led into the entire reason for the Senate being convened that day: President Clinton had been accused of sexual harassment. Although Graham went on to say that no one besides the parties involved and God really knew what happened, he was proud of a country "where you as a low-level employee can sue the governor of your state. And if that governor becomes president, you can still sue. The Supreme Court said 9-0, a shutout legally, Mr. President, you will stand subject to this suit." Was this truly a "big deal"? He believed it was:

> I would contend to you, ladies and gentlemen of the Senate, it became a big deal about being president when he raised the defense "You can't sue me now because I'm the president. I'm a busy man. I've got a lot going on." He used his office—or tried to—to avoid the day in court. But the Supreme Court said, "No, sir, you will stand subject to suit under some reasonable accommodations. [47]

Is it really that much of a burden to lay on a President to tell the truth in a judicial setting? Yet the President, countered Graham, seemed to believe it was too heavy a load. After lying in his deposition in the Paula Jones case, he did the same before a grand jury in August 1998. Even though we all have "human failings," Graham noted, the Senate should take action because President Clinton's actions were "so premeditated, so calculated, so much my interest over anybody else or the public be damned." The President had failed the character test, and Graham offered him this advice: "Don't cheat in a lawsuit by manipulating the testimony of others. Don't send public officials and friends to tell your lies before a federal grand jury to avoid your legal responsibilities. Don't put your legal and political interests ahead of the rule of law and common decency." He continued,

I don't want my country to be the country of great equivo-
cators and compartmentalizers for the next century. That's
what this case is about—equivocation and compartmentalizing
. . . We're asking no more of him [President Clinton] than to be
the chief law enforcement officer of the land. Follow your job
description. [48]

After his lengthy introduction, Graham laid out the history of recent
impeachments of federal judges. The foundation of his argument was
that there were not separate standards for judges and presidents. "When a
judge is impeached in the United States of America, the same legal standard . . . is applied to that judge's conduct as it is to any high official just
like the president. So, we're comparing apples to apples," he explained.

The first example he gave was the 1986 impeachment of Harry
Claiborne of Nevada, who was removed from office by a Senate vote of 90-
7. He was impeached for filing a false income tax return. Graham briefly
recounted the trial:

One thing they said in that case was, well, I'm a judge, and
filing false income tax returns has nothing to do with me
being a judge. And I ought not to lose my job unless you can
show me or prove that I did something wrong as a judge.

They were saying cheating on your taxes has nothing to do
with being a judge. You know what the Senate said? It has
everything to do with being a judge. And the reason you said
that is because you didn't buy into this idea that the only way
you can lose your job as a high government official under the
Constitution is to engage in some type of public conduct
directly related to what you do every day.

You took a little broader view, and I'm certainly glad you
did, because this is not a country of high officials who are tech-
nicians, this is a country based on character, this is a country
based on having to set a standard that others will follow willingly.[49]

Graham then turned to the case of Walter Nixon of Mississippi, an impeachment trial that was sent to the Senate in 1989. The Senate removed Nixon from office for perjury before a grand jury. He had tried to "fix a case" for the son of a business partner. He then lied about trying to do so. Graham explained,

> I guess you could say, what's that got to do with being a federal judge, it wasn't even in his court? It has got everything to do with being a high public official. Because if he stays in office, what signal are you sending anybody else that you send to his courtroom or anybody else's courtroom?
>
> The question becomes, if a federal judge can be thrown out of office for lying and trying to fix a friend's son's case, can the president of the United States be removed from office for trying to fix his case?[50]

Alcee Hastings of Florida, also in 1989, was another judge removed from his position by the Senate. This one had a little twist, though. "You know what's interesting about this case to me?" Graham queried. "He was acquitted before he got here." In other words, Graham explained, a court had declared Hastings not guilty of conspiring to take money to fix results in his own court, yet the Senate still found his behavior unacceptable:

> You know what the United States Senate and the House said? We believe your conduct is out of bounds, and we're not bound by that acquittal. We want to get to the truth, and we don't want federal judges that we have a strong suspicion or reasonable belief about that are trying to fix cases in their court.
>
> So, the point I'm trying to make is you don't even have to be convicted of a crime to lose your job in this constitutional republic if this body determines that your conduct as a public official is clearly out of bounds in your role.
>
> Thank God you did that.

> Beause impeachment is not about punishment. Impeach-
> ment is about cleansing the office. Impeachment is about
> restoring honor and integrity to the office.[51]

President Clinton, in Graham's view, had destroyed the honor and integrity of the presidency. The only remedy was to cleanse the office of its current occupant. He challenged the Senators by pressing the point that they could not live with themselves if they left a perjuring judge on the bench; therefore, they shouldn't be able to leave a perjuring President in office. The Constitution covers that. "The vice president will be waiting outside the doors of this chamber. Our constitutional system is simple and it's genius all at the same time. If that vice president is asked to come in to assume the mantle of chief executive officer of the land, chief law enforcement officer of the land, it will be tough, it will be painful, but we will survive and we will be better for it," he said.[52]

By focusing on the fact that the election would not really be overturned because Vice President Gore would immediately take up the mantle of the presidency if Clinton was turned out of office, Graham had made a telling point—so telling that the Senate Democrats were dispirited after his presentation. As Bob Bauer, lawyer for Minority Leader Tom Daschle, commented, "This guy's killing us." No longer did removal of the President seem so significant. As one analyst noted, Graham had made the unthinkable thinkable.[53]

Unfortunately, though, during the question-and-answer period, when Senators had their queries funneled through the Chief Justice, Manager Graham seemed to provide an out for any wavering Democrats. When the Manager team was asked if reasonable people could disagree that the President had to be removed from office for his misdeeds, Graham replied, "Absolutely." He continued, "I would be the first to admit that the Constitution is silent on this question about whether or not every high crime has to result in removal. If I was sitting where you are, I would probably get down on my knees before I made that decision. Because the impact on society is going to be real either way. You have to consider what is best for this nation." This effectively cut out the heart of the prosecution's argument and, tactically, has to go down as one of the most obvious missteps in the case. It provided cover for Democratic Senators seeking it. Other Managers attempted to counteract the response, but the damage had been done.[54]

Despite that comment, Manager Graham still believed personally that the President should be removed. During his closing argument on February 8, he made one last appeal to the Senators:

> If you have kept an open mind, you have fulfilled your job. If you have listened to the facts and you vote your conscience, you will have fulfilled your job. I will not trample on your conscience; I have said that before. I started this process with great concern, and I leave with a lot of contentment because I believe the facts have withstood the test of every type of scrutiny and demagoguery that have been thrown at them. They stand firm. Do you know what they are going to stand? They're going to stand the test of history. Some people suggest that history may judge you badly if you vote to convict this President. I suggest that will be the least of your problems. . . .
>
> Let me tell you what it all comes down to for me. If you can go back and explain to your children and your constituents how you can be truthful and misleading at the same time, good luck. . . .
>
> I want my country to go boldly into the next century. I don't want us to limp into the next century. I don't want us to crawl into the next century regardless of rule of law. No matter what you do, we will make it. But the difference between how you vote here, I think, determines whether we go boldly with the rule of law intact, or whether we have to explain it for generations to come.
>
> I leave with you an example that I think says much. General MacArthur was removed by President Truman, a very popular

fellow at the time. The reaction to the MacArthur dismissal was even more violent than Truman had expected. And for an entire year the majority of public opinion ranked itself ferociously against him. He said characteristically, as he felt that hostile poll, "I wonder where Moses would have gone if they had taken a poll in Egypt? And what would Jesus Christ have preached if they had taken a poll in the land of Israel? It isn't polls that count. It is right and wrong and leadership of men with fortitude, honesty, and the belief in the right that make epics in the history of the world."[55]

Looking Back

Graham has no regrets about his involvement with the impeachment, but that does not mean he is happy with some of the consequences. On the positive side, he believes the country came through the trauma well. He is pleased that the Managers "reinforced the idea that the Presidency is not a kingship, that we have reinforced a young generation of Americans, there are consequences to going too far." Prosecuting this case was necessary, he emphasizes: "If we had swept this under the rug and taken the political way out and followed the polls of the moment, then I think we wouldn't have a clear view of what this case was all about."[56]

He is particularly gratified with the leadership shown by Henry Hyde during the most trying of times. Republicans on the Judiciary Committee were a dispirited group after the 1998 elections, he recalls, not only because of the loss of House seats, but also because of the resignation of Newt Gingrich, followed the next month by Bob Livingston's resignation. Hyde, he says, rose to the occasion: "This is where I think he becomes a historic figure because there's no real Republican leadership around. All these guys are falling like flies, and people want to bury this in the back yard . . . And Henry, to his credit, called us right after the election and asked us how it would affect us personally. I remember very much in a conference call, every person, to a man, said press on. We knew it was tough, but we felt an obligation beyond our political careers to see where this thing takes us."[57]

The only regret to which Graham will admit is that his name will be forever linked to impeachment. His legacy will start off with that fact. "I didn't come up here to impeach the President. I came up here to change Social Security, protect the unborn, do all the things that a good fiscal and social conservative wants to do and have a debate with my liberal friends," he explains.[58]

The Republicans made some mistakes, he acknowledges. They allowed the process to get too partisan. For instance, his side of the aisle could have agreed on time limits for the hearings. The Democrats, however, exuded partisanship from the beginning, he believes. They "were just very hard to work with, very partisan. So that set a tone. . . . As the moderates in our party looked on the hearings, you could see the other side being very loud and shrill. You could see our side trying very hard to lay out a case."[59] Clearly, he sees a distinction between the outward actions of the parties: the Democrats were more concerned about saving the President than finding the truth; the Republicans were methodical in their investigation into the accusations, seeking to know the truth.

Charges of "playing politics" with the future of the President do not sit well with Graham. How could the Republicans' investigation possibly have helped them politically, particularly with the poll numbers strongly against them during the impeachment process? "If people said we did this for political reasons, then that makes no sense because it was the dumbest thing you could do politically at the time," he reasons. Although it may have been a politically "dumb" thing to do, he is proud of his party for doing what was best for the country:

> I knew that our political future as a Party was very much at risk, and we did it anyway. That's why I'm sort of looking back a year later, proud of the fact that we put our interest as a political group secondary to something. I can't tell you how many times I heard, as this vote was about to be cast, from people

from the northeast, more moderate districts from California and other places, "this may cost me my career, but I feel good about it." There were people going in there, putting that card in and voting yes, that were truly courageous.

Because when they cast that vote last year, in December of 1998, many of them thought—more than a few thought—it would be the end of their political career. It wasn't out of hatred of Clinton. There was no joy going, "Boy, I'm going to get that bastard, no matter what." None of that. They had a quiet, calm resolve that I've had a hard decision to make and I feel good about it. Those are the heroes of this case. Not some guy from the South who is a prosecutor by trade. But it's those people in the House, and some people in the Senate, who were in tough situations, who said, go forward, make people vote. I can't say there were many Democrats who rose to the occasion. [60]

Graham says he is most concerned for two groups: the young people of America and the future lawyers and judges. He wants the first group to understand that leadership requires honesty and that if you lie, you will pay a price. For the second group, the future lawyers and judges, he hopes "they will realize that our profession was on trial and that, as a profession, we passed. . . . The Chief Justice of the Supreme Court presided over a trial that, basically, will be a model for the ethical conduct of all lawyers to follow throughout the rest of the history of our country." Regarding the President, he adds, "It's important to me that the President should lose his law license. If the President does lose his law license—he's been fined by a federal judge—then I think a lot of people in my profession are going to see this as a wake-up call. We're going to try to clean our act up."[61]

Graham is happy to see that the public is, over time, grasping the truth:

No matter how good the rules are, and no matter how strong your justice principles are in terms of trying to get to the truth, human beings are involved in the process. Things go on inside a courtroom that are affected by things outside a court-room. An impeachment is very much that same way . . .

But, in the end, this is all gonna come out okay. A year after the trial, public opinion is that he *did* it. It wasn't because of some right-wing conspiracy of a bunch of zealots. It's because the President lied under oath, manipulated the evidence in a lawsuit where he was the defendant, in a way that would put the average person in serious legal jeopardy.

I think most Americans, 80 percent plus now, believe the President did commit perjury and obstructed justice. Over half the American people believe impeachment was warranted. That's up from 35 percent. So, it's my hope and belief that, over time, as the trauma of impeachment passes . . . that there will be more of a focus on the President being the author of his own fate.[62]

Chapter Ten Endnotes

[1] Statement of Congressman Lindsey Graham, House Judiciary Committee," 5 October 1998; available at http://www.house.gov/judiciary/graham.htm; accessed 28 April 1999.

[2] Lloyd Grove, "Rep. Graham's Southern Droll; GOP Lawmaker Keeps His Wit About Him on Judiciary Panel," *The Washington Post*, 7 October 1998, D1.

[3] The Impeachment Hearings: Opening Statements: Lindsey Graham, 11 December 1998; available at http://www.washingtonpost.com/wp-srv/politics/special/clinton/stories/graham121198.htm; accessed 1 April 1999.

[4] Ibid.

[5] Opening Statement of Lindsey Graham, Senate Impeachment Trial, 16 January 1999.

[6] Ibid.

[7] Questions and Answers, Senate Impeachment Trial of President Clinton, 23 January 1999; available at http://www.washingtonpost.com/wp-srv/politics/special/clinton/stories/questiontext1012399.htm; accessed 20 July 2000.

[8] Congressman Lindsey Graham, interview by author, tape recording, Washington, DC, 28 March 2000.

[9] Closing Argument of Hon. Lindsey Graham, Senate Impeachment Trial of President Clinton, 8 February 1999; available at http://www.house.gov/judiciary/grah0208.htm; accessed 9 February 2000.

[10] Ibid.

[11] Rebuttal Remarks of Hon. Lindsey Graham, Senate Impeachment Trial of President Clinton, 6 February 1999; available at http://www.washingtonpost.com/wp-srv/politics/special/clinton/stories/defensestext020699.htm; accessed 20 July 2000.

[12] Graham interview.

[13] Grove, "Graham's Southern Droll."

[14] Ibid.

[15] "Graham Still Sees Himself As Hometown Guy," *The Associated Press Political Service*, 27 July 1995.

[16] Graham interview.

[17] Grove, "Graham's Southern Droll."

[18] Guy Gugliotta, "GOP Rebels: Older, Bolder, More Influential," *The Washington Post*, 3 April 1998, A1.

[19] Dan Hoover, "Return to GOP Agenda or Step Down, Graham Says of Newt Gingrich," *Greenville (South Carolina) News*, 19 July 1997.

[20] Ibid.; also Grove, "Graham's Southern Droll."

[21] Graham interview.

[22] Ibid.

[23] Ibid.

[24] Ibid.

[25] Graham, House Judiciary Committee, 5 October 1998.

[26] Ibid.

[27] Graham interview.

[28] Robert Novak, "A Dirty Trick Overlooked by Starr," *Chicago Sun-Times*, 14 December 1998, 33.

[29] Graham interview.

[30] Ibid.

[31] The Impeachment Hearings: Opening Statements: Lindsey Graham, 11 December 1998.

[32] Ibid.

[33] Ibid.

[34] Ibid.

[35] Lizette Alvarez, "Conservative Ally of Clinton Turns Against the President," *The Cleveland Plain Dealer*, 12 December 1998, 9A.

[36] Graham interview.

[37] McLoughin, *The Impeachment and Trial of President Clinton*, 174.

[38] Chris Collins, "Graham Says DeNiro Called Him to Lobby for Clinton," *Gannett News Service*, 15 December 1998.

[39] "Graham Says He Could Support Censure If Senate Holds Full Trial," *The Associated Press Political Service*, 29 December 1998.

[40] Chris Collins, "Rep. Graham Tells Senate Clinton Must Be Removed," *Gannett News Service*, 16 January 1999.

[41] Chris Collins, "Garrulous House Manager Lindsey Graham Nervous About Talking Before Senate," *Gannett News Service*, 13 January 1999.

[42] Ibid.

[43] Graham interview.

[44] Schippers, *Sellout*, 13.

[45] Graham interview.

[46] Opening Statement of Lindsey Graham, Senate Impeachment Trial, 16 January 1999.

[47] Ibid.

[48] Ibid.

[49] Ibid.

[50] Ibid.

[51] Ibid.

[52] Ibid.

[53] Baker, *The Breach*, 313.

[54] Ibid., 342-43.

[55] Closing Argument of Hon. Lindsey Graham, Senate Impeachment Trial of President Clinton, 8 February 1999.

[56] Graham interview.

[57] Ibid.

[58] Ibid.

[59] Ibid.

[60] Ibid.

[61] Ibid.

[62] Ibid.

CHAPTER ELEVEN

Asa Hutchinson:
The Other Man from Arkansas

It was 1984. The Arkansas State Police were closing in. They had set up and secretly tape-recorded five cocaine deals. Then they confronted the dealer; he was being charged with distribution of cocaine. The perpetrator tried to deny any involvement, but when told he had been tape-recorded, he knew he no longer could act innocent. The governor's brother, Roger Clinton, was busted.

Clinton was sentenced, in January 1985, to two years in prison. He also testified, with immunity, in other cocaine-related cases. One of the others sent to prison, partially by Roger Clinton's testimony, was Dan Lasater, a close friend of both Clinton brothers "who set out lines of the white powder at his lavish parties."[1]

The federal prosecutor for that case was Asa Hutchinson, the Reagan-appointed chief prosecutor for all of western Arkansas from 1982 to 1985.[2] Hutchinson, looking back on the Clinton conviction, believes that he helped stem a burgeoning cocaine crisis in the state. According to Hutchinson, Roger Clinton's attitude also had been a problem: "Here the brother of the governor was saying, 'Hey, nobody touches me, look who I am!' And people had come to think it was all right." Hutchinson concluded, "The case was important in showing people they couldn't do that."[3]

Bill Clinton, prior to his impeachment, had said for years that his brother's conviction helped turn Roger's life around. The President and

Hutchinson even talked about it once. Hutchinson remembers, "I flew down on Air Force One back to Arkansas to examine the damage from the (1997) tornadoes, and during that trip we had a very casual visit and the president remarked that that prosecution probably saved his brother's life. . . . The prosecution was very tough on the family, and then-Governor Clinton responded to it as a loving brother would. I haven't followed Roger that closely, but I know he's made an effort to change directions."[4]

The Republican prosecutor did send Democrat Bill Clinton's brother to jail, but he simply was doing his job after the State Police investigation. He referred to Clinton as a loving brother and recognized how hard the case had been on the Clinton family. And friends of the President say he never held the conviction against Hutchinson.[5] Partisanship, in this instance, does not appear to have been the motivation for either person.

Early Political Career

Asa Hutchinson was born in Benton County, Arkansas, on December 3, 1950, sixteen months after his brother, Tim, who held Asa's House seat before him and who, as a Senator, sat in judgment not only on President Clinton's future, but also on the arguments of his brother. Both Hutchinsons helped tend their family's 279-acre cattle and chicken farm, then attended the same college, Bob Jones University in South Carolina, where Asa received an accounting degree.[6] After his undergraduate years, he attended the University of Arkansas and emerged with a law degree.

The Hutchinsons grew up in a Christian home, evidenced by their attendance at Bob Jones. "Faith is not something you have in a closet," according to Asa Hutchinson. "It is something you take with you every day. If it doesn't impact the way you live and the way you conduct your-self, it really has little worth." Neither is one's faith relegated only to careers associated directly with the church: "I think that you can have a ministry as a lawyer or in any secular field if you're seeking God's will and direction in your life. He [God] always wants us to be involved in ministry. So, as a lawyer, I always look for ways to impact society—public life—for the better and consistent with my faith."[7]

Hutchinson opened a private law practice in Bentonville in 1977 and continued in that capacity until his appointment as U.S. Attorney for the Western District of Arkansas in 1982, returning to private practice in 1986. But he did not wish to stay purely private, so he became more politically active, guided by his faith.

Hutchinson believes that faith "leads you in trying to be involved in different arenas. It led me into starting a Christian school or helping along that line; led me into very active youth group work. It also led me into being involved in building the Republican Party in Arkansas. I was a County Chairman. It's an outgrowth because you say, hey, there's a need out here to have a better political system, different ideas espoused, and a debate on public policy issues to talk about things I believe in. So, it leads you—it has an impact in your desire to make a difference and to be involved in public life."[8]

In what was considered a longshot for a political novice, Hutchinson challenged Dale Bumpers for his U.S. Senate seat in 1986. Although Bumpers easily won reelection with 62 percent of the vote, Hutchinson did impress his own Party with the campaign he ran, particularly by the way he conducted himself in a debate with Bumpers. In 1990, he tried again, this time in a race for the state's attorney general post. Although he lost once more, his vote total did improve to 47 percent.

Despite the two losses, Hutchinson remained devoted to politics, serving as Chairman of the state Republican Party from 1990 to 1995. When brother Tim ran for Congress in 1992, Asa took a leave of absence from his chairmanship to manage his brother's successful campaign, but then returned to his former position.

Appointment as House Manager

Bill Clinton's Arkansas legacy touched Asa Hutchinson's political life directly in 1996. The Whitewater investigation caught Governor Jim Guy Tucker in mail fraud and conspiracy, forcing him to resign from office.

This initiated a chain of events that led to Hutchinson being elected to Congress. When Tucker resigned, Republican Lieutenant Governor Mike Huckabee withdrew from his Senate race to become Governor. Tim Hutchinson, who simply was going to run for reelection to the House, decided instead to go for the Senate, leaving his House seat open. Asa, who had settled earlier on a race for state representative, chose rather to run for his brother's vacant national seat. Without Whitewater, Asa Hutchinson might never have entered Congress, never have accepted an assignment with the Judiciary Committee, and, of course, never have taken on the role of House Manager.

Hutchinson's concept of God's sovereignty in the affairs of men perhaps led him to see God's hand in the events that allowed him to serve in Congress. In a sense, Hutchinson looks upon the role of Congressman as a ministry:

> I've been given an extraordinary opportunity and it's an opportunity that comes by the providence of God. If you don't take advantage of those opportunities consistent with your faith and being obedient, then you're not doing what you should be doing. If you do, you really are having a ministry in terms of impacting others. I guess, at the same time, the only thing you have to be careful of as a person of faith involved in the public arena is that you don't simply impose your standards on the public will whenever there's not general support for it. You have to be careful at some points along that line. When it comes to life issues, I make sure my voters know exactly how I believe, that I'm gonna vote this way as a matter of conviction. But then there are other issues that might be a little bit grayer and you look a little bit more to what the public sentiment is as well as searching your own convictions.[9]

He did not seek appointment to the Judiciary Committee, but willingly accepted the assignment because "my mission in life is to uphold justice. I think that's very close to God's heart. It's part of my being."[10]

When he accepted a spot on the Committee, he had no idea that it would lead to impeachment proceedings and his very prominent role in them. When Henry Hyde broached the subject of his being a House Manager, Hutchinson was reluctant. His first inclination was to say no because he knew he might suffer politically for his involvement. Upon further reflection, he changed his mind:

> I thought, you know, what are you about? It's the cause of justice, it's equal justice, it's the principle of the rule of law. Surely there are some things in life, some principles, that you ought to be willing to give up your seat in Congress for—even if the risks are that extraordinary politically. So, after a lot of thought and debate, I accepted that responsibility. But it was not without a lot of reluctance.[11]

The task would be strenuous, he knew, and it would require wisdom: "I grew up in a home that took the Bible seriously and believes that whenever you lack wisdom, you can ask God and He gives to all men liberally. Whenever you're going through something so critical that impacts our nation, you've got to bathe it in prayer every day and seek God's wisdom in it."[12] This was the faith he took into the political battle.

Some Democrats wanted Hutchinson to excuse himself from the Manager team. "The Democrat Party in Arkansas was making news statements saying I had a conflict because my brother was a member of the 'jury,' so to speak, in the Senate, and that there was a conflict. That got some national play because of that, and it was something I had to address," he remembers.[13]

Hutchinson talked to both Republicans and Democrats in his district and came away with the strong impression that they wanted him to proceed. "They believed I could add a measure of fairness to the presentation and conduct myself in a proper manner," he concluded.[14]

When the new Congress convened in January 1999, the Manager team had to be reappointed. Some Democrats attempted at that time to remove Hutchinson. According to Democratic spokesman Jim Jordan, "In any legal system in the civilized world, it would be considered simply unethical for a prosecutor to argue a case on which his brother is a juror." There was another factor beyond this argument: Hutchinson was considered by the Democrats to be "one of the best legal minds on the House impeachment team."[15] Nixing him from that team could only help their cause, but their attempt was unsuccessful in the Republican-dominated House.

For his part, Hutchinson refused to discuss the case with his brother, even though they shared an apartment in Pentagon City, Virginia. "For the last six months, we've intentionally stayed away from talking about it," Hutchinson noted at the time.[16] Brother Tim remarked, "Asa's holed up in his bedroom working all day and all night. . . . He took a lonely card table and set it up in his bedroom as a desk. It's covered with papers." Asa even felt that Tim would be his "toughest critic."[17]

If the Democrats were truly concerned about the ethics of the situation, they also could have pushed for the exclusion of Democratic Senator Barbara Boxer from the trial. Senator Boxer's daughter was married to Hillary Rodham Clinton's brother, Tony Rodham. The Boxer family regularly celebrated holidays with the Clintons.[18] That conflict of interest, though, never was mentioned.

Hutchinson did receive criticism for standing by his appointment: "There were a couple of editorials in some papers. But then there were some cartoons. There was one cartoon that had a caricature of me stabbing Bill Clinton in the back. There was another caricature of me coming back to Arkansas, with Arkansas sort of a cabin, and the door was shut and barred from my entrance."[19]

Not all the criticism came from political foes. "The immediate reaction of people who really liked me and supported me was, my goodness, why do you want to do this? This is not good for your political career. This is pushing it too far. So far, you've had to do this because you're on the Committee; you didn't have any choice. But now, you're just going way too far. This is bad judgment. That was the immediate reaction," he recalled.[20] Hutchinson, though, felt he had to remain faithful to his responsibility.

One can reasonably ask if it was principle that led Hutchinson to remain steadfast or whether it was, in fact, personal animus toward President Clinton. After all, they had battled politically within Arkansas for many years, and Governor Clinton had won at every turn. Hutchinson denies, however, that his involvement in the impeachment was motivated by animosity toward the President:

> If you look back during his first run for President in 1992, I was state party chairman. The national media consistently called me, getting my comments on the President, all the Gennifer Flowers allegations, all these other rumors came to me about prosecuting his brother and was there cocaine in his past—all of these things. I never, never went into his personal life in those comments, in contrast to a lot of other people. I said, I'll talk about the public policy issues and the disagreements there. But I really think that my demeanor was one of fairness and not of animosity toward him. I didn't have that in my heart as this whole thing started.[21]

Debate in the House

Prior to the Judiciary Committee vote to proceed with an impeachment inquiry, Hutchinson commented publicly about the possibility. On October 16, he told an audience at the University of Arkansas Law School that he did not yet know how he would vote on the matter of impeachment. He considered the case "open" and believed that it would be "a very honest inquiry." He also felt that although the impending impeachment was going to be a "difficult process," it was not a constitutional crisis and the state of the union was still strong, as the President had claimed in his previous State of the Union speech. "Does that not speak volumes about the strength of our Constitution, about the strength of our democracy, and about the resilience of our republican principles and institutions? . . . This is not about Arkansas, it's about the Constitution and upholding the rule of the law. What's good for our country will be good for Arkansas," he told his audience. [22]

Earlier that same month, he had remarked in the Judiciary Committee that the real issue was the rule of law. Lawyers in the Nixon White House had not valued or respected the rule of law, but Hutchinson's professors at the University of Arkansas at the time had drilled it into their students "that lawyers should have the highest ethical standards . . . that we have a high responsibility to seek the truth in the courtroom and that we should never allow a fraud to be committed upon the court." He also noted that one of those professors was William Jefferson Clinton. He then asked, "Is the rule of law less significant today than 25 years ago? Is unchecked perjury—if proven—less of a threat to our judicial system today than when Watergate was the example?"[23]

The problem was that the Independent Counsel's Report stated that the President had committed perjury, while the President denied any such thing. How could one determine the truth without an investigation? "It is the answer to this question that we must ultimately decide," he explained. "And if we are to reach a fair and honest conclusion, it is necessary that we inquire further."[24]

He continued,

> The cynics will proclaim our work today a partisan struggle. There is no surprise in this. . . .
>
> Let me assure you that this is not about following our party but following the law and the Constitution—wherever that path may lead. It is not about which party has the votes, but it is about which position is closest to the concepts of justice, equity and historical precedence. Partisan loyalties must be checked at the door of this great institution we all serve; now we must look to our consciences. . . .
>
> Our duty is not to punish anyone, and our challenge is to avoid pettiness, but our goal should certainly be to determine whether a breach of the public trust has occurred, and if so, how do we best repair it. As the Prophet Nehemiah devoted his

life to rebuilding the wall around Jerusalem in times of old, let this Committee commit itself to the maintenance of the wall of the public trust.[25]

After the Congressional elections, the loss of Republican seats did not deter Hutchinson's concern for the rule of law. In comments to the Constitution Subcommittee on November 9, he alluded to the challenge of proceeding in the wake of the election, but he felt that the hearing might have even greater significance, particularly "to sharpen our focus and to remind us of the principles of our founding fathers and of the unavoidable judgment of history."[26] He kept returning to the rule of law and the consequences of setting it aside in this case:

> If this committee ignores an act of perjury by the president, what impact will that have on the next generation, on our rule of law and our justice system? I would not be on this committee if I did not have a love for the law and a belief that any citizen can seek justice with complete confidence that intentional falsehoods under oath are not acceptable. If we conclude that perjury was committed but we take no action, what will a jury do when asked to uphold the law and find someone guilty of lying under oath?[27]

Hutchinson clearly saw damage to the entire judicial system if the President were guilty, yet not called to account for it. Why should juries find other people guilty of perjury if the President could commit the same offense without penalty?

Public officials should be held to a higher standard than other citizens, Hutchinson believed. He then pointed to the fact that federal sentencing guidelines do impose additional penalties on "those who abuse a position of public trust." Who, in America, has a higher position of public trust than the President? "Some have concluded that perjury is an impeachable offense for a federal judge but not for president because there should be a *higher* standard for impeaching the President of the

United States. If that reasoning were adopted, we would in effect be setting a *lower* standard for the President than any other office in the land. Is that right policy? Is that the right message for our country? . . . The seriousness of this situation requires us to set aside any influence of partisanship and to proceed with these hearings with open minds, to look past the rhetoric and toward the facts," he argued.[28]

Hutchinson's call for the President to be investigated and brought to account for his actions if guilty was not a call for the House to punish him. That, according to the Congressman, would have been unconstitutional: "My reading of the Constitution tells me that this process is not about punishment, but rather protecting the public trust." He continued, "There are some who say that alternative punishments, such as censure or fine, may have public appeal as a way out, but there is a growing consensus of scholars who point out that such alternatives have no Constitutional basis and would violate the separation of powers, setting a dangerous precedent for future proceedings. For those on the other side of the aisle who call out for punishment, I would ask *how* and *under what authority?*"[29]

In his closing remarks to the Committee, Hutchinson reemphasized his concern for constitutionality: "I do not believe that the unpleasantness of the present circumstances justify [sic] playing fast and loose with the Constitution for the sake of expediency. To do so would be to imperil the very system of justice upon which our great nation was built."[30]

Prior to the Judiciary Committee's vote on the four articles of impeachment, a vote was taken on the feasibility of censure. No Republican voted for that action. When questioned by a reporter, Hutchinson again stressed that there was no constitutional provision for censure; the only option given to the House was impeachment. He was disappointed that not one Democrat on the Committee voted in favor of an impeachment article. He was concerned over the appearance of partisanship. Yet he believed he had no choice but to cast his vote in favor of impeachment: "I wish it could have resulted in a different outcome. But I have to follow the law and this is not something we can turn away from."[31]

During the Committee's debate on the impeachment articles, Hutchinson used his opening statement to differentiate between the personal aspects of the issue and those that were legal and constitutional. He freely acknowledged that there were qualities President Clinton possessed that he admired. He thought it was a "unique opportunity" for Arkansas to have one of its own elected President. He even offered that everyone should extend compassion and encouragement to the President "when he expresses regret for his actions and requests forgiveness for his conduct." But that was the personal side; the House was under obligation to debate the question of impeachable actions, during which, Hutchinson cautioned, Members were "not to be guided by . . . sympathies or prejudice, but by the facts and the law." [32]

Why was Hutchinson in favor of impeachment? First, the President's testimony established "a pattern of false statements, deceit, and obstruction. By committing these actions, the president moved beyond the private arena of protecting embarrassing personal conduct and his actions invaded the very heart and soul of that which makes this nation unique in the world, the right of any citizen to pursue justice equally." Neither the President nor his lawyers, Hutchinson asserted, had the right to determine who could or could not seek justice, yet President Clinton "took it upon himself to deny the right of a fellow American, in this case a fellow Arkansan, equal access to relief in the courts. The president's lawyers have declared such a lie to be a small one. But I cannot see how denying the rights of a fellow citizen can be considered of small consequence." [33]

Hutchinson also noted, "The evidence not only shows the president giving perjurious statements, but he continues his assault on the judicial system by soliciting and encouraging false statements by others." His actions, by violating a court oath as well as his constitutional oath, had damaged the State and "the integrity of government." Hutchinson was concerned about the message future presidents would receive from the outcome of this situation:

I have no trouble in setting a benchmark that future presidents cannot willfully and repeatedly lie under oath in an official judicial proceeding without jeopardizing their office. On the contrary, I have a great deal of trouble in lowering the standards to say to future presidents, "Lying under oath, no matter how often and no matter how intentional, is considered acceptable conduct."[34]

If the Congress were to fail to act in this instance, Hutchinson feared that as a people, we would "quietly embrace and even aid in the gradual subversion of our core belief that we are a nation of laws and that all of us, regardless of wealth or power, deserve equal treatment in the eyes of the law." He continued,

> It is reminiscent of every criminal case that I have prosecuted to hear the president's lawyers attack the prosecutor, blame this committee, criticize the process, and refuse to take responsibility. I concede his lawyers that tactic. But I have also urged them to show me compelling facts rebutting the long trail of evidence suggesting that the president lied under oath and obstructed justice. This they have not done to my satisfaction. . . .
>
> In the next few days I will cast some of the most important votes of my career. Some believe these votes could result in a backlash and have serious political repercussions. They may be right. But I will leave the analysis to others. My preeminent concern is that the Constitution be followed and that all Americans, regardless of their position in society, receive equal and unbiased treatment in our courts of law. The fate of no president, no political party, and no member of Congress merits a slow unraveling of the fabric of our constitutional structure. As John Adams said, we are a nation of laws, not of men. . . .
>
> Our nation has survived the failings of its leaders before, but

it cannot survive exceptions to the rule of law in our system of equal justice for all. There will always be differences between the powerful and the powerless. But imagine a country where a Congress agrees the strong are treated differently than the weak, where mercy is the only refuge for the powerless, where the power of our positions govern [sic] all of our decisions. Such a country cannot long endure. God help us to do what is right, not just for today, but for the future of this nation and for those generations that must succeed us.[35]

Above all, Hutchinson wanted the Constitution to be followed and wished to ensure that no one, including the President, should be above that fundamental law.

His statement also touched upon the issue of private versus public conduct, indicating that President Clinton's actions were not purely private. Hutchinson recognized that some actions of a public official are private and that it would not be appropriate for all private conduct to be considered grist for the impeachment mill. But neither could all private conduct be relegated to untouchable status. He offered an example: "If right after Pearl Harbor, the President said, well, I'm not worried about it and went and took a long vacation on some beach somewhere and just did not engage—in a sense, that's private conduct. He's not done anything against the Constitution necessarily, but he's neglected his responsibilities. So, a lot of times, private conduct causes you to neglect your responsibilities. Private conduct can be something that's damaging to the office of the Presidency." Yet Hutchinson also was quick to note that in President Clinton's circumstances, "it was not his private conduct that was an issue. I did distinguish it. I looked at the public conduct and the impact on the public office . . . Whenever you are giving testimony under oath in a proceeding, is that private conduct? I mean, I guess you can say it's private conduct, but it's certainly a very public act that has public responsibilities and public consequences."[36]

As the articles of impeachment moved from the Judiciary Committee to consideration by the entire House on December 18th and 19th,

Hutchinson entered into the debate forcefully. When Democrats argued that a censure vote should be allowed instead of a vote for impeachment only, he laid out the case for impeachment by stressing the willful nature of the President's actions. "Prior to his testimony," Hutchinson reminded his colleagues, "there was a uniform warning across this land. . . . Mr. President, whatever you do, do not lie to the grand jury. . . . Despite these warnings, the committee found that the president went before the grand jury, took an oath to tell the truth, and then intentionally provided false statements." And, Hutchinson noted, this was not an isolated incident:

> The facts establish a pattern of false statements, deceit and obstruction, and by committing these actions, the president moved beyond the private arena of protecting personal embarrassing conduct and . . . invaded the very heart and soul of that which makes this nation unique in the world, the right of any citizen to pursue justice equally. The conduct obstructed our judicial system and at that point that became an issue . . . of national consequence.[37]

When Republican Congressman Ernest Istook of Oklahoma noted that President Clinton did not bring forward any witnesses in the Judiciary Committee hearings, even when invited to do so, Democrat Marty Meehan of Massachusetts objected: "The gentleman from Oklahoma just said that we gave the president an opportunity to call witnesses, to prove his innocence. Since when is the burden of proof in this country on the person being accused? You have the obligation to provide a case before the Committee on the Judiciary, and you did not provide a single material witness in this case. Not one witness." Hutchinson felt he had to correct Meehan's statement:

> I want to respond to the gentleman from Massachusetts. He did have one thing right, and that is the burden of proof is on those going forward with impeachment. But that burden of proof was met with 60,000 pages of documents, an indepen-

dent review by the Committee on the Judiciary, and . . . there has not been one challenge to the evidence.[38]

The evidence was sufficient for most Republicans; two articles of impeachment passed.

The Senate Trial

For the Senate presentations, Henry Hyde placed Hutchinson on the group of Managers that had the task of detailing the exact offenses of which the President was accused. This was the group that would lead off the presentations. If these Managers did not capture the Senators' attention from the start, all would be lost. Hyde was convinced that the Arkansas Congressman would be able to accomplish that feat with his methodical handling of the material. Hutchinson focused specifically on the evidence for the article charging obstruction of justice. He began his presentation with a short apologetic for his participation in the trial, concluding, "In this journey on earth there is nothing of greater consequence for us to devote our energies to than to search for the truth, to pursue equal justice and to uphold the law. It is for those reasons that I serve as a manager."[39]

Hutchinson's presentation painstakingly detailed how the President tried to influence the course of events—his attempt to get Monica Lewinsky a job, his coaching of his secretary, Betty Currie, regarding what she should say to the grand jury, his concealment of gifts, and his false statements to his aides. "In this case, at every turn," Hutchinson recounted, "the President used whatever means available to evade the truth, destroy evidence, tamper with witnesses and take any other action required to prevent evidence from coming forward in a civil rights case that would prove a truth contrary to his interest. He obstructed the administration of justice before the United States District Court and before the federal grand jury." Hutchinson pointed to what he called the seven pillars of obstruction and concluded, "The seven pillars of this obstruction case were personally constructed by the President of the United States. It was done with the intent that the truth and evidence would be suppressed in a civil rights case pending against him. The goal was to win, and he was not going to let the judicial system stand in his way." [40]

His closing appeal to the Senators spoke of truth, justice, the Constitution, principles, and faith:

> At the beginning of my presentation, I tried to put this case into perspective for myself by saying this proceeding is the same as what takes place in every courtroom in America—the pursuit of truth, seeking equal justice and upholding the law. All of that is true, but we know there is *even more* at stake in this trial. What happens here affects the workings of our Constitution; it will affect the Presidency in future decades, and it will have an impact on a whole generation of Americans. What is at stake is our Constitution and the principle of equal justice for all.
>
> I have faith in the Constitution of the United States, but the checks and balances of the Constitution are carried out by individuals. Individuals who are entrusted under oath with upholding the trust given to us by the people of this great land. If I believe in the Constitution that it will work, then I must believe in you.
>
> Ladies and Gentlemen: I trust the Constitution of the United States, but today it is most important that I believe in you.
>
> I have faith in the Senate of the United States. You have earned the trust of the American people and I trust each of you to make the right decisions for our country. [41]

Hutchinson's presentation was masterful. According to one analyst, he "captivated the senators by spinning out the tale of obstruction of justice day by day, and sometimes minute by minute, methodically recounting each meeting, each phone call, each court action, and how they all seemed to fit together into a pattern of illegal behavior."[42] For some Senators, explained the analyst, this was the first time they had seen how the evidence all flowed together to make a convincing case:

> For many of them, it was a shock, especially for Democrats, who in their own minds had instinctively dismissed the case as weak. Listening to Hutchinson outline the sequence of events, building his case for obstruction of justice brick by brick, the senators were struck by the power of the evidence. Senators milling around the Democratic cloakroom afterward were morose and grim-faced. Senator Russ Feingold, the Wisconsin Democrat, walked out of the chamber thinking, There may actually be a case here. Fellow Democratic senator Dick Durbin of Illinois thought to himself that he might actually have to vote for conviction.[43]

During the question-and-answer period when Senators could have their questions relayed to both the prosecution and the defense through the Chief Justice, Hutchinson dealt with the significance of having live witnesses at this trial. He pointed out that both the President and his counselors had "denied each and every allegation under the two articles that have been submitted to this body. I focused on the obstruction of justice, and each of the seven elements of the obstruction of justice has been denied by the president. This puts it all in issue."[44] The only solution, he urged, was to call live witnesses to try to figure out who was telling the truth. Despite pleas from the entire Manager team, the Senate refused to entertain any live witnesses. All that they were allowed to show were three videotaped depositions. Hutchinson led the questioning of Vernon Jordan in one of the depositions. However, without the "live" feature, the testimony did not make as great an impression.

When a motion for dismissal of the case was presented, Hutchinson argued against the move. "[T]o dismiss the case would be unprecedented from a historical standpoint," he began. In addition, "it would be damaging to the constitution, because the Senate would fail to try the case; it would be harmful to the body politic because there is no resolution of the issues of the case; but, most importantly, it would show willful blindness to the evidentiary record."[45] It was beyond comprehension, to Hutchinson, that the Senate would not see this through to a conclusion. The motion did not succeed.

In his closing argument, the Congressman tried to rally the Senators to the Managers' cause, citing the vote of Edmund Ross in the Andrew Johnson impeachment. He urged them to follow Ross in eschewing political expediency. It might be to their political detriment, but it would reflect political courage. "I appear before this body as an advocate," he acknowledged. Yet he was not receiving any tangible benefit to do so. "I am not paid for this special responsibility. But I am here because I believe the Constitution requires me to make this case. The facts prove overwhelmingly that the President committed obstruction of justice and perjury," he stated. In his final words to the Senate, Hutchinson asked the members to see that justice is done:

> As the late Federal Judge Orin Harris of Arkansas always said from the bench to the jury when I was trying cases—and I hated his instruction because I was the prosecutor—but he would tell the jury, "Remember, the government never wins or loses a case. The government always wins when justice is done." Well, this is the Congress, and this is the Senate. And it is your responsibility to determine the facts and let justice roll down like mighty waters.[46]

Hutchinson's sense of justice did not prevail, but he also had told the Senate that he would not criticize its final decision and that he would respect the institution whatever the outcome.

Principle vs. Partisanship

How does Hutchinson answer charges of partisanship in his prosecution of the President? "It's one of those things that's hard to respond [to]," he mused. "It's like trying to prove that you didn't do something. It's difficult to answer, other than look at my conduct, look at what I say. My words mean something. Try to look deeper into the heart." He then pointed to his prosecutorial history: "When I was United States Attorney, the first public official I prosecuted was a Republican for corruption in office. I also wound up prosecuting some Democrats. When it comes to justice, there is really not any partisan divide there. Anybody who knows me and my history sees that reflected. So, I mean, again, it's a very difficult charge to answer, but I think you have to look at everyone's conduct. I think it was done out of a sense of commitment to some important principles."[47]

He also identifies certain mistakes made by Republicans. Congress, he says, never should have released all the material in the Starr Report without a thorough review first. It made the Managers' job more difficult because it decreased the shock value to the general public. If details had been presented first in the hearings, point by point, perhaps the public might have been more receptive to the impeachment proceedings. A related mistake was releasing the videotape of the President's testimony to the Grand Jury; that tape would have had greater impact if it had been introduced in the hearings. Hutchinson also felt that witnesses should have been called into the Judiciary Committee hearings. He advocated strongly for that, but he did not prevail.

A mistake that touches directly on the partisan issue was not working out "a bipartisan agreement on the structure of the Judiciary Committee hearings. We were real close to time limits that the Democrats wanted. We could have worked out a bipartisan foundation for that that I think would have been satisfactory. But we didn't do that, and I think that was an error."[48]

Although the Managers operated under difficult circumstances in the Senate, Hutchinson believes they did a much better job there than they had done in the House. And he has no regrets over having served as a Manager: "I felt like I helped our country through a very difficult time in the way I handled it in the Senate, as well as in my public discourse. So, it was just one of those rare times in life you feel you did something good for democracy, you did something good for the republic. No matter how long you serve in Congress, those feelings might not come along that often. ... The people in my district have supported me in it; I think [they] eventually saw my heart attitude and said, you handled it in the right way."49

Hutchinson hopes that this impeachment experience has taught Americans that our republic is strong and that America is able to persevere:

> That our founding fathers were right in setting up a procedure to follow and that when you follow it, our democracy is stronger, our republic is stronger, and that we can survive even enormous challenges to our system. All the doomsayers said the economy was going to collapse, the Supreme Court couldn't function, the Senate would be stalled for months and months and months, and this was going to hurt the Presidency and everyone. The fact is, none of those things happened. People around the world looked at the United States and said, my goodness, what a testimony toward equal justice. Even the President must be held accountable.
>
> If we had not done that, then I think our principles of justice would have been diminished. So I think the lesson is that what a marvelous republic we have, a balance-of-power system that works, and we made it work in a respectful way. ...
>
> There are just very few times in history that you will see political leaders simply make a statement that we're going to follow our principles and we're not going to follow the polls. That's an extraordinary time. That's exactly what happened.
>
> I'll never forget the day after the election. We had a conference call with the Members of the Judiciary Committee led by Henry Hyde. In essence, he said, well, yesterday, gentlemen, we took a shellacking at the polls. But we always said the election didn't have anything to do with our responsibilities, so let's proceed forward. And everybody said, you're right, let's go.

It was literally a shock to every political pundit and every media person out there. They thought it was dead after that election because they thought it was all about politics. And that demonstrated that it wasn't. It's a rare time in our country, and I think people eventually saw that.[50]

Chapter 11 Endnotes

[1] David Maraniss, *First in His Class: The Biography of Bill Clinton* (NY: Simon & Schuster, 1995), 422.

[2] "Arkansas Congressman Introduces First Article Against Clinton," *The Associated Press Political Service*, 18 December 1998.

[3] Maraniss, 423.

[4] Kelly P. Kissel, "A Decade Ago, Asa Hutchinson Prosecuted Roger," *The Associated Press Political Service*, 14 September 1998.

[5] Ibid.

[6] "Arkansans' Paths Converge at Trial: Asa Hutchinson Makes Case Against Clinton; Brother Tim is a Juror," *The Baltimore Sun*, 14 January 1999, 1A; "Asa Hutchinson," The Associated Press Political Service: AP Candidate Bios, 11 October 1996. Basic biographical information in the following paragraphs comes from this same source.

[7] Congressman Asa Hutchinson, interview by author, tape recording, Washington, DC, 29 February 2000.

[8] Ibid.

[9] Ibid.

[10] Ibid.

[11] Ibid.

[12] Ibid.

[13] Ibid.

[14] Peggy Harris, "Arkansas Democrats Ask Hutchinson to Decline Prosecutor Role," *The Associated Press Political Service*, 21 December 1998.

[15] Kathy Kiely, "The Brothers Hutchinson: An Impeachment Conflict?" *USA Today*, 6 January 1999.

[16] Ibid.

[17] "Arkansans' Paths Converge at Trial."

[18] Ibid.

19 Hutchinson interview.

20 Ibid.

21 Ibid., 4-5.

22 "Rep. Hutchinson Undecided on Clinton Case," *The Associated Press Political Service*, 16 October 1998.

23 Statement of Congressman Asa Hutchinson, House Judiciary Committee, 5 October 1998; available at http://www.house.gov/judiciary/hutchinson.htm; accessed 28 April 1999.

24 Ibid.

25 Ibid.

26 Remarks of Congressman Asa Hutchinson to the Constitution Subcommittee, Hearing on the History of Impeachment, 9 November 1998; available at http://www.house.gov/judiciary/22411.htm; accessed 16 April 1999.

27 Ibid.

28 Ibid.

29 Ibid.

30 Ibid.

31 Chuck Bartels, "Asa Hutchinson Stands By Impeachment Votes," *The Associated Press Political Service*, 12 December 1998.

32 The Impeachment Hearings: Opening Statements: Asa Hutchinson, 11 December 1998; available at http://www.washingtonost.com/wp-srv/politics/special/clinton/.../hutchinsonstext121198.htm; accessed 1 April 1999.

33 Ibid.

34 Ibid.

35 Ibid.

36 Hutchinson interview.

37 McLoughlin, *The Impeachment and Trial of President Clinton*, 169-70.

[38] Ibid., 193.

[39] Opening Statement of Hon. Asa Hutchinson, Senate Impeachment Trial of President Clinton, 14 January 1999; available at http://www.house.gov/judiciary/hutsenate.htm; accessed 12 April 1999.

[40] Ibid.

[41] Ibid.

[42] Baker, *The Breach*, 303.

[43] Ibid., 305.

[44] McLoughlin, *The Impeachment and Trial of President Clinton*, 346.

[45] Ibid., 359.

[46] Closing Argument of Hon. Asa Hutchinson, Senate Impeachment Trial of President Clinton, 8 February 1999; available at http://www.house.gov/judiciary/hutc0208.htm; accessed 9 February 2000.

[47] Hutchinson interview.

[48] Ibid.

[49] Ibid.

[50] Ibid.

CHAPTER TWELVE

Bill McCollum:
For the Record

A Member of Congress attends many meetings in his home district—so many that they can become a blur. There are some meetings, though, that are easier to remember than others. Representative Bill McCollum of Florida remembers one such meeting. It was early in the morning with approximately fifty or sixty UPS workers, probably in September of 1998, shortly before the Independent Counsel sent all those boxes of evidence to the House of Representatives. McCollum asked them, as he usually did at meetings with constituents, what they were thinking about. He recalls,

> One of the men piped up and said that he didn't think we should impeach the President. I said, okay, that's fair. What does everybody else think? Let's have a show of hands or some-thing. It was pretty overwhelming that the group didn't think the President should be impeached. So I then asked them why did they think that, if in fact (I didn't know it at the time), the President had committed crimes of perjury and obstruction of justice and things that were pretty serious. Did they think nothing should happen? Because other people would certainly have problems with that. You couldn't be head of a corpora-tion; you couldn't expect to keep your job. You couldn't expect to be the Admiral in charge of the Navy anymore if you did anything like this. Their response was, "Oh, we don't think

what he did was right. If you could remove him in a week, that would be great. That would be fine. . . . But we're just tired of seeing this on the television screens every night, and we don't want to see it anymore. We don't want to fiddle with it any more; we don't want the nation to go through it; we don't want the government to be involved with it. We just don't want to hear about it anymore." It was a consensus.[1]

Mused McCollum, "I think that predilection was there on the part of a lot of Americans of just being tired and tuned out *before* the House of Representatives ever received the paperwork that initiated this inquiry in the first place, before we ever were charged to do anything."[2] In other words, the third strike was on its way toward home plate before the batter even got into the batter's box.

But Bill McCollum was not about to strike out without taking a swing, just in case a home run could be hit, no matter how unlikely. He says he never has shied away from controversial decisions. While others avoided serving on the Judiciary Committee because of the controversial nature of some of the issues it tackled, McCollum claims that never has bothered him. "I've always believed in voting the way I think is right," he related. "I believe that if you take a position and you decide what it is based on your best judgment as a legislator after you've researched everything and you understand it, and it happens to be different maybe from what popular opinion is at the moment, that's the way it is. You just vote your conscience and vote what you believe is right."[3]

Career Path

A Floridian since his birth in 1944, Bill McCollum strayed from his native state only while serving in the armed forces. He received both his bachelor of arts and law degrees from the University of Florida, earning the latter in 1968. From 1969 to 1972, he served in the Navy's Judge Advocate General's Corps, continuing in the Naval Reserve until 1992.

Upon leaving active military duty in 1972, McCollum returned to Florida and joined the law firm of Pitts, Eubanks, and Ross in Orlando. Although he had held no local or state elective office, he decided to run for Congress in 1980, successfully capturing the House seat that he still held as the impeachment drama unfolded.

By 1998, McCollum had achieved a significant leadership role in the House. He held the chairmanship of the Judiciary Committee's Subcommittee on Crime, chaired the Select Committee on Intelligence's Subcommittee on Human Intelligence, Analysis, and Counterintelligence, and was Vice Chairman of the Banking Committee. Along the way, he co-chaired hearings investigating the Branch Davidian incident in Waco, Texas, and he was chosen as one of the fifteen Members of the House to serve on the House Committee to investigate the Iran-Contra affair. The latter two assignments put him on the front line of major controversies.

McCollum served with Henry Hyde on the Iran-Contra investigation, and both heartily defended Oliver North during his questioning by the Committee. They received much criticism from liberal sources for their stance. A Freedom of Information Act suit revealed that Robert McFarlane had briefed four Republicans, including Hyde and McCollum, in 1985 about attempts to help the Contras financially through third-party contributions from other countries. The *St. Petersburg Times* insisted that their silence on this matter "helped keep the diversion scheme secret from the congressional leaders who legally should have been informed of it."[4] *The New Republic* opined, "Their silence sheds light on more than their hollow rhetoric and posturing; it exposes their dishonesty with their colleagues and their willingness to hide their complicity evading the law. ... Do McCollum and Hyde ... still believe that their professed patriotism puts them above the law? Gentlemen, start your alibis."[5]

The accused Congressmen sent a reply to *The New Republic* in which they called the allegations "old and discredited." The allegations, they retorted, were "patently untrue, unwarranted, and unsupported. They are in fact refuted by publicly available information, which your publication could and should have known about." Never did Mr. McFarlane or any other official brief them about "illegal contra aid activities," they claimed. They also took issue with the word "illegal" and charged the magazine with publishing "an egregious falsehood that is far below a minimum standard of editorial responsibility."[6] McCollum, stating his views more specifically in his rejection of the Committee's majority report, steadfastly maintained that while President Reagan had "made a major error of judgment" in failing to deal openly with his disagreements with Congress, it was unclear whether the restrictions Congress had placed on aid to the Contras applied to the National Security Council. Ultimately, McCollum believed the congressional restrictions had been unconstitutional and should have been fought.[7] Therefore, he believed that he was acting in accord with the Constitution and with integrity. Accusations that he was playing fast and loose with the truth were unfounded, he would say, because of his belief system.

"I am a Christian," McCollum states, and he says that his faith has given him his basic values. He rejects moral relativism: "I just don't buy into that. Never have." He does not consider his stance on Iran-Contra to have been contradictory to his values. He was standing for what he believed was right, in accord with the Constitution and the law. Further, he believes that "there are certain absolutes in life." While it may be difficult at times to carry over those absolutes into all of a society's laws, he does draw a line over which one cannot cross:

> When it comes to government and laws that men make, while we may compromise the laws, there is no compromising those things that are basic values. They are there. They stem from the basic law that we wrote about, our Founding Fathers did, the laws of man and nature, and why we came into being as a nation as the greatest free nation in the history of the world.[8]

Iran-Contra, in McCollum's view, was an attempt, albeit clumsy at times, to allow another people to experience the freedom that America enjoyed.

The Congress was getting in the way of one of America's most basic values, in his estimation.

The 1995 Waco hearings also had the potential of dividing along partisan lines, and with McCollum serving as co-chair, he could have become a lightning rod for partisan attacks. Yet it did not turn out that way. When talk of impeachment surfaced in the atmosphere of these hearings, McCollum simply would say, "This is not our job. Our job is to get it [information] all out, let it all hang out." He claimed to have no preconceptions: "Without a clear accounting . . . there cannot be a restoration of confidence in law enforcement. We have to go through this process." [9]

When the process ended, the report, while faulting Attorney General Reno for her "highly irresponsible" decision to force an end to the standoff, still concluded that David Koresh had to bear the ultimate responsibility for the deaths that resulted. McCollum's investigation did not uncover the federal conspiracy that many conservatives felt was the impetus behind the government's actions.[10] Even the *New York Times* acknowledged that the co-chair had handled himself responsibly.[11] Thus, a purely partisan divide was averted by a fair process conducted by someone who could have scored tremendous political points with his ideological colleagues if he had come to a different conclusion.

Two years before the House had to deal with the cartons of evidence amassed by Ken Starr, McCollum's Crime Subcommittee was seeking ways to change the Independent Counsel law. A bill passed the subcommittee that tried "to eliminate what many legislators perceive as the excesses of the current Whitewater investigation . . . and the previous Iran-Contra probe." Chairman McCollum commented at the time that this was "an effort to see if we [can] come up with some reasonable bipartisan compromise."[12] The law had been an irritant to both parties, and he sought a solution. But no solution was found before he had to face the evidence supporting President Clinton's misconduct.

The House Inquiry

I do believe . . . that when it comes to the United States and its constitutional structure and the framework that we live under to enable us to be free, and we see the separation of powers into the executive, legislative, and judicial branches, that anything which undermines the fundamentals of the system we have, undermines basic freedom. And it undermines the American system. That bothers me and that's what I think the impeachment trial was really all about. Granted, Bill Clinton did make moral transgressions, in my judgment, that I don't condone in his behavior, but, to me, the issue, the question in front of Congress, at least, [was not] dealing with his personal behavior or those moral values that he violated in that non-governmental sense. Rather, what we were confronted with were those basic structural precepts which allow us to function and keep the democratic system.[13]

Those were the sentiments, Congressman McCollum said, that guided him as he considered the evidence for President Clinton's guilt. His concern was the American system of government, not the President's moral transgressions alone. Making that point was the primary battle that had to be fought throughout the impeachment process.

In the beginning, as the House was considering whether to go forward with an inquiry, those who thought the matter needed serious attention already were climbing a steep hill in public opinion. "The President's men went out, and his operatives and his various talking heads, I think, in a network of absolute public relations brilliance, were able, in a fairly short order, to capitalize on this underlying sentiment that many Americans felt about being tired of it and not wanting to see any more of it, of rallying people in large numbers to vocally oppose," McCollum noted with the benefit of hindsight. "And this strong public opinion about dealing with this subject was even stronger once there was a revelation of some of the explicit material in the Independent Counsel's report ... I think, at that point, it became very clear in a matter of a few weeks that there was going to be great difficulty in gaining a conviction in the Senate if, indeed, the President were impeached."[14]

As the Judiciary Committee hearings reached their climax—votes on the articles of impeachment—Representative McCollum knew where he stood. "The United States is the greatest free nation in the history of the world," he told the Committee. "The foundation of this greatness is our justice system. Instead of settling our disputes with guns and knives or paying off protection rackets, as occurs in much of the rest of the world, any American who's injured may go to court and get a fair resolution of a dispute based on the law and the facts."[15]

He then turned to the issue of perjury specifically, remarking that people go to court expecting witnesses to tell the truth: "That's what we mean by the term 'rule of law.' Without truthful testimony, justice can't be rendered and the system doesn't work." Truthful testimony, he noted, is so crucial that Federal Sentencing Guidelines provide harsher punishments for those convicted of perjury and obstruction of justice than they do for those who are convicted of bribery. "Under the Constitution, impeachable offenses are 'treason, bribery, and other high crimes and misdemeanors.' If our courts, for good reason, punish perjury and obstruction of justice more severely than bribery, how could anyone conclude they're not impeachable offenses?" he asked. "Bribery and perjury both go to the same grave offense, the undermining of the administration of justice."[16]

The most pernicious aspect of the case before the Committee was that this crime of perjury—that most damaging of all offenses in the administration of justice—had been committed by the chief law enforcement officer of the nation, as well as the commander in chief of the military. "If we tolerate such serious crimes as perjury and obstruction of justice by the president of the United States and fail to impeach him," McCollum warned, "there will be grave, damaging consequences for our system of government." He continued,

If he has committed these crimes and is not impeached, a terrible message will go out across the country that will undermine the integrity of our court system. We will not only send the message that there is a double standard and that the president of the United States is above the law in these matters, but also a message that these crimes are not as serious as some people once thought they were. More people in the future will likely commit perjury in the courts than would be the case if the president were impeached.

Furthermore, it will be far more difficult in the future for congresses to impeach federal judges for perjury, and the like, which we've done in the past. And there's bound to be repercussions in our military, where the commander in chief is treated quite differently from officers and other enlisted personnel who would be routinely removed from duty and discharged from the service for activities the president has admitted to, not to mention the crimes themselves, which no doubt would get a military officer a court-martial. . . .

. . . His conduct constitutes a great insult to our constitutional system and subverts our system of government.[17]

Moreover, in McCollum's estimation, the Committee was not dealing with merely one of two isolated incidents; rather, this President had "engaged in a whole pattern of conduct over an extended period of time" that concealed the truth, obstructed justice, and tampered with witnesses. There really was no other recourse: "Some have suggested that we're ill-served by the time that would be consumed in the trial of these matters, but having examined the evidence thoroughly, I don't agree. Just the opposite is true: to fail to impeach the president, knowing what I know . . . I think would be dereliction of duty on my part. . . . To do otherwise would undermine the rule of law, undermine our constitutional system of government."[18]

When the matter went to the full House, Congressman McCollum participated actively in the debate. Democrat Steven Rothman of New

Jersey objected to the articles of impeachment because "the founders specifically rejected proposals to allow impeaching the president for poor character or for morally bad behavior. . . . The president," he insisted, "can only be impeached for treason, bribery, or high crimes or misdemeanors against the state." McCollum felt a correction to his colleague's views was needed:

> Mr. Speaker, I simply want to respond to one of the comments the gentleman from New Jersey just made about the level to which it has to be . . . before we impeach a president. . . . It certainly does not have to be presidential powers only. If the president of the United States committed murder, if he committed a lot of other crimes, it seems to me that those would be perfectly impeachable, and if we are talking about perjury, which rises to the level of bribery . . . it seems abundantly clear that perjury is impeachable.[19]

As the debate continued, Democrat Charles Rangel of New York asked a question for which he provided his own answer: "What has this president done to cause so much hatred, so much animosity?" he wondered. "And for those of you that say this is not about sex, I agree with you: This is about getting rid of the president of the United States. . . . You brought hatred to this floor. You can see it in the eyes, you can see it in the language, and people will walk lockstep and vote as Republicans and not as Members of the United States Congress." McCollum responded,

> Mr. Speaker, I simply want to express concern over the gentleman from New York's statement that there was hatred over here on our side of the aisle with regard to the president. That is just not really true, in all honesty and sincerity . . . I have personally talked with Members who have made their decisions only in the last few days after they have gone over the record who really truly did not want to impeach this president and have no hatred at all. It is an objective concern that perjury and obstruction of justice and the crimes are so over-

whelming this president committed that they made that decision.[20]

McCollum, even in retrospect, believes that the Republicans "went at this with a very open mind. A lot of people don't accept that, but I certainly did. And I believe from what I saw, everybody did." Judiciary Committee members and many of the undecided Republicans went over to the Ford Building where all the material was kept under strict security arrangements. They spent hours perusing the material, trying to decide if the evidence was sufficient. McCollum continued,

> I recall distinctly, once we recommended impeachment as a Committee, before the House voted, we had some Members that could be said to be moderate Republicans who questioned this more than others might have and certainly were not prepared to vote for impeachment initially. They came back to Washington the week of that vote and were persuaded to go over and look at some material for themselves that was not all public. They came away concluding, as we did, that indeed the President had committed these crimes and it was very serious. Therefore, they felt compelled to go ahead with the impeachment.[21]

Commenting further on Democrats' charges of hatred toward President Clinton as the motivation for Republicans' actions, McCollum simply said,

> Well, I tell people, as I told them from the very beginning, that I have no ill will or malice toward Mr. Clinton. I, obviously, am from a different political party. I believe that anyone objectively looking at this would have considered what I considered in the same way, and should have. That is, if you have the Chief Executive Officer of the nation, the chief legal officer of the nation, the head of the military, your commander

in chief, who has committed crimes that would constitute grounds for immediate removal if you were in any major subordinate position to him, then ignoring them just because he's the President of the United States strikes me as being something terribly corrosive to the system of law that we have in this nation that allows us to protect our freedom.[22]

That is why Bill McCollum voted for impeachment. The House agreed with him—barely—and the scene shifted to the Senate.

Presenting the Evidence

"I don't think anyone would volunteer to be a House Manager. I don't think anybody would really want to do that role," Manager McCollum related more than a year after the ordeal ended. The role did have its positives, he acknowledged; it gave him the opportunity to use his lawyerly skills once again, and it allowed him to advocate for a position that he believed was right. "But it's not a position, I would think, that anybody would say they really wanted to do, you know: 'I want to impeach the President of the United States.' You *don't* ever want, society doesn't want to do that, and you certainly don't want to embroil the nation in a controversy. You don't want to put yourself and your family through all that. But it's something I had an obligation to do, and I was in that position of singular leadership and asked to do it by Henry Hyde. And I did it," he said.[23]

While McCollum denies that he thought the outcome was a foregone conclusion, he knew from the start, in meetings to discuss the Senate rules, that removing the President from office was going to be one of the hardest tasks he had faced. Normally reserved and gentlemanly, he came back from one meeting with the Senate leadership frustrated to the point that he wondered whether the effort would be worth it. "We are another House of the Congress. They're treating us like we're an embarrassment," he told his fellow Managers. "They don't even want to see us in there. I suggest that we walk on the floor of the Senate and refuse to participate in this charade."[24] These were strong words emanating from strong emotions, yet he ultimately agreed that to follow his suggestion would not achieve the goal they all sought.

After Managers Bryant, Hutchinson, and Rogan presented the evidence against the President on the first full day of the Senate trial, McCollum began the second day with a summary of that evidence, the objective being to help the Senators digest all the material they had heard. As nearly all the Managers did, McCollum started by asserting that he bore no animosity toward the President. "But I happen to believe that allowing a President who committed crimes of perjury and obstruction of justice and witness tampering to remain in office would undermine our courts and our system of justice," he admitted.[25]

This all began, he reminded his audience, with President Clinton's attempt to hide his relationship with Monica Lewinsky from the Paula Jones attorneys in a legal deposition. McCollum then anticipated the defense's approach: "His lawyers will argue to you next week that everything he did to keep the relationship hidden was legal. They will say he may have split a few hairs and evaded answers and given misleading answers, but it was all within the framework of responses and actions that any good lawyer would advise his client to do. They will also say that if he crossed the line technically anywhere, he didn't knowingly or intentionally do so. Oh, how I wish that were true! We wouldn't be here today. But, alas, that's not so." And as he did in the House, he pointed to the fact that perjury and obstruction of justice merited greater punishment in the criminal law than bribery.[26]

As he reviewed the evidence, he again urged the Senators to be aware of the tactics of the other side: "I implore you not to get hung up on some of the absurd and contorted explanations the President and his attorneys try to make to get around his obvious and apparent criminal behavior. . . . When you are thinking about all of this, keep in mind the whole context, not just some compartmentalized portion that might be subject to word games."[27] The reference to "word games" was in the context of the highly publicized (and largely ridiculed) presidential comment about what the meaning of the word "is" is. McCollum knew it could not hurt to remind Senators of that exchange under oath.

At the completion of his summary, McCollum stated what he considered to be the obvious conclusion that each Senator ought to reach: "I believe that when you finish hearing and weighing all of the evidence you will conclude as I have that William Jefferson Clinton committed the crimes of obstruction of justice, witness tampering and perjury; that these in this case are high crimes and misdemeanors; that he has done grave damage to our system of justice and leaving him in office would do more; and that he should be removed from office as President of the United States."[28] Although Manager McCollum believed the Senators should come to that conclusion, he knew the key would be live witnesses, and that was going to be a struggle.

Originally, the Managers wanted to bring at least ten to fifteen witnesses to the floor of the Senate. When they made that proposal in a meeting with Senate leaders, they were shut out immediately. Hyde reminded the Senators present that Senate rules provided for a real trial— with live witnesses. According to David Schippers, the Judiciary Committee's Chief Investigator, who was in that meeting, Democrat Joe Biden of Delaware responded simply, "We make our own rules."[29] In the Managers' minds, this was a far cry from the very concept they were trying to uphold—the rule of law. The Managers were reduced to trying to argue for at least three live witnesses, rather than the original number they wanted. Even that, they found, would not be allowed.

During the question-and-answer period after the initial presentations from both sides, McCollum tried to make the case for the witnesses. "We need to bring in witnesses to resolve conflicting testimony," McCollum argued, "to give you a true picture of the president's scheme to lie and conceal evidence for the other obstruction of justice charges and certainly for the last perjury charge. They are more complex. They are more dependent on circumstantial evidence and inferences you logically have to draw." Paper evidence was not as persuasive as live testimony—that was the case he was attempting to make:

And that is why you need to hear from Monica Lewinsky, Vernon Jordan and Sidney Blumenthal, to tell you about these things themselves.

When you do, you are just plain going to get a different flavor; you are going to feel the sense of this. We believe you will find at the end of the day, once you have done that . . . the president is guilty of the entire scheme we presented to you in every detail beyond a reasonable doubt. . . .

I am not going to be the one describing what Monica Lewinsky is going to show you if she comes in here. . . . I can tell you that she herself will convey this story to you in a way that it cannot be conveyed off a piece of paper. . . .

I suppose that is why the White House counselors are so afraid of our calling any witnesses. They don't want you to have the opportunity to see that, an opportunity you can only get the full flavor of if not only you let us take the depositions, but you at least let us call her live here on the floor. . . .

They know that the written record conceals this. There is no way to lift that out. There is no way for you to see the relationship, how she responds to the questions, how she answers, how she conducts herself in making it very apparent what the president's true meaning and intent was.[30]

Despite McCollum's best attempt, and the attempts of the other Managers, the Senate allowed only three witnesses—on videotape, not live. That spelled the end of the case, in McCollum's estimation. He had not given up hope, as long as there was the possibility of live witnesses. With that ruled out, he knew the chances of removal were less than slim. "The reason I wasn't convinced of that until then is because I always felt, up to that point, that if we were able to present the American public with the drama of this in the sense of having Monica Lewinsky testify and be cross-examined, and some of the other key witnesses, the public would focus in on it and reevaluate it," McCollum explained. He knew the public was, to a great extent, tuned out; live witnesses could change that, and public opinion might give the Managers the impetus they needed:

> I had hopes that by making a presentation of the case as you would in a regular trial, you would rivet the public's attention. They would pay attention to the details, and they would actually wake up to the reality that what we were talking about was criminal behavior that was just intolerable. But that never happened. Barring that happening, I think it was very clear the Senate wasn't going to convict. . . . Everybody, by that time, knew the outcome, except maybe for the votes of one or two Senators.[31]

Knowing the outcome ahead of time could have dampened the enthusiasm for proceeding, but McCollum insists that was not the case: "I felt that we had a duty to perform to uphold the rule of law." He continued,

> And the rule of law in this country is very important, and I think the precedents we set and the fact that we didn't simply roll over was important to go through the trial. The impeachment itself was important. It was very historic. The President was impeached. He was only the second President in history to be impeached. He obviously wasn't convicted and wasn't thrown out of office, but I think all of us engaged in this realized that we had a duty to perform and that we had to do our very best. We made the arguments and put them on the record and historians could review them, and students and scholars in the future. Hopefully, some good would come out of this. Maybe the nation would never face precisely this again, but at least there would be a record, and lessons could be learned, and the debate would have been fully fleshed out.[32]

McCollum's final attempt at fleshing out the debate came in the closing arguments on February 8. He was convinced that most Democratic

Senators agreed that the President was guilty, but he also thought that they were not going to convict because of party loyalty; so he decided to challenge them directly. "Notwithstanding the clever and resourceful arguments that White House counsel have made to you today, and in the past few weeks," he began, "I suspect that most of you—probably more than two-thirds—believe that the President did, indeed, commit most, if not all, of the crimes he is charged with under these articles of impeachment. I suspect that a great many of you share my view that these are high crimes and misdemeanors."[33] Even so, he understood that they were not prepared to vote for conviction. Instead, they were ready to acquit the President unless persuaded to do otherwise. So he pleaded with them to hear the facts one more time.

After reviewing the evidence again, McCollum asked the Senators to consider the consequences of not removing President Clinton from office. The first consequence would be "a precedent of doubt as to whether perjury and obstruction of justice are high crimes and misdemeanors in impeaching the President." If acquittal were the result, would any future President even be considered for removal for such actions? "Is that the record you want?" he asked.[34]

The second consequence would be to set different standards for impeaching a President and a federal judge—and the former would be lower than the latter. "So while the Constitution on its face does not make a distinction for removing a President or removing a judge," he reminded them, "if you vote to acquit, believing that the President committed perjury and obstruction of justice, for all times you are going to set a precedent that there is such a distinction."[35]

The third consequence would be to set aside constitutional requirements for the sake of the popularity of the incumbent, thereby putting public opinion above constitutional obligation. "Can you imagine how damaging that could be to our constitutional form of government," he argued, "to set the precedent that no President will be removed from office for high crimes and misdemeanors unless the polls show that the public wants that to happen? Would the Founding Fathers have ever envisioned that? Of course not. Our Constitution was structured to avoid this very situation."[36]

The rule of law was the fourth victim. McCollum asked some practical questions: "What damage is done for future generations by a vote to acquit? Will more witnesses be inclined to commit perjury in trials?" What about juries? Will they now decide not to convict people for perjury and obstruction of justice? He continued,

> To vote to acquit puts the President on a pedestal which says that, as long as he is popular, we are going to treat him differently with regard to keeping his job than any other person in any other position of trust in the United States of America. . . .
> Are you going to put on the record books the precedent that all who serve under the President and whom he has appointed will be held to a higher standard than the President? What legacy to history is this? What mischief have you wrought to our Constitution, to our system of government, to the values and principles cherished by future generations of Americans? All this because—I guess this is the argument—Clinton was elected and is popular with the people? All this, when it is clear that a vote to convict would amount to nothing more than the peaceful, orderly, and immediate transition of government of the Presidency to the Vice President?
> William Jefferson Clinton is not a king; he is our President. You have the power and the duty to remove him from office for high crimes and misdemeanors. I implore you to muster the courage of your convictions, to muster the courage the Founding Fathers believed that the Senate would always have in times like these. William Jefferson Clinton has committed high crimes and misdemeanors.
> Convict and remove him.[37]

Bill McCollum gave his best argument—for the record.

Reflections—For the Record

McCollum has neither great happiness nor regrets for his involvement in the impeachment. "It's an experience I had," he says simply. "I haven't had a lot of time to reflect. I haven't written any memoirs. I only occasionally encounter the subject matter because someone raises it with me." Yet some reflection has occurred, and he probably has thought about it more than he realizes.

For instance, he relates how one of the consequences he dreaded has begun to manifest itself:

> I don't know how many attorneys have come up to me over the months from the beginning of this event to the present time and said to me: "It's much harder now for me to convince my clients that they have to tell the truth when they're under oath in court, especially if they're domestic relations clients and they're talking about their spouses, child support, divorce in general. It's very hard to convince them that they have to tell the truth. Why should I, say the clients, if the President doesn't get any punishment for that?" So I think that is a very serious matter . . . and that's the part of this that is the most onerous.[38]

A more positive reflection has to do with his fellow Managers, for whom he says he has the utmost respect. He uses a military analogy to describe his feelings. If you had to take a hill, "with these fellas, you never had to look over your shoulder, you never had to look back. We were a team. There was a strong sense that we were doing what was right and what was necessary. It wasn't a desire to get the President. It was a desire to do what was right for the judicial system to protect the rule of law. We all felt equally strong about it, and nobody wavered." The pressure was intense, at times, not to follow through—they received a lot of angry calls to their offices. "But nobody ever doubted. Nobody ever flinched. So, in that sense, I'm proud of the team I served with. I think what we did was right and honorable and correct," he said.[39]

McCollum maintains faith in the American people. He believes that they "respect those who are in public office who don't put their finger in the wind all the time to just see what public opinion is, but rather do what they truly believe is right." The impeachment endeavor was an "extreme test" of his belief, but he continues to hold to it. He also hopes that Americans have learned that the American governmental system is strong:

> We're not fragile. We're not going to fall apart because we have a challenge to the President. It isn't a challenge to the Presidency; it's a challenge to a single individual. Our Founding Fathers presented a framework for deciding these matters which was absolutely brilliant, not perfect. Our system isn't perfect; it's just the best system of government ever devised by man. It preserves, if properly done, the framework that allows us to have freedom. We need to preserve that for our children and our grandchildren so they can have a better quality of life, or at least as good as ours, and hopefully better. . . .
>
> . . . I think we had an airing, as the Founding Fathers would have expected us to, of the grievances. They were done deliberately. They were done by the procedures and processes that were set forth. While the outcome was not as I personally would have preferred it to be, the system worked.[40]

Bill McCollum's faith, both in the American system of government and in the good sense of the American people, apparently came through the impeachment experience intact.

Chapter 12 Endnotes

1 Congressman Bill McCollum, interview by author, tape recording, Washington, DC, 11 April 2000.

2 Ibid.

3 Ibid.

4 Editorial, "Whom Was McCollum Representing?" *St. Petersburg Times*, 4 July 1990, 22A.

5 "Unindicted Co-conspirators," *The New Republic*, 23 July 1990, 10.

6 "Dangerous Liaisons," *The New Republic*, 13 August 1990, 4.

7 Lee H. Hamilton and Daniel K. Inouye, *The Iran-Contra Affair: Supplemental and Additional Views*, Chapter 12, *Views of McCollum*; available at http://www.elibrary.com/s/edumark/getd; accessed 19 May 1999.

8 McCollum interview.

9 Sean Piccoli, "Some Heads Could Roll after Waco Hearings," *The Washington Times*, 24 July 1995.

10 Geert De Clerq, "Reno Faulted for Handling of Cult Siege," *Reuters*, 11 July 1996.

11 "McCollum's Handling of Waco Hearings a Pleasant Surprise," *Minneapolis Star Tribune*, 5 August 1995, 16A, quoting a *New York Times* editorial.

12 "Panel OKs Changes to Independent Prosecutor System," *National Journal*, 20 September 1996.

13 McCollum interview.

14 Ibid.

15 The Impeachment Hearings: Opening Statements: Bill McCollum, 10 December 1998; available at http://www.washingtonpost.com/wp-srv/politics/special/clinton/stories/mccollumtext121098.htm; accessed 1 April 1999.

16 Ibid.

17 Ibid.

18 Ibid.

19 McLoughlin, *The Impeachment and Trial of President Clinton*, 178-79.

[20] Ibid., 196-97.

[21] McCollum interview.

[22] Ibid.

[23] Ibid.

[24] Schippers, *Sellout*, 12-13.

[25] Opening Statement of Hon. Bill McCollum, Senate Impeachment Trial of President Clinton, 15 January 1999.

[26] Ibid.

[27] Ibid.

[28] Ibid.

[29] Schippers, *Sellout*, 17.

[30] McLaughlin, *The Impeachment and Trial of President Clinton*, 362-63.

[31] McCollum interview.

[32] Ibid.

[33] Closing Argument of Hon. Bill McCollum, Senate Impeachment Trial of President Clinton, 8 February 1999; available at http://www.house.gov/judiciary/mcco0208.htm; accessed 9 February 2000.

[34] Ibid.

[35] Ibid.

[36] Ibid.

[37] Ibid.

[38] McCollum interview.

[39] Ibid.

[40] Ibid.

CHAPTER THIRTEEN

James Rogan:
Principle above Politics—
Honor above Incumbency

As one enters the Capitol Hill office of Congressman James Rogan of California, one can see Rogan's love of politics exude from the very walls—literally. One looks almost in vain for empty space on his walls, which are decorated with every type of political memorabilia. Pictures on his bookcases also dominate the scene. One, in particular, draws one's attention. It features President Bill Clinton with a little girl on either side of him. Those girls are Rogan's daughters. "Every time I've ever met him," Rogan commented, "he's always been gracious to me, to my wife, to my family. This was pre-impeachment, but, I mean, he's holding my little girls in this picture. I mean, he's always been very gracious."[1]

James Rogan's first contact with Bill Clinton occurred in 1978. Rogan, at that time a Democrat and applying to law schools, was attending a Democratic midterm convention in Memphis. The moderator at that convention was the young governor-elect of Arkansas. He fascinated Rogan. "He was glib, he was smart, he was sharp, he was in control," Rogan remembered. When the convention ended, he walked up to Clinton, introduced himself, and began to talk politics. Rogan told the rising young star that Rogan himself also would like to run for office someday. "Bill Clinton spent, I don't know, ten or fifteen minutes, encouraging me, talking to me about law school, talking to me about what a good background that would be, asking me about myself," Rogan said.[2]

Clearly, Rogan had been impressed by what appeared to be a caring individual.

Twenty-one years later, this second-term Congressman, now a Republican, was called upon to explain to the United States Senate why this caring individual should be removed from office. His personal feelings toward Bill Clinton had not changed, but now he carried a governmental responsibility that could not be avoided. "My faith doesn't lead me to be judgmental against anybody," he reasoned. Whenever a reporter would ask him a question that might allow him to insult President Clinton personally, Rogan would instead quote the Bible. "I always made the press a little nervous when I would quote scripture to them, so I liked to do it," he admits. He kept two things in mind at all times. First, he always considered the effect anything he said might have on Chelsea Clinton: "I want to be mindful that I am talking about some young lady's father." Second, he remembered the biblical admonition to remove the beam from one's own eye first: "It would be very easy to have moralized and criticized the President and to have attacked him and to have focused upon the sliver in his eye." He continued,

> But I know my heart; I know what the Bible says is true: I am a sinner saved only by grace through faith. My sin condemns me to death, and it is only through Jesus that I am saved. It isn't my job to judge the President. It was my job to carry out my constitutional obligations and respect the rule of law.
>
> If I had taken a pass on voting to impeach this President who used the power of his job and, beyond the power of his job, abused his office by committing perjury and obstructing justice and suborning perjury—crimes that were committed merely to protect himself from political embarrassment and political consequences—if I had voted against defense of the Constitution to protect myself from political consequences, then I would have been guilty of the same offense he was. I had to take my oath of office seriously, even when I didn't believe the President took his seriously.[3]

Thus, according to Rogan, seeking to remove the President from office was not a personal thing; it was a matter of conscience, of taking seriously the oath of office that he recited when he entered Congress. He believes the entire Manager team felt the same. The Managers even prayed together for President Clinton. "Ed Bryant led us in prayer a couple of times. He led us in prayer in the Committee Room, when we were beginning the debate on impeachment. He led us in prayer the first day of the trial. We prayed for wisdom. We prayed for guidance. We prayed for God's mercy on us. We prayed for the President and for his family. This was not a bitter, angry, hostile mob of people out to hurt the Constitution or hurt the President," he remembered.[4]

What brought this former Democrat to the place where he was standing on the floor of the United States Senate, arguing that a man with whom he had a cordial relationship should be removed from the highest office in the land? Of all the House Managers, James Rogan's personal odyssey may be the most unique.

Rough Beginnings

Rogan's background is not the type that most people might imagine for a conservative Republican lawmaker. The basic facts are that he was born in 1957 in San Francisco. But he relates, "My father was a bartender who got my mother pregnant and left. My mom was a convicted felon. I was the oldest kid. We were all on welfare and food stamps. I dropped out of high school to go to work in the tenth grade and never did go back and finish."[5] His home situation was so bad that his grandparents had to take him in, but they both died before his ninth birthday. He was shuttled off to a great-aunt, who died before he became a teenager. Then, at twelve, he finally lived with his mother for the first time. She kept getting in trouble with the law, served a jail term, later violated her probation, and was sent back again. According to her son, "She cheated or she misrepresented herself to get additional benefits [on welfare] or food stamps."[6]

When he quit school, Rogan worked nearly every job imaginable: "I was a bartender, I was a bouncer for three days at a pornographic theater, I was a janitor, I scrubbed toilets, I sold vacuum cleaners door to door—I took every job I could find."[7] If social conditions determine one's life, then James Rogan had no chance of going anywhere in the world. Yet he was not forever scarred by his early influences. In fact, the situation seemed to have little effect on him. "I think if you are loved and, even if you're poor, if you have friends in similar circumstances, you never feel like you are abused or that life is insurmountable," he reflected later. "I never felt I had a hard childhood, but as I got older, people said to me, 'Boy, you overcame a lot!'"[8]

Family circumstances such as Rogan's are not normally breeding grounds for future Republicans. He was a Democrat from the time he could first understand politics. He loved history, and as he read, he realized that no matter where one starts in life, one still could achieve great heights. "What dawned on me is that through the political process, it really didn't matter what kind of background one came from. Political history is covered by people from very humble means. Upon reflection, that may have been part of the attraction," he believes now.[9]

The high school dropout decided to become a lawyer. He worked his way through junior college, then attended the University of California, Berkeley, and finally, the UCLA Law School. Upon completion of his law degree in 1983, Rogan worked for a couple of years as a corporate lawyer, then turned to the public realm as a Los Angeles Deputy District Attorney, where he labored from 1985 to 1990. Along the way, two life-changing decisions occurred—one political, the other religious.

Rogan had been working his way up the ladder of the Democratic Party, becoming a member of the Los Angeles County Central Committee. The Party was the Party of his grandparents, but the more he examined it, the more doubts he entertained. "I really started doing a lot of soul searching about where I had come from, what my Party, the Democrats, had done to families, particularly poor families, by making them dependent on government and convincing them there was no concept of individual responsibility connected with governmental favors.

I saw the personal destructive nature of what welfare did to families, what illegitimacy did to families, what drugs and crime and dropout rates and all those other pathologies involved."[10] He concluded that the policies the Democratic Party was promoting were not beneficial and that he could no longer support them. His conservative views led him into the Republican Party.

The political change actually occurred after the religious change; the latter probably had a lot to do with the former. By the mid-1980s, Rogan had risen from poverty to become a corporate lawyer, "making more money than I could have ever imagined." Yet he remembers feeling empty:

> I couldn't figure out why I felt "ucky" inside, why all of these material things that I had achieved did not fill this big empty hole in me. And I met this young woman who sang in the church choir who wouldn't go out with me because I wasn't a Christian. But she did invite me to church, and I started listening to the service and listened to a tape from a fellow ... Chuck Colson, who quoted Pascal and it hit me like a ton of bricks. He quoted Pascal, who said that every man has a God-shaped hole in him and you can't fill it with anything else. You can try sex, you can try drugs, money, power—it doesn't fit. So I became a Christian and turned my life over to the Lord. That was about fourteen years ago [i.e., 1986].[11]

For Rogan, the religious conversion was not merely a change of mind; it changed the way he lived and provided him with new priorities:

> I personally couldn't do this job if I were not a Christian. The pressures of time and power and all of the surrounding attributes that go with any high-profile position like this would have me living such an unreasonable life—and that's not the objective I really want. If I had been elected to Congress in my twenties instead of my forties, I would have had a totally different take on this job. I would have been very much under the power and the title and the women, and

every now and then maybe write a bill just so I could write home about it—essentially just living a big party life.

Coming here now as a Christian with two little girls and a wife, I understand things about this job that I didn't understand in my twenties. I didn't understand what a terribly family-unfriendly job this is. I didn't understand how much pressure there is on marriages, and what a high degree of divorce there is among Members of Congress, and what a great degree of alienation there is between Members of Congress and their own children who, essentially, grow up sometimes fatherless, if we let this job do that to us. It's like being a hamster on a wheel. We keep running faster and faster, trying to keep up with the obligations of the job. The world just goes faster, and we miss all of the things surrounding us.[12]

Armed with a new and vibrant faith, and with an altered political philosophy, Rogan was ready for the next phase in his life.

California Politics

Rogan's switch from a Democratic Central Committee member to a Republican in 1988 made him somewhat of a trophy convert for Republicans. In 1990, Republican Governor George Deukmejian appointed Rogan to a judgeship on the Glendale Municipal Court, making him the youngest sitting judge in California at that time.[13] He held court for four years until the resignation of a Republican state legislator in his district opened the door for a try at elective office.[14] He ran as part of a seven-candidate field, with both Democrats and Republicans vying to finish the term. Some of his Republican opponents tried to paint him as a turncoat who had switched parties to obtain a judgeship. They called it a character issue. So he not only had to deal with Democratic opposition, but Republican as well. Rogan countered that his credentials and integrity had both been well tested. Surprisingly—to him—he won 53.9 percent of the vote and became state representative for the 43rd District.[15]

In November of that same year, 1994, Rogan had to run again in the regular general election. Again he met an in-house challenge from Republican Peter Repovich, who claimed that Rogan was too conservative. Repovich blasted Rogan's ties to the "Christian Right" and complained that his opposition to abortion would "drag the party to defeat."[16] The Democratic Party felt the same and tried the identical tactic. Democratic challenger Adam Schiff decried the money Rogan was receiving from the "Christian Right." He also ridiculed Rogan's support for the teaching of creationism in public schools.[17] But in spite of the efforts of both Republican and Democratic detractors, Rogan won again.

Barely a year after his first victory, James Rogan had made a name for himself in the California General Assembly. He was respected for his judicial manner and developed a reputation as a mediator in a highly fractured legislative body. One reporter called him "that rare breed of right-wing Republican: a born-again, conservative Christian who is not an immediate turnoff to liberal Democrats." Rogan commented at the time, "I have a good working relationship with almost everybody. This is—for better or worse—a house which is essentially evenly divided and is, therefore, a house that must learn to work together."[18]

Republicans had gained a one-vote majority in the Assembly for the first time in two decades. Some Republicans viewed this turn of events as an opportunity to get even—but not Rogan. He desired to build bridges instead: "We cannot be so vain," he told his colleagues, "as to perceive a bare majority as an overwhelming mandate that would allow us the comfort of ignoring what our friends on that other side have to say." One GOP staffer commented, "The guy practically oozes fairness." More than one Democrat was surprised to find Rogan on their side on certain issues such as stronger domestic violence laws and stiffer penalties for carrying concealed firearms.[19]

Democrat Sheila Kuehl, who became the legislature's first openly lesbian member, considered Rogan a reasonable man. "He listens. When he discusses bills, he often takes a very reasoned approach. He'll come over to ask for your vote and argue the sensibility of the bill. I like a member who approaches the matter as though it has some intellectual content," she said. Another Democratic Assemblyman, John Burton, commented wryly, "He's a very decent, bright and able young man, albeit misguided in his political philosophy. At one time he was a decent Democrat, but he must have fallen on his head—and that's what made him a right-wing Republican."[20]

Rogan's ability to work with both sides of the aisle made him the perfect candidate for majority leader in the next term, despite his relative youth and inexperience. As colleagues began touting him for the job, he remained philosophical: "Of the 79 people in the Assembly, if you scratched 78 of them deep enough, you'd find the desire to be Speaker. I'm that 79th one."[21] If the meek shall inherit the earth, Rogan experienced at least a scaled-down version of the maxim when he won the role of majority leader less than two years after his first election to the legislature. He developed an amicable relationship with his counterpart on the Democratic side, minority leader Richard Katz, who said of Rogan, "Jim is a hard-core ideologue. But he's a friendly hard-core ideologue."[22]

Even as he was sworn in as majority leader, everyone knew that his time in that post would be limited. The congressional seat in his home district, the 27th, was being vacated, and Rogan decided to run for Congress. Why did he choose to give up his position at that time? He concluded that the opportunity to join the "Republican Revolution" in Congress "was just too tempting to let slide . . . If I really want to be on the front lines for the fight ahead, Washington is the place to be."[23]

Running in a congressional district that boasted a higher Democratic registration than Republican, Rogan knew that he might be throwing away a promising political career. The district, though sending a Republican to the House for the past thirty-four years, was changing demographically. Bill Clinton had beaten George Bush in the district by 9 percent in 1992, and it was obvious that Bob Dole was going to fare no better in 1996. Rogan, though, had not only his credential as majority leader in the California Assembly, but had just been awarded, in a *California Journal* magazine poll, the "No. 1 rating for integrity" and been named "best Assembly member of the year."[24] The race was about as close as a race can get, but he came out the winner with 50.1 percent of the vote. His 1998 margin was nearly the same. In the midst of the impeachment battle, he joked with his fellow Managers, "In '96, we weren't impeaching him. I got 50.1 percent. In 1998, we are impeaching him and I got 50.8 percent. So obviously it's a political winner."[25] After only two years in politics, James Rogan was on his way to Washington.

The Impeachment Path

Unlike most of the other Managers, Rogan did not seek to be on the Judiciary Committee when he arrived in Congress. Henry Hyde wanted him on the Committee, but Rogan preferred the Commerce Committee where he could work on trade issues. "I had already made my reputation in criminal justice and in the law as a judge and as a D.A., and as a state legislator. I really didn't feel I needed to add to my résumé in that regard. I wanted to focus on other issues," he said. Hyde continued to talk with him and told him about the Judiciary Committee's Subcommittee on Intellectual Property. Rogan realized that might be good for him after all; his district encompassed the Hollywood studios and a number of high-tech companies. "Intellectual property was our lifeblood of those industries—copyrights, patents, and trademarks. Piracy alone in the movie video industry costs us billions of dollars a year," he reasoned.[26] So he told Chairman Hyde that he would be interested in the next opening on the Committee.

That opening came in a tragic and unforeseen way. Congressman Sonny Bono, a member of the Intellectual Property Subcommittee, was killed in a skiing accident in January 1998. Hyde approached Rogan to take Bono's place. Because Commerce and Judiciary were exclusive committees—normally, one person cannot serve on both—Hyde had to get a waiver from Speaker Gingrich to allow Rogan to serve. "I think it was on January 19th or 20th that Gingrich, I think the 19th, Gingrich approved it—somewhere like the 20th, I think, the waiver was granted, the 21st the Lewinsky story broke," Rogan remembered. This made the press wonder. Rogan explained,

> So it was virtually contemporaneous. With my ascension to the committee, the Lewinsky story broke. The press descended on me, all of them wanting to write their spin. The spin was that "now they're beefing up the committee with this ex-gang murder prosecutor to impeach the President." All of these reporters would gather outside my office every day, and they would shove their microphones in my face, and they would shout the same question: "Isn't it true you're on this committee to impeach the President? That's why you were appointed." And I would smile and say, "No, I'm just here to work on copyrights, patents, and trademarks." Then they would all laugh and go off and write their story that I was there to impeach the President.
>
> The truth is, it was never contemplated by me. I didn't run for Congress to impeach the President. I ran for Congress to work on a whole bunch of issues. The President wasn't on my radar screen in any way at that time.[27]

Shortly afterward, in March, Gingrich gave Rogan an assignment. Knowing that Ken Starr might give the House evidence in the coming months, the Speaker assigned the Congressman the task of producing a report on previous investigations of presidents and "offer[ing] his thoughts on the legal and political options available to the House."[28] The Watergate model did not apply fully, so Rogan had to work from scratch:

> I went around to a number of current and former Members of Congress—on both sides, Democrats and Republicans—who had dealt with investigations of the Executive Branch. And the hypothetical I posited to them . . . turned out to be prescient. I

said, "Suppose we just got a phone call, and the phone call advised us that moving trucks have just pulled up to the front steps of the House of Representatives and have dumped off boxes of information that are a referral from Judge Starr's office. How do we proceed?" That's exactly what happened. It was funny.[29]

What about the vast right-wing conspiracy touted by the First Lady after the Lewinsky matter became public knowledge? Rogan laughed at the thought: "If there was a vast right-wing conspiracy, it bypassed me. Newt Gingrich, the Speaker of the House, purposefully kept a hands-off approach, both privately and publicly, on impeachment." Why was this? According to Rogan, because he counseled Gingrich to stay out of it. When he interviewed Speaker Gingrich as part of his assignment, he asked him regarding the possible impeachment, "How would you foresee your role?" Rogan recalled,

> He started off by saying, well, as the Speaker, I would call a press conference and Chairman Hyde and I would do this and Chairman Hyde and I would do that, and when we finished I said, "Why are you in the equation? Why is the personal pronoun 'I?'" He looked at me slightly befuddled that I would even ask such a question. He said, "I'm the Speaker of the House. I'm the titular leader of the Republican Party. I'm an officer of the Congress. I'm the Speaker. It would be my job to move this forward." I said, "You are all of those things and more. You are in the constitutional line of succession, and that makes you the one person in the House of Representatives with a constitutional conflict of interest if you involve yourself in this."[30]

In order to convince Gingrich that he had to stay out of the fray, Rogan related a story he had heard when he had interviewed Peter Rodino, who had chaired the Judiciary Committee during the Richard Nixon impeachment inquiry. Rodino told Rogan what Carl Albert, Democratic Speaker of the House during Watergate, had determined at that time. According to Rodino,

> Albert told his caucus, he said, "Listen, I'm the Speaker of the House. Agnew's on the ropes, I'm right now two heartbeats away from the Presidency. If Agnew falls, I'm one heartbeat away. I'm in the constitutional line of succession. If I do anything out of the ordinary, it will look like I'm trying to engineer a coup to position myself and will call my office and myself into suspicion. And so I have to step out of this mix altogether. I have a conflict of interest. From here on out, whenever anybody asks me about impeachment, my response is going to be, 'Talk to Chairman Rodino of the Judiciary Committee. We're not creating some new form—the Republicans will attack it. We're going to send it right to Judiciary.'"
>
> And I said that's what my recommendation to him [Gingrich] was. The light bulb just, I could see it just went off. He said, "You're right." A couple of days later, a few days later, he gave an interview to one of the local newspapers here on the hill, *Roll Call*, and it was almost verbatim what Carl Albert had said. Gingrich said in the interview, "I'm in the constitutional line of succession. I have a constitutional conflict of interest. If any of you wants to talk to me about impeachment, my response to you is talk to Chairman Hyde. It's going to the Judiciary Committee. That's the regular order." And so that's what happened.[31]

Rogan felt it was necessary to set the record straight on that point because some analysts had been speculating that Gingrich had backed off because of intimidation concerning his own extramarital affair that was going on at the same time. Rogan does not believe that had anything to do with Gingrich's hands-off approach. Later, after the election, when

Gingrich stepped down as Speaker, the press started to focus on Majority Whip Tom Delay as the "bad guy." Rogan doesn't buy that perspective either:

> The press had to find a new person to demonize. That's really when they started demonizing Tom Delay. They started saying his nickname is "The Hammer." Well, I had served in this place for two years and was one of Delay's whips. I never once heard anybody call Tom Delay "The Hammer." It was this creature of the media that just got invented.
>
> The skinny was that "The Hammer," Delay, was banging away behind the scenes trying to drive this impeachment. One of the President's lawyers later told me that they viewed me— and I'll just tell you what he told me, I'm not trying to inflate my own position on the Committee because I don't necessarily agree—but one of the President's lawyers told me that they referred to me on the Committee as "the domino." They called me the domino because they felt if they could swing me on the Committee, I could take between five and eight votes with me and kill articles of impeachment. Assuming, for the sake of argument, that my influence extended even to half that— where I could have taken a few votes with me—if there was anybody that Tom Delay should have come and pressured or put the screws to—or even remonstrated with—it would have been one of his own whips.
>
> . . . Tom Delay, to my recollection, never once—I can tell you emphatically—he never pressured me, he never called me in to have a discussion with me. I don't remember him ever discussing impeachment with me. . . .
>
> . . . If he was out there hammering people, I never saw it. So I'm very skeptical about this whole press-generated spin about this being some kind of, you know, crazy conspiracy driven by Delay. It's historically not true.[32]

Although Rogan had been involved in preparing for a possible impeachment, no one knew for certain that an inquiry would be approved. After the delivery of the Independent Counsel's evidence, the Judiciary Committee opened hearings on whether an official inquiry should be conducted. In those hearings, Rogan took the opportunity to try to place the discussion on a higher level than mere politics. "I shall speak of it not as a Republican, but as an American," he began. "To use or manipulate these proceedings for any partisan advantage would be a national tragedy of manifest proportions. In times like these, each of us is obliged to check our party affiliation at the door. . . . The common bond that connects us, each to the other, is our mutual oath of allegiance to the Constitution of the United States. We must view this oath with nothing short of reverence."[33]

He entered these proceedings, he insisted, "with no fixed conclusions as to whether the president committed potentially impeachable offenses." He understood, from his background as both a prosecutor and a judge, the meaning of presumption of innocence, a presumption that had to be passionately respected and defended. Neither was he present to pass judgment on Bill Clinton's personal lifestyle. "However, it is both our purpose, and our legal obligation, to review the president's alleged conduct within the framework of the rule of law, and whether such conduct violated his obligation to faithfully execute the law," he explained. American jurisprudence has always upheld the maxim that no person is above the law, Rogan reminded the Committee. "Yet despite the two centuries of tremendous sacrifice for this legacy, the ghosts of patriots past cannot compel us to maintain the standard that no person is above the law. Each generation ultimately makes that choice for itself," he reasoned. The sobering task for the Committee, he concluded, was to seek the truth no matter how much discomfort it might bring: "In so doing, we will honor our constitutional duty, and we surely will fulfill our ultimate obligations both to conscience and to country."[34]

The full House did vote for the inquiry to begin. There was much wrangling between the parties concerning how long the inquiry would last. Some Republicans wanted an open-ended investigation, looking for more evidence to come from Ken Starr that was beyond merely the Paula Jones and Monica Lewinsky mess. Democrats, on the other hand, wanted a truncated inquiry limited to the latest allegations. Meanwhile, Republican losses in the 1998 congressional elections had created some hesitancy in the ranks for proceeding. In the midst of all that inter-party bickering and Republican insecurity, Rogan made a statement to his fellow Republicans on the Judiciary Committee that put it all into perspective. Rogan had barely scraped by in the election, returning to the House by the slimmest of margins, yet he challenged his colleagues to stand by their convictions:

> You know, my race [for reelection] was probably one of the ones in which the whole question of what we are doing here was a major issue. No, it was actually the *only* issue. I was attacked by my opponent constantly for being involved in the impeachment. . . . The people of my district sent me here to do my duty, and by God, I'm going to do it. We are not surrogates; we are Representatives. We have to be worthy of our office. We have to be prepared to lose our seats if that results from doing our duty.[35]

A man is judged by his willingness to go beyond mere words. Rogan had demonstrated that willingness in his last election, so his words had the ring of credibility. His actions continued to support his words, even as votes on the articles of impeachment approached. He remembered, "It would have been very easy for me to let that cup pass to somebody else." Rogan continued,

> In fact, a very, very, very, very high ranking Member of the Republican leadership came to me and said to me on the eve of the impeachment vote, "I have to worry about your re-election. If you vote to impeach the President, it may cost you your seat. We've got the votes on the Committee to impeach him,

and we have the votes on the floor to pass the articles. I'm convinced we have the votes. We don't need your vote." And so he never said the magic words; he just let his voice drop with that "and so," and he gave me a look. But I knew what he was saying. I just responded that I appreciated his concern about me, but I had a job to do. I didn't tell him how to do his job, and he couldn't tell me how to do my job.[36]

Rogan refused the offer to let the cup pass.

"Our committee undertakes its task in an era where the deceitful manipulation of public opinion no longer is viewed as evil, but as art," Rogan declared just prior to the Committee votes on articles of impeachment. "Propaganda once invoked images of dictators enforcing mind control over the masses. Now we readily bathe ourselves in spin and we confer the degree of 'doctor' upon those who administer the dosage," he lamented. Enough was enough. "In this very sobering hour, the time has come to strip away the spin and propaganda and face the unvarnished truth of what this committee is called upon to review," he stated.[37]

The impeachment issue was not about the sex life of the President; it was about lying under oath. In doing so, the President had undercut sexual harassment laws—laws that he was obliged, as President, to uphold. And a simple statement of sorrow over past actions would not suffice. "Fidelity to the presidential oath is not dependent on any president's personal threshold of comfort or embarrassment. Neither must it be a slave to the latest polling data," he added. Even more disturbing, in Rogan's eyes, was the willingness of some for purely partisan purposes to embrace "a thoroughly bastardized oath, so long as the offender expresses generalized contrition while at the same time rejecting meaningful constitutional accountability."[38]

George Washington had pledged that his public policies "would be grounded in principles of private morality." Washington had offered himself as a servant of the law, not as a ruler of men. He had established the idea of the rule of law. After recounting Washington's principles, Rogan then contrasted Washington's era with today's:

Two hundred years later, in an era of increasing ethical relativism, it seems almost foreign to modern ears that the first speech ever delivered by a president of the United States was a speech about the relationship between private and public morality. George Washington was not perfect. He certainly was no saint. But soldiers knew his bravery on the battlefield. His national reputation for truthfulness was unquestioned. Washington, a very human being with very human flaws, still could set by personal example the standard of measurement for the office of the presidency.

Today, from a distance of two centuries, Washington stands as a distant, almost mythical figure. And yet President Clinton and every member of the Congress of the United States have a living personal connection to him. Like Washington, each of us took a sacred oath to uphold the Constitution and the rule of law.[39]

The rule of law, Rogan continued, was more important than a sound economy because without it, "all contracts are placed in doubt and all rights to property become conditional." The rule of law was more important than national security because without it, "there can be no security and there is little left defending." President Clinton's "repeated and lengthy pattern of felonious conduct" could not simply be "wished or censured away." Rogan finished his statement with what he called a "heavy heart," but he could not back away from his oath, an oath that "obliges me to do what the president has failed to do—defend the rule of law, despite any personal or political costs."[40]

Rogan took an active part in the debate on the floor of the House, as the full House vote on the articles of impeachment drew closer. He was part of a rapid-response team: "Our job was to be familiar with the 60,000 pages of documentary evidence and respond to factual inaccuracies that were raised by the other side. It was a very grueling and very time-consuming process."[41] The other side kept him busy.

Steny Hoyer of Maryland complained, "It is not a case of bribery. And, as so many scholars of all political and philosophical stripes have testified, it does not amount to high crimes and misdemeanors." Rogan responded, "Lawyers did not just show up one day and begin to question the president's personal lifestyle . . . Now, in a desperate last-ditch attempt to insulate this president from any constitutional accountability for his conduct, his defenders are forced to trivialize felony perjury. How trivial is perjury to the person who loses a child-custody case or goes to prison because perjured testimony was offered as a truth in a court of law?"[42]

A short time later, he returned to the issue of perjury: "Some of our friends on the other side have indicated that perjury is not an impeachable offense under the Constitution. I remind them of the testimony of the former Democratic attorney general of the United States, Griffin Bell. . . . General Bell testified that Blackstone identified a series of . . . 'crimes against justice,' and those crimes included perjury. General Bell concluded, 'I am of the opinion, my conclusion, is that those crimes are high crimes within the meaning of the impeachment clause.'"[43]

When Major Owens of New York commented that no prosecutor would go forward with this type of perjury case, Rogan was quick to inform the Congressman that "under the Clinton Justice Department, since President Clinton became president, some 700 people have been tried and convicted for perjury and perjury-related crimes. As we speak today, Mr. Speaker, some 115 people sit in federal prisons as a result of their conviction on perjury charges." And when another Democratic Congressman accused Republicans of staging a coup d'état, Rogan could scarcely believe what he was hearing. "Mr. Speaker," he countered, "[to] suggest that holding a president accountable after committing perjury in a criminal grand jury proceeding amounts to a coup d'état or will bring blood on the floor demeans the level of this debate."[44]

Rogan recalls one moment of great candor from "a senior Democrat from a northeastern state." While the House was proceeding through the vote on the first article of impeachment, this senior Democrat took Rogan aside for a little talk:

He said, "You know Jimmy, if they put us all under oath, we'd all be guilty of perjury." And I said, "What do you mean?" He said, "Well, what I mean is we—meaning the Democrats— we all want the son of a bitch to leave and you all want the son of a bitch to stay." What he meant by that was Bill Clinton was hurting his party in the polls and was going to hurt Al Gore.

The best thing that could have happened for the Democrats would be for the Republicans to impeach him and remove him from office because then Al Gore—this is what he was telling me—Al Gore would become the President, he would give a speech like Gerald Ford did ("our long national nightmare is over"), people were already weary of the scandals, and they would have said, yes, of course, give this new President a clean slate—breath of fresh air—and Gore would have cruised to re-election.

The other side of that, he was saying, "You Republicans really don't want him impeached or removed because you're gonna wrap him like a millstone around our neck in the 2000 Presidential election and cost Gore the presidency, perhaps." That was an interesting political dynamic at play where, if you scratched the partisan surfaces deep enough around many of the Democrats, they'd just as soon would have seen him kicked out and the Republicans would just as soon have seen him stay.[45]

Regardless of the direction many Congressmen, in their hearts, might have wanted the vote to go, the final tally was almost totally partisan. The difference, though, was that many Republicans had been won over by the evidence they had seen in those boxes from the Independent Counsel, while scarcely any Democrats even bothered to view the evidence.

Presenting the Evidence

Rogan was not sure at first if he was going to be one of the Managers. Although he had taken a leading role in the House inquiry, he was a junior member of the Judiciary Committee. But when he returned to his office on the day the House voted in favor of two articles of impeachment, he found a large envelope on his desk. Inside was a book put out by the Senate entitled *Rules and Precedents for Impeachment Trials in the United States Senate*. Attached was a cover note from Henry Hyde requesting that he familiarize himself with these rules. "I turned to my Chief of Staff," remembers Rogan. "I said, 'I think this means I'm going to be a House Manager.'"[46]

Hyde gave Rogan one of the key spots as part of the evidentiary team, the group that would go first in making the case, specifically pointing out the charges and walking the Senators step-by-step through each offense. Rogan's task was to show exactly how the President had committed perjury. He stood in the well of the Senate on January 14, 1999, and laid out the facts. "In a judicial proceeding, a witness has a very solemn obligation to tell the truth, the whole truth, and nothing but the truth," he began. "Perjury is a serious crime because our judicial system can only succeed if citizens are required to tell the truth in court proceedings. If witnesses may lie with impunity for personal or political reasons, 'justice' is no longer the product of the court system, and we descend into chaos. That is why the United States Supreme Court has placed a premium on truthful testimony and shows no tolerance for perjury."[47] Rogan continued along the same line:

> When the president made that solemn pledge, he was not obliging himself to tell the "partial" truth.
>
> He was not obliging himself to tell the "I didn't want to be particularly helpful" truth.
>
> He was not obliging himself to tell the "this is embarrassing so I think I'll fudge on it" truth.
>
> He was required to tell the truth. The whole truth. And *nothing* but the *truth*. And he swore to do it in the name of God.[48]

Before the grand jury, noted Manager Rogan, President Clinton failed to tell the whole truth in four general areas. The first area was the nature of his relationship with Monica Lewinsky. According to Rogan, President Clinton even had the audacity to authorize Dick Morris to conduct a poll on whether the public would forgive him if he perjured himself: "Once he got the bad news from Dick Morris that his career was over if he perjured himself, he told Dick Morris, 'we'll just have to win.'" Beyond that, Rogan informed the Senators, "during his grand jury testimony, the president actually suggested he had a *right* to give less than complete answers. Why? Because he questioned the *motives* of Mrs. Jones in bringing her lawsuit. If this standard is acceptable, what does that do to the search for the truth when an oath is administered in court to one who *claims* to question the 'motive' of an opponent? This suggestion has *no* basis in law and is destructive to the truth-seeking function of the courts" (emphasis added).[49]

The second area of falsehood had to do with prior perjuries in the Jones deposition, falsehoods he repeated during his grand jury testimony. The third area of falsehood was with respect to the false affidavit filed by Monica Lewinsky in the Jones case—"an affidavit that he knew was false," Rogan said. Finally, he committed perjury, according to Rogan, when he testified falsely about his "blatant attempts to influence the testimony of witnesses, and his involvement in a plan to hide evidence that had lawfully been subpoenaed in the civil rights action brought against him." Rogan's presentation was punctuated throughout with video clips of the President's testimony under oath.

Manager Rogan closed with an appeal:

> Posterity looks to this body to defend in a courageous way the public trust and take care that the basis of our government is not undermined. . . .
>
> If the witnesses that make the case against the president— who incidentally are *his* employees, *his* top aides, and *his* close friends—if all these people are lying, then he has been done a grave disservice. He deserves not just acquittal; he deserves the

profoundest of apologies.

But if the evidence is true—if the chief executive officer of our nation used his power and influence to corruptly destroy a lone woman's right to bring forth her case in a court of law— then there must be constitutional accountability. And by that I mean the kind of accountability the Framers of our Constitution intended for such conduct, and not the kind of accountability that satisfies the temporary mood of the moment.

Our Founders bequeathed to us a nation of laws, not of polls, focus groups, and assorted talk-show habitués.

America is strong enough to absorb the truth about their leaders when they act in a manner destructive of their oath of office.

God help our country's future if we ever decide otherwise (emphasis added).[50]

Rogan's presentation had worked well with Hutchinson's, making Democratic Senators uneasy with their determination not to remove a Democratic President. This may have been the high point of the trial for the Managers. When live witnesses were ruled out and they had to depend on three videotaped and edited depositions only (Rogan questioned Sidney Blumenthal), they knew they were fighting a losing battle. All that remained were the closing arguments.

Rogan had worked so long and so hard that he requested to be taken out of the lineup for the closing arguments: "We had been in trial every day and staying up all night preparing for the next day. I would catch an hour or two of sleep here and there during the day. But the very last day I told Henry, 'I've spoken enough. Let some of the people that haven't had a lot of air time do the closing arguments.'" But Hyde refused; he wanted Rogan to be one of the final speakers. So he prepared again:

I went on this couch—somebody came in at four in the morning and took a picture—I still have the picture of me with my glasses on and my jeans, bleary-eyed at 4:30 in the morning, just feverishly laboring away. I wrote it myself. I had staff here all night with me. I would give them chunks to retype while I'm working on a new chunk, and I'd take it back, and I'd cut and paste and tear it apart. When I was done, it was a fifteen-minute speech. I was really thanking the Lord because I was praying "Lord, I just don't have it in me to write one more speech. I can't do it. I've got writer's block—whatever you want to call it—I need you to help me with this. You've gotta unlock whatever's blocking me from being able to put [down] another word."

   ... When I finished it, I thought it was very good. I was able, in a few pages, to articulate—really, to summarize—what this whole proceeding meant to me constitutionally, historically, factually, and personally.[51]

At least, that was what he intended. But something happened that convinced him he had to alter his plan.

Asa Hutchinson had just completed his closing argument, and the Senate had called a break before hearing from Rogan, Graham, and Hyde one more time. In that fifteen-minute break, Rogan had wandered back into the Marble Room just behind the Senate floor to prepare himself for his final presentation. He remembers a TV set being on in the room:

   I can't remember what channel, but there were a bunch of talking heads on TV. I stood and I watched and I watched somebody say, "You know, Dale Bumpers was right." Dale Bumpers had come and given this passionate, lengthy defense of Bill Clinton earlier in the trial. Dale Bumpers said, "These guys just don't care about the humanity of the trial. They don't care about the personal aspects. They don't care about this man and his family and what they've gone through." I only had about eight minutes to go now before I was up in probably the biggest speech of my life, my final closing argument of the impeachment of the President.

I had in a loose-leaf notebook about fifteen pages of my read-ing copy—fifteen pages because it was double-spaced and eigh-teen-point font so I could do it without my glasses. And I just thought to myself, I saw that person say that and I thought, "Son of a gun." I took my speech and I pulled a grease pencil out of my briefcase. I "x'd" out the first eight or nine pages, two-thirds of my speech—"x'd" it out. I walked on the floor, and I spoke extemporaneously.[52]

What did he say? He told the Senators about the first time he had met Bill Clinton at that Democratic Convention back in 1978. He let the Senators know how much that encounter had meant to him at the time. "And so I stood there on the Senate floor recounting that story, and I looked at all the Members of the Senate, and I said, you know, the point was, this is personally very painful for me. I've never forgotten twenty-one years ago the graciousness of then-Attorney General Bill Clinton taking the time for a young man who was interested in him and interested in the process. . . . I told that story because I didn't want that woman to be able to say that again on television—that we didn't pay attention to the human element. We paid attention to it very much," he insisted.[53]

Rogan was able to conclude with some of his prepared remarks. He returned to a familiar theme: no person is above the law. The House of Representatives had upheld that standard. It also had "jettisoned the spin and the propaganda." How would the Senate respond? "Now it is your unhappy task to make the final determination, face the truth, and polish the Constitution, or allow this Presidency, in the words of Chairman Henry Hyde, to take one more chip out of the marble," Rogan said. He stressed also the significance of the oath that a President takes to execute the laws faithfully: "The Founders did not intend the oath to be an afterthought or a technicality. They viewed it as an absolute requirement before the highest office in the land was entrusted to any person." Rogan ended with a call to principle and honor:

On the day the House impeached President Clinton, I said that when they are old enough to appreciate the solemnity of that action, I wanted my little girls to know that when the roll was called, their father served with colleagues who counted it a privilege to risk political fortunes in defense of the Constitution.

Today, I am more resolute in that opinion. From the time I was a little boy, it was my dream to one day serve in the Congress of the United States. My dream was fulfilled 2 years ago. Today, I am a Republican in a district that is heavily Democratic. The pundits keep telling me that my stand on this issue puts my political fortunes in jeopardy. So be it. That revelation produces from me no flinching.

There is a simple reason why: I know that in life dreams come and dreams go. But conscience is forever. I can live with the concept of not serving in Congress. I cannot live with the idea of remaining in Congress at the expense of doing what I believe to be right.

I was about 12 years old when a distinguished Member of this body, the late Senator Ralph Yarborough of Texas, gave me this sage advice about elective office:

Always put principle above politics; put honor above incumbency.

I now return that sentiment to the body from which it came. Hold fast to it, Senators, and in doing so, you will be faithful both to our Founders and to our heirs.[54]

History's Judgment

"If you look around my office, you see a lot of political memorabilia," Congressman Rogan noted. "I started collecting this stuff when I was ten years old because I really am, at heart, a political historian. That's a labor of love for me. I'm a Congressman right now, but I'm a historian forever." Evidence of that love for history lies in the fact that he kept a diary during the impeachment proceedings, a "very copious diary," he calls it. He acknowledges that most Congressmen have stopped this practice "because they're afraid they'll have their diaries subpoenaed for something." He kept the diary anyway, primarily because he wanted to offer a contemporaneous record of what happened behind the scenes during the impeachment. "At the end of the day, I don't really think anybody is going—one hundred years from now—[to] remember my name. They'll remember the fact that Clinton was impeached. But I wanted them to have an accurate record . . . because I knew that there were going to be revisionist histories going to work on this before it even was completed. So far, that's proven to be the case," he said. He intends to give his diary to the National Archives someday.[55]

In the meantime, for the historical record, does he have any regrets over his involvement with the impeachment? "I regret that America had to live through this, and I deeply regret that the President conducted himself in a manner where he showed such disrespect for the law [and] that he allowed our country to be mired in this for as long as we did," he responded. A second regret is what this has done to the children of America. Rogan is astonished, when he goes to speak at schools now, that even elementary-age children ask questions such as, "Did Bill Clinton have oral sex with Monica Lewinsky? Why did Bill Clinton lie? How come if I lie I get into trouble?" Rogan calls this a pain that never goes away—being "asked these questions by small children that never should have been exposed to [this]."[56]

Those are regrets for the sake of the country, but what about personal regrets? "From a personal perspective, as I said earlier, this may cost me my re-election. I just assumed going into it that it was going to cost me my re-election. The fear factor doesn't exist with me," he answered. He says he was prepared for that possibility and made his decision ahead of time to be true to his conscience. He is proud to have served with Henry Hyde and the rest of the Manager team. He knows that being associated with this effort could come back to hurt him professionally, but again he claims that that does not bother him: "I wouldn't care if it cost me my professional reputation because I assumed that those same masters of personal destruction who turned their guns on people like Juanita Broderick and Paula Jones and Ken Starr and others would do the very same thing to me. I wouldn't care if it cost me my life. We were averaging twelve death threats a day in my office during this. There are times when you have to do what Ralph Yarborough told me when I was a kid, and I quoted him in my closing argument: put principle above politics and put honor above incumbency."[57]

Rogan proved again that his actions back up his words. He was asked to be the keynote speaker for a tribute to Ken Starr. To most people, this would be the ultimate act of political suicide. However, Rogan again insisted on doing what he felt was right:

> I called my campaign folks, and I said, you know, I've been invited to do this, and they all laughed. They thought I was joking. They thought I was just trying to get their goat. I said, no, I'm in earnest and it's gonna be broadcast on C-Span. They were unanimous in telling me not to do it because they are trying to politically position me as far away from this unpopular subject back home as possible. They are having a hard time doing that because they happen to work for somebody who thinks that what he did was the right thing and is proud of answering the call of duty.
>
> So I called my campaign consultant, Jim Nygren, and I said, you know how every couple of years I call you (he's done every campaign since my first assembly race) and I tell you I'm about to do something that you're just absolutely going to hate? This is one of those calls. He did hate it. But my wife and I talked about it, and she said, how will you feel if you turn this down because you're worried about how it will play back home? I said, Ken Starr is one of the finest men to ever serve in government during my lifetime. He is an honorable man. He is a distinguished public servant. He has been beaten up by

bullies, by dirty bullies, and he never fought back because he thought it was beneath the dignity of his office and his obligation. I don't like bullies. That's what they were. I would feel dirty and cowardly if I didn't do it. She said, how will you feel if you do it? I said, I will feel honored to have been asked to speak on behalf of a man I respect so much. She said, I think you've just answered your own question.

And I did. I spoke, and I was honored to be there.[58]

What should the American public learn from this impeachment? First, says Rogan, the public needs to realize that imperfect people run government. But the lesson does not stop there. Those imperfect people "are called upon to rise above their imperfections." They are not in Washington, DC, to serve only the constituents who elected them, but must also "render service to the ghosts of patriots past." He challenges Americans with this thought:

In a dark hour of our country's history, in an extremely politically charged motivation, whether people in the future think it was a good idea or a bad idea to impeach the President, I hope people at least know, or have a sense, that at that critical hour there were men and women who were prepared to do what the voters tell us in the final analysis they want us to do: be prepared to follow your conscience instead of the polls. I hear that all the time from voters: "We want people who are going to follow their conscience, not the polls." We followed our conscience; we didn't follow the polls. I will leave it up to the voters to determine whether they mean it when they say it.[59]

Chapter 13 Endnotes

[1] Rogan interview.

[2] Ibid.

[3] Ibid.

[4] Ibid.

[5] Ibid.

[6] Cynthia H. Craft, "Rogan Bridges Partisan Gap: Conservative Glendale Assemblyman Wins Respect from Both Parties for His Reasoned Discourse," *Los Angeles Times*, 14 May 1995, 1.

[7] Rogan interview.

[8] Craft, "Rogan Bridges Partisan Gap."

[9] Ibid.

[10] Rogan interview.

[11] Ibid.

[12] Ibid.

[13] Craft, "Rogan Bridges Partisan Gap."

[14] The legislator, Pat Nolan, resigned after pleading guilty to one count of political racketeering. He was sent to prison. John Schwada, "GOP Leaders to Ask Rogan Foes to Quit Race," *Los Angeles Times*, 5 May 1994, 1.

[15] John Schwada, "Glendale Judge Wins Race for Seat in Assembly Elections," *Los Angeles Times*, 4 May 1994, 1.

[16] John Schwada, "GOP Leaders to Ask Rogan Foes to Quit Race."

[17] John Schwada and Cynthia H. Craft, "Schiff Probes Political Weakness in Rogan's Financial Muscle," *Los Angeles Times*, 7 October 1994, 5.

[18] Cynthia H. Craft, "James Rogan May Be GOP's Savior: The Conservative Freshman Assemblyman from Glendale Has a Knack for Getting Along," *Los Angeles Times*, 10 July 1995, 3.

[19] Ibid.

[20] Craft, "Rogan Bridges Partisan Gap."

[21] Craft, "James Rogan May Be GOP's Savior."

[22] Henry Chu, "Assembly Chiefs Share Drive, Not Agenda: James Rogan, Richard Katz Take Charge As Their Capitol Exits Near," *Los Angeles Times*, 29 January 1996, 1.

[23] Ibid.

[24] Nancy Hill-Holtzman, "Kahn and Rogan Both Vying for Centrist Vote: Despite His Conservative Credentials, Republican Rogan Campaigns As a 'Clinton-esque' Moderate," *Los Angeles Times*, 27 October 1996, B1.

[25] Baker, *The Breach*, 161.

[26] Rogan interview.

[27] Ibid.

[28] Hugo Martin, "Rogan Asked to Help Get the House Ready for Clinton-Starr Wars," *Los Angeles Times*, 27 March 1998, B5.

[29] Rogan interview.

[30] Ibid.

[31] Ibid.

[32] Ibid.

[33] Statement of Congressman James E. Rogan, House Judiciary Committee, 5 October 1998; available at http://www.house.gov/judiciary/rogan.htm; accessed 28 April 1999.

[34] Ibid.

[35] Schippers, *Sellout*, 107-08.

[36] Rogan interview.

[37] The Impeachment Hearings: Opening Statements: James Rogan, 11 December 1998; available at http://www.washingtonpost.com/wp-srv/politics/special/clinton/stories/rogantext121198.htm; accessed 1 April 1999.

[38] Ibid.

[39] Ibid.

[40] Ibid.

[41] Rogan interview.

[42] McLaughlin, *The Impeachment and Trial of President Clinton*, 175-76.

[43] Ibid., 177.

[44] Ibid., 182, 194.

[45] Rogan interview.

[46] Ibid.

[47] Opening Statement of Hon. James Rogan, Senate Impeachment Trial of President Clinton, 14 January 1999; available at http://www.house.gov/judiciary/rogansenate.htm; accessed 12 April 1999.

[48] Ibid.

[49] Ibid.

[50] Ibid.

[51] Rogan interview.

[52] Rogan interview.

[53] Ibid.

[54] Closing Argument of Hon. James Rogan, Senate Impeachment Trial of President Clinton, 8 February 1999; available at http://www.house.gov/judiciary/roga0208.htm; accessed 9 February 2000.

[55] Rogan interview.

[56] Ibid.

[57] Ibid.

[58] Ibid.

[59] Ibid.

CHAPTER FOURTEEN

James Sensenbrenner: Taking a Stand

Wisconsin Congressman James Sensenbrenner received a unique Christmas present in December of 1997. While in a Capitol Hill liquor store, Congressional Liquors, Sensenbrenner decided, "on an impulse," to put $2 down on the Quick Cash lottery. The impulse was more for fun than fortune; the Congressman already was a millionaire. At the time ranked the twenty-second richest Member of Congress, he certainly did not need the extra cash. When he looked at the lottery number in the paper the next morning, he thought he had won $10. It took him eleven days from the date of his lottery purchase to stop by the store to pick up his winnings. But he had not seen the numbers accurately. He had not won $10, but rather $250,000. The liquor store worker "thought I'd faint, but I just took a deep breath, turned and said, 'What's the most expensive bottle you got here?'"[1]

Suddenly, after nineteen years as a Congressman, Sensenbrenner was a celebrity. But he was a little irked that it took winning a lottery for people to notice him. As he told one reporter, "I'm chairman of the Science Committee involved in updating American science policy and the role of Government, academic and the private sector. I'm deep into the Medicare issue, the space program, the year 2000 problem. I've been grilling Janet Reno on the Judiciary Committee. So why don't you give me as much attention on these important issues as on the fact that lightning just struck me?" He then related, while laughing, "The guy said he was writing this story for the same reason people watch 'Geraldo' in the middle of the afternoon."[2]

If Representative Sensenbrenner really wanted to be noticed for his work in the Congress, he did not have to wait much longer. One month after purchasing that lottery ticket, the Lewinsky scandal hit the headlines. A few months later, the Judiciary Committee, on which he sat, was neck deep in an impeachment inquiry that the entire nation noticed.

Background and Congressional Career

Born in Chicago in 1943, James Sensenbrenner went west to receive his bachelor of arts degree from Stanford University, graduating in 1965. His first congressional experience came that same year when he served as a staff assistant to California Congressman J. Arthur Younger. He then earned a law degree from the University of Wisconsin in 1968 and made that state his permanent home. Sensenbrenner set up a law practice, but that did not stop him from setting his sights on politics. He served in the Wisconsin Assembly from 1969 to 1975, then in the state Senate from 1975 to 1979. It was in 1978 that he ran for Congress and was elected with 61 percent of the vote. His winning percentages ever since have been consistently high—in 1998, even with impeachment underway, he received a vote of confidence from 91 percent of the electorate.[3] Except for Henry Hyde, Sensenbrenner has served longer in Congress than any of the other House Managers.

He has a reputation as a strong conservative. Those who love him, love him unconditionally. Those who do not—do not. He is admired by his constituents and respected by colleagues for his "principled, uncompromising positions." As one Republican colleague commented, "You always know where Jim stands. Some are taken aback by that. Some are more accustomed to the politicians who talk out of both sides of their mouths, and Jim Sensenbrenner is not one of those types." Others, though, view him as "arrogant, abrasive and unable to work with his colleagues." One unidentified Democratic Congressman complained that Sensenbrenner was "not a consensus-builder. He doesn't seek to work with his allies or his opponents to find common ground. He tends to be quarrelsome and contentious." Another Democratic critic said, "Jim Sensenbrenner is a very smart, articulate man with almost no sense of proportion. He doesn't know when to pick and choose his fights. When he happens to be on the right side of an issue or when he's got something important to say, because he's mouthed off on so many other issues, he's diminished his impact." Whether admirer or critic, both agree that he has been hard working, intelligent, and honest—worthy of notice for more than winning a lottery.[4]

Sensenbrenner claims not to be bothered by such criticisms. For most of his congressional career, he has been part of the minority where, he says, "there are two ways to get your point across. One is to let people know where you stand and stick by your principles, and that's what I have done. One of the reasons why Congress is held in such low repute, in my opinion, is that there are too many folks out here who go along to get along . . . The other way is to attempt to grovel to get a few crumbs. That means groveling with people who have raised the national debt to $4.5 trillion and in my opinion are spending this country's future into oblivion. If I had to do that, I wouldn't be in this business."[5] He believes his electoral triumphs come from being faithful to his word:

> I think a lot of my political success is based not on agree-
> ment with everything I do because there's no way that every-
> body in somebody's district can agree with every vote their
> representative casts, but the fact that I do my homework, I'm
> thoughtful, I listen, I take a stand, and when I've taken a stand,
> I live up to my commitments.[6]

Sensenbrenner has been solidly conservative on social issues, adamantly opposed to abortion and the legalization of homosexual marriages. In 1993, when shootings at abortion clinics provided momentum to the Freedom of Access to Clinic Entrances Act, Sensenbrenner, while condemning the violence, opposed the bill because it "unfairly tramples free speech and violates the constitutional rights of those on just one side of the abortion issue." In an opinion piece in *USA Today*, the Congressman argued,

> This bill makes it a federal crime to "physically obstruct" access to an abortion clinic and allows those "physically obstructed" to bring a lawsuit in federal court. It does not distinguish between violent and peaceful protest and does not apply to those protesting on the other side of the issue or any other issue.
>
> The First Amendment to the US Constitution was intended to protect free speech by all Americans, not just "politically correct" speech.
>
> I wonder how supporters of this bill would have reacted 30 years ago if Congress had enacted special federal criminal laws which applied only to anti-Vietnam War protesters, civil rights marchers or striking workers.
>
> My guess is "not favorably"—to put it mildly.[7]

Sensenbrenner also was one of the original sponsors of the Defense of Marriage Act, which freed states from recognizing same-sex marriages licensed by other states. "Marriage is a principal founding block of society," he said at the time. "Every religious tradition for 5,000 years has given preferential consideration to heterosexual marriage, as have the laws of all of our states and every foreign country." Many of America's social problems, he believed, stemmed from the disintegration of marriage and the family. "We should not make a major change in social policy at a time when the American family is under attack," he warned.[8]

As Chairman of the Science Committee, Sensenbrenner has had to deal with some other hot ethical issues. One of these has been the issue of human cloning. He critiqued the Clinton Administration's approach because it declared "that human cloning is immoral only because it is currently unsafe." That rationale was not good enough, according to the Congressman: "Cloning humans is unethical and immoral. Ethics and morals are not transient."[9]

He takes these stances on social issues because of his religious beliefs. "You really can't divorce your values from how you reach decisions, whether they be religious values or other values which are not religious in nature," he has determined. Sensenbrenner is a practicing Episcopalian, but his conservative views sometimes conflict with the more liberal political stance of that denomination. At one time, says Sensenbrenner, the bishops of the Episcopal Church in Wisconsin "wrote a letter that practically excommunicated me for introducing a bill that abrogates certain parts of the alien treaties which have since been used to expand Indian gambling, which I am opposed to." His written response was to ask the bishops how they would react if the Catholic Church "attempted to excommunicate a pro-abortion elected public official. I said they would absolutely go through the roof. So I don't mind disagreeing with the stated policy of my denomination when I think it is wrong."[10]

Sensenbrenner has been on the Judiciary Committee ever since he entered Congress in 1979. He asked for the assignment precisely because he wanted to be where the social issues were debated. "It's also a committee that requires a fair amount of detail work because of the complexity of many of the items that are under the Judiciary Committee's jurisdiction," he added. "You don't get a lot of people wanting to find out the nuances of the bankruptcy law, for example."[11]

Being on the Judiciary Committee during the 1980s also gave him impeachment experience. Three federal judges were removed from the bench during that time. In the case of Nevada judge Harry Claiborne, Sensenbrenner played a leading role in starting the impeachment. He was angry that Claiborne, who already was in prison for tax fraud, was still collecting his federal salary. "Every day Judge Claiborne continues to draw his salary it makes a mockery of our judicial system," Sensenbrenner declared. On the House floor, he called for the Congress "to uphold the integrity of the judiciary and prevent erosion in public confidence in judges."[12]

Together with Henry Hyde, Sensenbrenner, in 1988, introduced the impeachment resolution that led to the removal of Alcee Hastings from his judgeship in Florida. Although a U.S. District Court acquitted Hastings of conspiracy to accept a bribe, the House still believed there was ample evidence that he took part in the plot and committed perjury at his trial. Another imprisoned judge, Walter Nixon of Mississippi, convicted of perjury, was removed in 1989. Sensenbrenner served as the lead Manager for that case.[13] "Clearly the judge is not fit to sit upon the federal judiciary, and we must perform our constitutional duty to impeach him," he said.[14] All of these impeachments prepared him for the big one that arrived on the Judiciary's doorstep in 1998.

Even after that rash of impeachments in the 1980s, Sensenbrenner was concerned with the ongoing problem of federal judges collecting their full salaries and benefits while in prison. In 1993, the National Commission on Judicial Discipline and Removal developed recommendations for how Congress could streamline the process of removing federal judges from office. The Commission, though, failed to recommend suspending the salaries and benefits of judges convicted of crimes. That did not go over well with the Wisconsin Congressman, who called the continuation of their salaries an insult both to taxpayers and to the judicial system. Sensenbrenner favored a constitutional amendment that would give the Supreme Court the authority to remove federal judges convicted of crimes and eliminate their salaries and benefits. "I support life tenure for judges," Sensenbrenner acknowledged, "but only if they don't abuse the public trust."[15]

The next year, Sensenbrenner made it clear that he was not concerned about judges only. When Democratic Congressman Dan Rostenkowski was in the midst of a legal battle that would determine whether he would be serving prison time, Sensenbrenner prepared resolutions for expulsion and censure to present to the House. He was concerned that "Rostenkowski could plead guilty to a felony and still keep his office. Felons don't belong in Congress," he concluded.[16]

Concern for integrity and fiscal responsibility work in tandem for Sensenbrenner. The National Taxpayers Union Foundation, in 1994, conducted a study of all budget-related votes of all federal lawmakers.

James Sensenbrenner came out on top as the greatest "saver" in Congress. If Congress had always voted Sensenbrenner's way, the study revealed, federal spending would have been cut by $72.6 billion. According to Paul S. Hewitt, executive director of the foundation, "Many members of Congress are less than sincere in their pledges of fiscal probity." Representative Sensenbrenner commented, "Voters can use this study to recognize members of Congress who do more than just talk about reducing spending, but actually vote that way."[17]

The Impeachment Saga

The Judiciary Committee met in early October 1998 to discuss the opening of an official impeachment inquiry. Sensenbrenner, in his statement at this hearing, noted that the Committee was embarking on a task "second only in gravity to Congress' power to declare war." The debate, he said, was not about the President's affair and lies to his family, his staff, his Cabinet, or to the American people. It was, instead, "about Judge Starr's finding that the President violated his oath to tell the truth, the whole truth and nothing but the truth in a successful attempt to defeat Paula Jones' civil rights suit against him." Sensenbrenner asked,

> What's the difference between lies about an affair to family and friends and those made under oath during legal proceedings?
>
> Plenty. Our legal system is based upon the courts being able to find the truth. That's why there are criminal penalties for perjury and obstruction of justice.
>
> Even the President of the United States has no license to lie. Deceiving the courts is an offense against the public in that it prevents them from administering justice . . .
>
> . . . That is an offense against the public, made even more serious when a poor and weak person seeks the protection of our civil rights laws against the rich and powerful.

The President denies all the allegations. Someone is telling the truth and someone is lying.

An impeachment inquiry is the only way to try to get to the bottom of this mess. It will give Congress and the American public one last chance to get the truth and the whole truth. If this inquiry uncovers the whole truth, we will have gone a long way to putting this sad part of our history to rest.[18]

Prior to the opening of the official inquiry, the 1998 elections took place. Sensenbrenner, in his safe district, had no worries, but the Republican Party, as a whole, was plenty worried by the results. There were qualms about progressing with the impeachment inquiry. Sensenbrenner noted, though, the resolve of the Republican members of the Judiciary Committee:

The day after the election, Chairman Hyde polled the Republican members of the Judiciary Committee on whether we ought to stop or whether we ought to keep on going. The vote was unanimous. We felt that this was a duty. None of us supported the Independent Counsel statute when it was re-authorized in 1994. But given the fact that the statute did require a referral if the Counsel found evidence of impeachable activity, I think that imposed an obligation on the Judiciary Committee to review the evidence and either determine that impeachable activity occurred and write articles of impeachment, or determine that it didn't occur and essentially dismiss the case. So we had to make a decision, I think, one way or another pursuant to a law which all of the Republicans believed was significantly flawed.[19]

To critics in his home district, the Wisconsin Congressman responded that he was simply doing his duty: "I said there are certain things you have to do, regardless of what the political consequences were." And to those who accused him of unjust partisanship, he responded, "When we receive evidence that an official subject to the impeachment clause, as the President is, has possibly committed an impeachable offense, I think we have to proceed regardless of the political affiliations of the respondent in the matter or the majority in the committee. We were no more partisan or no less partisan than the Rodino Judiciary Committee was in 1973 and 1974 during the Richard Nixon impeachment."[20]

Neither was the impeachment inquiry a personal vendetta against a President that he and other Republicans detested. Any conviction for a criminal offense would come later in the court system. The Republicans simply were following the Constitution. Sensenbrenner noted,

> If you look at the debates in the Constitutional Convention of 1787, it was quite clear that the Framers indicated, or decided, that the impeachment process was to cleanse an office of someone that had soiled it, rather than to impose a criminal sanction. The end of the impeachment clause that limits the punishment upon conviction in the Senate to removal from office but says that anyone removed is subject to indictment, trial, and punishment as prescribed by law means that the criminal justice process is not a part of the impeachment process. Impeachment is not to be used to determine whether or not someone committed a crime, but just to get someone who had violated the public trust out of there and to allow someone else to take over.[21]

As the Judiciary Committee prepared to vote on the articles of impeachment, Sensenbrenner, in his opening statement, did his best to convince his Democratic colleagues that impeachment was essential. He began with an appeal for the children of America. The toughest questions he had had to answer in the past eleven months, he said, were from parents wanting to know what to tell their children. "Every parent tries to teach their children to know the difference between right and wrong, to always tell the truth, and when they make mistakes, to take responsibility for them and to face the consequences of their actions," Sensenbrenner explained. President Clinton had not helped the parents of America. "No amount of government education programs and day-care facilities can reverse the damage done to our children's values by the leader of our country," he remarked.[22]

He realized, of course, that being a poor leader was not sufficient grounds for impeachment, but the President had gone beyond that—he had undermined the rule of law. Making a false statement under oath to a grand jury had been the basis for removing Walter Nixon from the federal judiciary in 1989; why should it change now for the President? "To accept the argument that presidential lying to a grand jury is somewhat different than judicial lying to a grand jury and thus not impeachable is wrong. It sets the standard for presidential truthfulness lower than for judicial truthfulness. The truth is the truth, and a lie is a lie, no matter who says it. And no amount of legal hairsplitting can obscure that fact," argued the Congressman.[23]

While President Clinton had acknowledged that his relationship with Monica Lewinsky was wrong, he had not "owned up to the false testimony, the stonewalling, the obstructing the courts from finding the truth, and the use of taxpayer-paid White House resources to hide and perpetuate his lies." An apology for private conduct was one thing, but it could never take the place of accepting the consequences for one's actions. In Sensenbrenner's view, the President was continuing to lie. He concluded his statement by emphasizing again what he considered the heart of the matter:

> What is on trial here is the truth and the rule of law. Our failure to bring President Clinton to account for his lying under oath and preventing the courts from administering equal justice under law, will cause a cancer to be present in our society for generations. I want those parents who ask me the questions to be able to tell their children that even if you are the president of the United States, if you lie when sworn "to tell the truth, the whole truth and nothing but the truth," you will face the consequences of that action, even when you don't accept the responsibility for them.[24]

In the full House debate on the articles of impeachment, one of the strategies employed by the Democrats was to get a vote on censure instead. When faced with this tactic, Sensenbrenner gave a little history lesson from the Richard Nixon impeachment. At that time, it was the Republicans who were pushing for censure rather than impeachment. When the Republican leader of the House, John Rhodes, asked Speaker Tip O'Neill for permission for a censure vote, O'Neill responded, "I am bitterly opposed to that." Sensenbrenner continued, "I think that my friends on the other side of the aisle should listen to their former Speaker one last time, because on this one, he is right."[25]

Later in the debate, Sensenbrenner defended the Judiciary Committee on the fairness of its proceedings: "Mr. Speaker, the president's lawyers had up to 30 hours to present their defense. Mr. Starr had 12 hours . . . The Democrats had almost two-thirds of the witnesses before the committee. They called 28 witnesses, the Republicans called 15, and they shared two. The chairman, the gentleman from Illinois [Mr. Hyde], asked the White House to present evidence that would exonerate the president, and they did not."[26] For Sensenbrenner, it was time to move on to the Senate. The majority agreed.

In the Senate

That James Sensenbrenner would be one of the House Managers was not in question. As senior member of the Judiciary Committee, next to Chairman Hyde, he naturally would have this assignment. His experience with judicial impeachments also was significant in his selection.

Sensenbrenner's presentation followed Henry Hyde's opening statement. At first, Hyde had thought of giving his Wisconsin colleague the honor of opening the trial, but then concluded that as lead Manager, he should set the tone and the direction. Hyde's oratorical skills would be needed to grab the attention of the Senators right from the start. Even Sensenbrenner himself knew that he lacked trial lawyer experience. He joked with his fellow Managers, "Did I ever tell you about the time I handled an uncontested divorce case and lost?"[27] When he asked Hyde how long he should speak, he was told that the only precedent was in the Andrew Johnson trial. "The opening argument was three days long. I promised to be more concise," Sensenbrenner said.[28]

When Hyde finished his opening remarks, Manager Sensenbrenner began his presentation by focusing on the rule of law. "Some have commented this expression is trite," he noted, "but, whether expressed by these three words, or others, the primacy of law over the rule of individuals is what distinguishes the United States from most other countries and why our Constitution is as alive today as it was 210 years ago." The Congress, he continued, had trusteeship of "that sacred legacy"; the decision of the Senate would let the country know whether that legacy would be strengthened or diminished. He realized that the process would be long, difficult, and unpleasant, but the Senators had to keep in mind that it was essential to go through this process "to maintain the public's trust in the conduct of their elected officials—elected officials, such as myself and yourselves, who through our oaths of office have a duty to follow the law, fulfill our Constitutional responsibilities, and protect our Republic from public wrongdoing."[29]

In this case, the President of the United States sought to deny a person her civil rights in court. "Our civil rights laws have remade our society for the better," he reminded his audience. "The law gives the same protections to the child denied entry to a school or college based upon race as to an employee claiming discrimination at work. Once a hole is punched in civil rights protections for some, those protections are not worth as much for all. Many in the Senate have spent their lives advancing individual rights. Their successful efforts have made America a better place. In my opinion, this is no time to abandon that struggle—no matter the public mood or the political consequences."[30]

This entire impeachment trial, the Manager noted, did not have to happen. It was occurring because of the unwillingness of the President to tell the truth. "It is truly sad when the leader of the greatest nation in the world gets caught up in a series of events where one inappropriate and criminal act leads to another, and another and another. Even sadder is that the President himself could have stopped this process simply by telling the truth and accepting the consequences of his prior mistakes. At least six times since December 17, 1997, William Jefferson Clinton could have told the truth and suffered the consequences. Instead he chose lies, perjury, or deception," Sensenbrenner explained.[31]

Sensenbrenner was able to add a personal note to his litany of the President's actions. He told about being approached by a Wisconsin circuit court judge just a few months earlier while the details of the Starr Report were being discussed by the nation. "He said that some citizens had business in his court and suggested that one of them take the witness stand and be put under oath to tell the truth. The citizen then asked if he could tell the truth, 'just like the President,'" Sensenbrenner recalled.[32] How, Sensenbrenner asked, will the courts be able to administer justice if that attitude prevails? And when such an attitude is encouraged by elected officials, what will be the consequence? He continued,

Whenever an elected official stumbles, that trust is eroded and public cynicism goes up. The more cynicism that exists in government, its institutions, and those chosen to serve in them, the more difficult the job is for those who are serving.

That's why it is important, yes vital, that when a cancer exists in the body politic, our job—our duty—is to excise it. If we fail in our duty, I fear the difficult and dedicated work done by thousands of honorable men and women elected to serve not just here in Washington, but in our state capitals, city halls, courthouses and school board rooms will be swept away in a sea of public cynicism. We must not allow the beacon of America to grow dim, or the American dream to disappear with each waking morning.[33]

The country, warned Sensenbrenner, was going through "an impassioned and divisive debate," and the Senate "now finds itself in the midst of the tempest." The job was being made even more difficult due to the omnipresence of public opinion polls showing that the President was still a popular figure. They were diversions, "subsuming the true nature of this grave and unwelcome task." The Senate, he instructed, was now going to have to "sift through the layers of debris that shroud the truth." He knew that this would be painful at times. "But beneath it lies the answer," he insisted. "The evidence will show that at its core, the question over the President's guilt and the need for his conviction will be clear. Because at its core, the issues involved are basic questions of right versus wrong—deceptive, criminal behavior versus honesty, integrity and respect for the law." He concluded,

> Our legacy now must be not to lose the trust the people should have in our nation's leaders.
>
> Our legacy now must be not to cheapen the legacies left by our forebearers.
>
> Our legacy must be to do the right thing based upon the evidence.
>
> For the sake of our country, the Senate must not fail.[34]

Four weeks later, in closing arguments, he got one more chance to convince the Senators, even though, by that time, no real hope for conviction remained. Perhaps that is why Sensenbrenner chose to focus, at the beginning of his talk, on the motives of the Managers. "The news media," he remarked, "characterizes the managers as 13 angry men." They are partially correct, he said, but off the mark as to the reason for the anger. "We have not spent long hours poring through the evidence, sacrificed time with our families and subjected ourselves to intense political criticism to further a political vendetta. We have done so because of our love for this country and respect for the rule of law and our fear that if the President does not suffer the legal and constitutional consequences of his actions, the impact of allowing the President to stand above the law will be felt for generations to come," he explained. Then he became even more personal:

The *Almanac of American Politics* has called me "a stickler for ethics." To that, I plead guilty as charged because laws not enforced are open invitations for more serious and criminal behavior. This trial was not caused by Kenneth Starr, who only did his duty under a law which President Clinton himself signed. It was not caused by the House Judiciary Committee's review of the independent counsel's mountain of evidence. Nor was it caused by the House of Representatives approving two articles of impeachment, nor by the Senate conducting a trial mandated by the Constitution.

Regardless of what some may say, this constitutional crisis was caused by William Jefferson Clinton and by no one else. President Clinton's actions, and his actions alone, have caused the national agenda for the past year to be almost exclusively concentrated on those actions and what consequences the President, and the President alone, must suffer for them.[35]

One of the biggest hurdles the Managers faced, in Sensenbrenner's estimation, was that President Clinton had committed so many egregious acts, and had repeated them so often, that it was easy to overlook the significance of the grand jury testimony. Sensenbrenner was concerned that the perjury committed in that testimony was not getting the attention it deserved, so he reminded the Senators again of the case of Judge Walter Nixon, who, in 1989, was removed from the bench for perjury. The vote had been 89-8. Forty-eight current Senators had voted for that removal. Vice President Al Gore, who had been a Senator at the time, had cast one of those aye votes. What had changed? "To boot a Federal judge from office while keeping a President in power after the President committed the same offense sets a double standard and lowers the standard of what the American people should expect from the leader of their country," he concluded.[36] Yet not one Democratic Senator who had voted for the removal of Judge Nixon decided to apply the same standard to a sitting President.

Ruminations

Manager Sensenbrenner actually did not think that the Senate acquittal had been a foregone conclusion. Since some influential Democratic Senators like Robert Byrd and Patrick Moynihan had spoken publicly about the seriousness of the charges, he had hoped that others could be swayed as well. But "the White House spin machine and political machine got to them, so the President ended up being acquitted simply because the Democrats voted in a block 'not guilty' in the Senate, ignoring the Constitution, the law, and the evidence," he reflected sadly. Now Sensenbrenner is concerned that a future President in trouble will "use the Clinton playbook in order to get off the hook." Regardless of the outcome, he was thankful for the opportunity "to lay out the case against the President in a forum where we weren't interrupted every thirty seconds by Maxine Waters or Barney Frank yelling 'point of order.' The opening argument I made at the beginning of the trial was the first time where we were able to lay the case out against the President in a cogent manner free of interruption."[37]

He has no regrets because, as he puts it, "We did what was right." And he points to President Clinton being found in contempt of court and being fined more than $90,000 for lying during a deposition as at least a partial vindication. In addition, "I can say that to this day I can be practically anywhere in the country and, if people recognize me, I have complete strangers that don't even live in my district coming up to me and saying, 'Thank you for doing what you did because you stood up for the law.'"[38]

Sensenbrenner remains disturbed, though, "that people seem to want to separate out a public official's private life from his public stance." He particularly criticizes groups like the National Organization for Women, "who basically excused Clinton's terrible behavior toward women because he was 'so good on women's issues.' I don't think you can be good on women's issues if you don't respect women or a woman as an individual human being and treat that person with the respect that any human being deserves." As for the majority of the populace, Sensenbrenner says,

As time has gone on, more and more of them realize that this was not about sex. I said all along, you know, in town meetings and in press interviews, that the House of Representatives, and the Judiciary Committee in particular, should not be making judgments on whether William Jefferson Clinton is morally evil to continue to lead the United States in the free world. That is something that each of us have to make as an obligation to citizenship. Making difficult judgments as individuals isn't easy, and it isn't fun. In this case, I guess because Clinton was not facing an election, it was something that could be postponed and didn't have to be made. So because the people themselves did not have to decide through the election process whether they wanted Clinton to stay as President of the United States, they kind of had this schizophrenic view, saying that "we disapprove of his personal behavior but we give him a good job approval rating." I don't think I could be able to get away with that in my district.

He adds, maybe a little wistfully, "Perhaps the American people, in the end, will end up appreciating [us] doing what was right rather than taking a poll to find out what to do."[39]

Chapter 14 Endnotes

1 Francis X. Clines, "A Politician Wins Notice by Winning the Lottery," *The New York Times*, 4 January 1998, 1:12.

2 Ibid.

3 Sensenbrenner Biography, AP Candidate Bios, *The Associated Press Political Service*; available at LEXIS-NEXIS Academic Universe; accessed 11 May 1999; Congress Watch, "Rep. F. (Jim) James Sensenbrenner, Jr."; available at http://abcnews.go.com/reference/congress/WI09.html; accessed 29 December 2000.

4 Patrick Jasperse, "Sensenbrenner: His Blunt Personality Draws Many Admirers—and Critics," *The Milwaukee Journal Sentinel*, 5 December 1993, A3.

5 Ibid.

6 Ibid.

7 Jim Sensenbrenner, "Protect Right to Protest," *USA Today*, 18 November 1993, 14A.

8 Frank A. Aukofer, "Pair Take Different Paths on Gay Issues," *The Milwaukee Journal Sentinel*, 19 May 1996, 7.

9 James Sensenbrenner, "Safety of Cloning Should Not Preclude Ethics or Morality," *Wisconsin State Journal*, 29 January 1998, 11A.

10 Congressman James Sensenbrenner, interview by author, tape recording, Washington, DC, 11 April 2000.

11 Ibid.

12 "Imprisoned Judge Given Choice: Resign or Face Impeachment," *The San Diego Union-Tribune*, 23 May 1986, A4.

13 Sensenbrenner interview.

14 "Impeached Judge Faces Ouster Effort in Senate," *The San Diego Union-Tribune*, 11 May 1989, A4.

15 Frank A. Aukofer, "Two Officials from State Trade Jabs in Move to Revise Process to Impeach US Judges," *The Milwaukee Journal Sentinel*, 4 July 1993, A11.

16 Pierre Thomas and Kenneth J. Cooper, "Rostenkowski Plea Accord Proves Elusive; Deal Would Avert Major Court Battle," *The Washington Post*, 24 May 1994, a04.

[17] Karen J. Cohen, "Anti-Spending Group Ranks Sensenbrenner No. 1," *The Milwaukee Journal Sentinel*, 2 September 1994, A8.

[18] Statement of Congressman James Sensenbrenner, House Judiciary Committee, 5 October 1998; available at http://www.house.gov/judiciary/sensenbrenner.htm; accessed 28 April 1999.

[19] Sensenbrenner interview.

[20] Ibid.

[21] Ibid.

[22] The Impeachment Hearings: Opening Statements: James Sensenbrenner, 10 December 1998; available at http://www.washingtonpost.com/wp-srv/politics/special/clinton/stories/sensenbrennertext121098.htm; accessed 1 April 1999.

[23] Ibid.

[24] Ibid.

[25] McLoughlin, *The Impeachment and Trial of President Clinton*, 176.

[26] Ibid., 191.

[27] Baker, *The Breach*, 302.

[28] Sensenbrenner interview.

[29] Opening Statement of Hon. James Sensenbrenner, Senate Impeachment Trial of President Clinton, 14 January 1999.

[30] Ibid.

[31] Ibid.

[32] Ibid.

[33] Ibid.

[34] Ibid.

[35] Closing Argument of Hon. James Sensenbrenner, Senate Impeachment Trial of President Clinton, 8 February 1999; available at http://www.house.gov/judiciary/sen0208.htm; accessed 9 February 2000.

[36] Ibid.

[37] Sensenbrenner interview.

[38] Ibid.

[39] Ibid.

CHAPTER FIFTEEN

Election 2000

In one episode of *The Wonder Years*, the Emmy-award-winning television series that played on the nostalgia of growing up in the turbulent 1960s and early 1970s, the program's beleaguered hero, Kevin Arnold, is trying his best to make up for his insensitivity to girlfriend Winnie Cooper. He buys an enormous stuffed bear and goes to her house, bear in arms, hoping this gift will allow him to ease his way back into her affections. She opens the door, they talk awkwardly, then she closes it again. Nothing was resolved. The omnipresent narrator in the series—Kevin at a later age reminiscing—comments, "The funny thing was, I was standing there with this huge bear in my arms the entire time, and neither of us ever mentioned it." That might be the perfect image to apply to the 2000 election. The bear would be the impeachment. No one, Democrat nor Republican, seemed to want to mention it directly; in fact, the word "impeachment" rarely was uttered. Yet it obviously formed the backdrop for the entire campaign, particularly for those who served as House Managers.

At the presidential level, election 2000 will go down as the election that never seemed to end. Recounts and court challenges dragged on until mid-December before George W. Bush emerged the victor. At the congressional level, however, the results for the former House Managers were known on election night. How did the impeachment—that unmentioned bear—play into those results?

At first, it appeared that the impeachment might become the centerpiece of the upcoming elections. Even before the Senate cast the final votes on the articles of impeachment, news stories circulated that President Clinton was so furious at Republicans in general—and the House Managers in particular—that he vowed to mount an all-out offensive against them in the 2000 election. Quoting anonymous advisers to the President, *The New York Times* described how Clinton "viewed winning back the House as almost as important an affirmation of his legacy as electing Vice President Al Gore as his successor." According to one adviser, "He knows the districts, he knows the candidates, and he doesn't like these people. He's obviously real hot on the managers." Another added, "It will be a personal crusade. . . . He [Clinton] says, 'It's the unfairness of this whole process—these right-wingers who tried to undo the election.'"[1] A top Clinton political strategist declared, "I would start with the House managers with malice aforethought and go after them day and night. They made his life miserable. The time has come for payback."[2]

The House Managers responded swiftly. "If he feels he has to vindicate himself by going after House managers, then he has to do that. All I can say is that we as a House, the majority, felt that we certainly didn't put him in this predicament. If anybody ought to be upset, it ought to be the American people, with the President, for doing those things," commented Ed Bryant. An equally even-tempered Asa Hutchinson told reporters, "It would be wrong for the Republicans to say we are not going to work with the President—and wrong for the President to say I will get even with Republicans."[3] "He can take his best shot," replied James Rogan. "I certainly regret that the President is spending his energies plotting revenge."[4] Fumed Chris Cannon, "This is the height of arrogance."[5] Bob Barr had more to say:

> This report does not come as a great surprise. When we began our effort to hold the President accountable for committing felonies in office, we knew he would attack us personally and politically. These new threats are par for the course, from a White House that has turned the politics of personal destruc-

tion into an art form with enemies lists, whispered comments to reporters, and political duplicity of staggering proportions. In fact, the White House offensive began months ago, with personal attacks against certain House Members, and continues today with efforts by the Department of Justice to discredit Judge Starr.[6]

Apparently, the President was furious that his words had leaked to the public. Immediately, the White House started another spin, casting doubt on the report, claiming that the Administration was smarter "than to campaign on a personal vendetta against the House members who prosecuted the case." Jim Nicholson, Republican Party Chairman, predicted vindication for all Republicans, stating, "Far from being ground under the heels of Bill Clinton's tawdry effort to celebrate his impeachment trial, these men and women will be rewarded by the people they represent and remembered as giants."[7]

In the months following the impeachment trial, the House Managers were treated as royalty in GOP circles. Their stand for the removal of President Clinton energized the Party's conservative base and helped in fundraising. In one sense, the loss in the Senate probably made them more honored within conservative ranks than if they had won because conservatives seem to have an attachment to those who fight for lost causes. "It's been an unbelievable experience for me," Lindsey Graham said just a little over one month after the trial. "I sit in an airport for five minutes reading a paper and half a dozen people come up and just kind of shake my hand and say, 'We're really proud of what you tried to do.'"[8] Graham also noted, "Among the party base, this is something that's seen as the party getting back to its principles."[9] By June of 1999, according to one reporter, the Managers were flying high:

So what if they lost the trial of the century? They're making speeches to packed houses. They're hot on the fund-raising circuit. And have they got juice with the House GOP leadership.

In the 114 days since President Clinton beat the Monica Lewinsky sex scandal rap in the Senate, the 13 House impeachment managers have thrown themselves back into their day jobs. And some are finding that carrying the GOP torch in that battle left them with valuable new friends and political muscle.

"Like any other thing in life, if you're a team member and you seem to have your stuff together," said Representative Lindsey Graham (R-S.C.), "people take care of you."

Graham and Representative Asa Hutchinson (R-Ark.) have hundreds of invitations pouring in from all over the country to speak at GOP fund-raisers.

Graham recently helped Hutchinson draw 1,100 avid Republicans to a Lincoln Day Dinner in Fayetteville, "the largest Republican Party gathering in the history of Arkansas," he said.

Impeachment ringleader Representative Henry Hyde (R-Ill.) wants all of his fellow managers to have fat war chests. So he's visiting each of their districts for thank-you fund-raisers . . .

After carrying the House GOP's water through the six-month impeachment battle, managers also have added leverage with their leadership.

When he asks colleagues for help, Hutchinson acknowledged, "They know who I am this time around.[10]

A Battleground 2000 poll, conducted jointly by Democratic and Republican pollsters in June 1999, showed that Republicans actually boosted their election prospects by impeaching President Clinton. Democrats, according to the poll, were suffering from "delayed voter disgust with Mr. Clinton's scandals." The Democratic pollster, Celinda Lake, said that Democrats had paid "a big price" for their defense of the President. "It has diminished our credibility on morality," she noted in her analysis of the poll results. The GOP, in the poll, had almost a "20 percentage-point edge over Democrats as best representing personal responsibility, honesty and faith in God." Bob Barr weighed in on the poll, stating that the findings "reflect precisely what I had been hearing before and during the entire impeachment process from constituents of mine and from citizens across the country. Now that the dust settled, the scandal is seen for what it is—a deep-rooted problem with this adminis-tration and those who blindly support it. The American people are deeply resentful of that."[11]

While the House Managers remained popular with the Republican base, and polls seemed to indicate that Republicans had a winning issue in the impeachment, both sides demonstrably distanced themselves from the issue by September 1999. As one reporter for *The Boston Globe* remarked, "It's been only six months. But the impeachment trial of President Clinton might as well have been six years ago, if the fledgling congressional campaigns for next year's elections are any sign. Despite gleeful predictions from Democrats this year that Republicans could lose their majority control of the House on the strength of anti-impeachment sentiments, the issue has all but disappeared. Democrats have backed off plans to campaign against Republicans on their role in impeachment. In the halls of Congress, the word 'impeachment' is rarely uttered."[12]

Yet even while both parties seemed to be running away from any direct reference to the impeachment, it always seemed to be hovering in the air. Democratic strategist Peter Bynum stated, "No one wants to revisit the impeachment nightmare. Yet every candidate running is holding up some kind of mirror to the impeachment, and everything they say is one or another reflection of what went on in the impeachment hearings."[13]

On the Republican side, George W. Bush would continually talk about restoring honor and dignity to the White House, implicitly calling up memories of impeachment, but he rarely addressed it directly. The GOP National Convention did not exactly highlight any of the House Managers. They did not get stage time. The Republicans hoped, instead, to take advantage of the unstated. As Bush strategist Ralph Reed commented, "Impeachment has had an impact on our politics by helping to create a pervasive and abiding hunger on the part of the electorate for a president that will restore dignity and honor to the office. One of the important subtexts of the 2000 campaign will be the extent to which the next president will restore our faith and confidence in the personal conduct of the person in the Oval Office."[14]

Democrats had to deal with "Clinton fatigue." Al Gore, living in the shadow of the Clinton presidency, impeachment included, felt the need to stress that he was his own man. Normally, if anyone has to declare that he is his own man, one might wonder why the declaration is necessary. Actions should speak louder than words. Commentator Charles Krauthammer, after watching day two of the Democratic National Convention, remarked, "In Tuesday's four main speeches—by Caroline and Edward Kennedy, Bill Bradley and Harold Ford—the word 'Clinton' hardly passed any lips. However much some Democrats still want him now, the party knows that, like Nixon, his near-term legacy is toxic."[15]

So, as election 2000 approached, impeachment was in the background. Any hopes that Democrats entertained of damaging the House Managers fell by the wayside, in most cases. Eleven of the Managers ran for reelection to their House seats, one resigned his seat to run for the Senate, and the other, Charles Canady, honored his pledge to remove himself from the House after serving four terms. How did those who ran for reelection fare?

The Safe Seats

Seven of the Managers—Hyde, Sensenbrenner, Gekas, Buyer, Bryant, Cannon, Graham, and Hutchinson—had little trouble retaining their House seats. They were in strong Republican districts, and in most cases, their prosecution of the President probably helped their reelection.

Henry Hyde

Having been elected every two years since 1974, Henry Hyde knew that he probably did not have to worry much in 2000. "On the other hand," he cautioned, "nothing is a foregone conclusion because times change, we're in an Internet world, and if people want to pour a lot of money into a race, it can change the dynamics ... So I am not complacent at all. I intend to run a very vigorous campaign. But I recognize the possibility of defeat. It's always possible, so I'm going to try and forestall it. If I lose, it won't be for lack of effort on my part."[16]

Although a conservative icon for his role in the impeachment, some commentators believe his reputation with the general public suffered the most of any Manager's. Prior to impeachment, he had been "a rare hybrid: a politician whose 'Hyde amendment' prohibiting the use of Medicaid funds for abortion put him at the center of one of society's most volatile debates but whose even-handed manner and intelligent humor won him the respect of many Democrats."[17] That reputation took a hit after the revelation of a decades-old affair and the acrimony of the impeachment hearings in the Judiciary Committee, although it would be hard to place the blame for that acrimony on Chairman Hyde.

He was so weary from the entire impeachment debacle that one close congressional friend believed he would not seek reelection. "He's not going to run," the source predicted. "I know that he's very defeated."[18] Hyde, though, turned his friend into a failed prognosticator when he determined to run after all. He handily won with 59 percent of the vote. That tally was down from 67 percent in 1998. Perhaps the impeachment did have a negative effect, but most politicians would accept those numbers gladly.

James Sensenbrenner

In 1998, Sensenbrenner had only token opposition in taking 91 percent of the vote in his Wisconsin district. The Democrats tried a little harder in 2000, but he still came away with a resounding 74 percent, the same percentage he had gained in 1996. He knew he had little to fear. Sensenbrenner's role in the impeachment strengthened his hold on his seat. He had commented prior to the election about the impeachment's impact, "I do have a safely Republican district, but I can go around to various social functions and picnics during the summer and people come up and say, I meant to write you a letter at the time but it slipped my mind, but I want to thank you now."[19] Obviously, impeachment was a plus for him.

George Gekas

Before Gekas won his congressional seat, it had been held by a Democrat. He always keeps that in mind. Although his victory margins have been large, he runs as if he could be upset in every race. "My ego tells me that I'm going to win," he stated more than eight months prior to the 2000 election. "My brain tells me that I'm going to campaign hard. So I'm going to do both. I'm going to campaign hard, and I'm going to win."[20] His prediction proved prophetic as he kept his seat by a margin of 72-28 percent.

Steve Buyer

"Serving in Congress is not the pinnacle of success," remarked Steve Buyer barely more than six months prior to the 2000 election. The best decision he made when he first won a congressional seat, he said, was to realize that he was elected to serve only two years: "That's it. That's my job. My job is only for two years. At the end of the first year, then, you have to make a decision on whether to run for reelection. When you decide that you only serve for two years, every judgment that you are faced with is easy to make if you're not counting on the job. So I only run for two years at a time."[21] He does not, therefore, see Congress as a lifetime appointment and, at some point, may decide to step down and follow another path.

In 2000, however, Buyer chose to run again. He knew he would be targeted. An editorial writer at *The Indianapolis Star* knew it also. The writer warned constituents in Buyer's district to expect "a noisy propaganda campaign" against the Congressman. "They'll be told Buyer arrogantly ignored the wishes of his constituents and was consumed by hatred in his zeal to prosecute Clinton on charges the majority of Americans had rejected," the writer explained. This would be an assault on Buyer's character, the editorial continued, but the voters needed to take into consideration that "it deeply bothered Buyer that he aggressively pursued a cause opposed by so many Americans, but he did it anyway because he believes it's more important to do what's right than what's popular." The editorial concluded,

> When it comes to right and wrong, Buyer sets a high and exacting standard, not a low one. Maybe that is a character flaw. But I know one thing. God help us if we succeed in ridding government of people with this particular character flaw.[22]

The people in Indiana's Fifth District decided that Buyer's "character flaw" was worth keeping, giving him 61 percent of the vote.

Ed Bryant

As with all the House Managers, Bryant's office was flooded with calls, letters, and e-mails throughout the impeachment proceedings. After the trial ended, that flood dwindled to a trickle. But he still was receiving congratulatory calls "like you would have if you'd made a good game out of it and stood for certain things, but the score was against you," he noted. He also continued to receive flowers. He kept them, but, he quipped, "We're throwing out anything that ticks. And we don't eat any brownies they send."[23] Through it all, he maintained a sense of humor.

Right after the end of the impeachment trial, Doug Horne, Chairman of the Tennessee Democratic Party, said, "We're going to try hard to remove Ed Bryant from office. We think he is beatable. All we need to do is get a good viable candidate and fund him well." He went on to say, in reference to Bryant's interview of Monica Lewinsky, "I think most Tennesseans would be embarrassed and somewhat appalled at his behavior. He just did a very poor job."[24]

Those were strong words, but nothing came of them. Democrats had a hard time finding that viable candidate, partly because Bryant sent signals that he was contemplating a run for governor in 2002. "Most everybody would prefer to wait until the seat becomes open," Shelby

County Democratic Chairman David Cocke acknowledged.[25] The other problem was the growing lock Republicans have demographically in his district. When the election dust settled, 70 percent of the electorate voted to return Bryant to Congress.

Chris Cannon

"I come from a district that really disliked what the President was doing," explained Chris Cannon. "It's a very constitutionally oriented group of people who care about their freedom and care about the sacredness of the institutions of the country." But he did have some concerns:

> I was out of my district for well over a year because of this whole thing. And people forgot that the reason I was gone was because of the impeachment. So where is this guy? Why isn't he around? Does he really care about us? Has he really become a Washington guy? . . . Now I'm spending a lot more time than I ordinarily would trying to make up for the time I didn't spend last year in my district. It's turning around, I will say. I walked into three meetings with 50 people each last night. This is my hometown, and I felt some antagonism when I walked in, like here's this guy who gets elected and just ignores us. After talking to them for a few minutes, they all became very, very warm. So we're making up for it, but it came with a cost.[26]

Cannon's belated attention to the people of his district paid off. In a five-person field of candidates, he took 59 percent of the vote and retained his congressional seat.

Lindsey Graham

Graham's ability to provide a good quote did not end with the impeachment trial. Speaking before a highly appreciative Republican audience in April of 1999, he commented, "I feel like Elvis in his fat period. My hour and a half of fame are over, but they can't stop applauding." On a flight to Atlanta, the pilot of the plane, a former Marine, left the cockpit to congratulate Graham and stood in the aisle chatting with him for twenty minutes. Quipped Graham later, "Everyone was getting real nervous watching us. So I says, 'Captain, this is great but maybe you should climb back into that cockpit.'"[27]

He never was too concerned about his reelection chances. "In South Carolina, if 'Clinton Fatigue' is an illness, we're the highest infected population in the nation," he had joked months before the election.[28] His assessment was correct; the electorate returned him to Congress with 68 percent of the vote.

Asa Hutchinson

From one perspective, Asa Hutchinson should have been the most vulnerable of all the Managers. How does one take on a President from one's own state—a state where that President had been a very popular governor—and survive? When one editorial cartoon depicted Hutchinson stabbing his state in the back and another showed the doors of the state shut and barred against him, it was not hard to sympathize with his concerns for his political future. "It was a high risk at the time," he remembers. "Any time you're in a close, marginal district, the rule is: Don't take risks that could come back and haunt you. Whenever you're going against 65 percent public opinion ... it's an extraordinary risk. It would almost be the definition of political suicide."[29] And to be sure, he was a target.

"I think it's completely clear that what the Republicans and Asa Hutchinson want is vengeance, not justice," an angry Democratic woman in Hutchinson's district fumed in the middle of the trial. She warned ominously, "They are very wrong in thinking people will forget what they've done. I honestly think it's going to go against them in the next election." A more sober assessment came from the Democratic Chairman in one of Hutchinson's counties: "If anything, I think he's getting high praise for the way he's done his job during this. Frankly, I don't think we can touch him."[30] The more sober assessment was the more accurate assessment.

Although Democrats tried hard to recruit a candidate with enough appeal to challenge Hutchinson, they were unable to do so. Of all the House Managers, Hutchinson was the only one to run unopposed in the election. "So much for the House assault on impeachment managers," noted National Republican Congressional Campaign Committee Chairman Tom Davis of Virginia. "Democrats are always looking for the silver bullet. First it was impeachment, then it was guns. But there isn't a silver bullet this year."[31]

More Competitive Races

Two other Managers who won their races had to face stiffer competition, although in both cases, the odds were in their favor.

Steve Chabot

According to Steve Chabot, he had reason to be concerned about reelection:

> There were two of us of the thirteen Managers that the press recognized as being the two most "vulnerable" House Managers. That was Jim Rogan and myself. We both have relatively tough districts for Republicans. There were three previous Members of Congress in my district before me that were all Democrats. They have made major efforts to try to knock me off in the past several elections, unsuccessfully. The mayor of Cincinnati ran against me last time, and I had one of the most high-profile races in the country. The AFL-CIO and other liberal national groups came after us very hard in the election prior to that. I think I was number six in the entire House in money spent against candidates. I beat an incumbent in the election before that to win the seat. So it's a challenging seat. President Clinton won my district both in '92 and in '96.[32]

Although recognizing the potential danger of linking himself too closely to impeachment in a district that could have gone either way, Chabot did not shy away from his involvement when he reached out to his supporters. Regional mailings featured his role in the impeachment. Henry Hyde also spoke at a fundraiser for him. In the six months following the Senate trial, he collected five times more than he had during the same time period two years earlier. At a campaign rally with George W. Bush, Chabot made a statement that reminded the audience of the President's troubles when he said, "We want prosperity without perjury."[33] He also was helped by disarray within the Democratic Party. Through it all, he held steadfastly to the belief that "Your best chance of getting re-elected is doing your best job."[34] Fifty-three percent of the Cincinnati-area voters agreed, sending Chabot back to Congress.

Bob Barr

Of all the Managers, Bob Barr was the one the Democrats wanted most desperately to beat. His foray into an impeachment inquiry, even before Monica Lewinsky was a household name, rankled Democrats at all levels—and many Republicans. Barr knew that he was going to be possibly the biggest target on the Republican side. But he appeared not to be bothered by his high profile. Perhaps he even basked in it. "They'll probably all be down there in force and with an awful lot of money," he mused eight months before the election. "My wife actually warned me about that three years ago, in early 1997, when I first started to look at this. She said, you know that they are going to come after you if you do this, if you proceed with this. She was absolutely correct," he admitted. "But it certainly hasn't changed anything that I will do, and it won't change anything that I will do. We'll just deal with it." He continued,

> I don't think it will have a direct impact in the election . . . I don't think that they will directly raise the issue of impeachment because I think they realize if they did, it's a losing issue in the 7th District. The people of the 7th District supported the impeachment process. So if they were to go out there,

whoever my opponent is, and say vote for me and vote against Bob Barr because he stood for impeachment, and vote for me because I don't think President Clinton should have been impeached, I think that would hurt them tremendously. They know that; they see the polling. I'm sure they do a lot of polling. But it will have an indirect impact because it has made my race very high profile. They will pour an awful lot of money into it. I think there will be a vindictiveness about the way they run their campaign that would not otherwise have been there.[35]

The Democrats felt that Barr was vulnerable because he won only 55 percent of the vote in 1998 against a very weak candidate who operated with a budget of only $13,000.[36] The Democratic opponent in 2000 was businessman Roger Kahn, who moved from Florida to Atlanta in 1998, and only after that bought a farm in Barr's district. In the campaign, Barr used that fact to promote the idea that Kahn was a carpetbagger whose primary goal was to unseat the incumbent Congressman rather than really become a part of the district.

Some Republicans pushed for Barr to change his image. They were concerned that he came across as too much of a bulldog. He said he would settle for what he called a "warm and fuzzy bulldog" image, but that Bob Barr would still be Bob Barr. "What you see is what you get," Barr remarked. "People really appreciate consistency."[37] As if to underscore that point, one of his campaign spots had Barr staring straight into the camera and saying, "You don't send me to Washington to smile. You send me to work, to speak strongly for the people of the 7th District. I hope you'll send me back."[38]

Despite spending nearly $3 million on the race, Democrat Kahn did not do much better than his underfunded colleague two years earlier. When the votes were counted, Barr had garnered 54 percent. He was heading back to Washington to work—not to smile.

The Casualties

Two of the House Managers did lose races, but the real question is how much that can be attributed to their role as Managers. Bill McCollum decided to go for the open Senate seat in Florida. If he had chosen instead to run again for his House seat, he probably would have won with ease. He already had served as a Congressman from that district since 1980. Republican Ric Keller won McCollum's open seat. Keller was a political newcomer considered the underdog against Linda Chapin, a former Orange County Commission Chairman.[39] If an unknown political entity could win against an established Democrat, there is little question that McCollum could have retained his seat. James Rogan, the other Manager who lost, had never won by more than 50.8 percent of the vote previously, so his district never was secure, with or without impeachment.

Bill McCollum

"I don't think the voters of Florida will decide the election on the basis of my role as an impeachment Manager," McCollum predicted in April of 2000. He continued,

I think they're going to decide on who they believe can best succeed Connie Mack and serve the people of Florida for Florida's unique interests in the next decade in the Senate, and who best represents the basic values of government that Connie stands for, his conservative political philosophy on all kinds of things ranging from government regulations and taxes to health care to Social Security and Medicare, education, defense, and so on. So I really think the down side to it [the Manager's role] is minimal, from what I observe. Yet I think the up side is there in a broader sense because I think most people respect me for doing what I believe was right and for standing on principle and not putting my finger to the wind to test the public opinion to decide something of such importance.[40]

When McCollum decided to enter the Senate race, he was not the choice of most state Republicans. Many GOP leaders in Florida privately wished for anybody but McCollum because they considered him too conservative. State Education Commissioner Tom Gallagher seemed a better choice to them, but McCollum surprised his own Party leaders by raising more money and picking up more Party endorsements. Finally, Gallagher dropped out of the primary race, leaving the nomination to the former House Manager.[41]

McCollum's Democratic opponent was Florida Insurance Commissioner Bill Nelson, who was more widely known throughout the state. McCollum and Nelson actually had been friends in their youth. They were fellow Key Club officers in high school, and they joined the same fraternity in college. Nelson, though, was a Democrat even at that time, and "McCollum was a Goldwater Republican who helped found the Campus Conservative Club."[42] Little did they know they would one day face each other in a US Senate race.

By all accounts, McCollum's role in the impeachment did help raise his visibility among Republican voters statewide. It also helped bring in financial resources that he normally would not have been able to command for a Senate race. "It was a huge advantage because it quickly gave us a base of support that we might not have had otherwise," the candidate admitted.[43] Yet all that quick cash did not translate into a lead in the polls. In mid-September, he was eight points behind Nelson in two polls, while another poll showed an eleven-point spread. One-fifth of Republican respondents in one of the polls said they were planning to vote for Nelson. The pollster provided this analysis: "McCollum's image is still too extreme for some moderate Republicans, and he's running out of time."[44]

President Clinton showed up in Florida to raise money for Nelson. Fundraising events that the President attended brought in over one million dollars, and Nelson had the opportunity to ride on Air Force One with the commander in chief. McCollum did not mention impeachment at campaign events. His campaign spokeswoman, Shannon Gravitte, explained that while McCollum "has never shied away from his role [in impeachment] . . . it's not a subject people on the campaign trail generally bring up for discussion. They want to look to the future." But when the President showed up for Nelson, McCollum felt it appropriate to remind his supporters of the impeachment in a fundraising letter. The letter stated, "With the exception of Hillary's New York race, my defeat is Bill Clinton's highest political priority. And he's still the Democrats' chief fundraiser and most shameless attack artist." The letter also claimed that Clinton was "driven by revenge to try to defeat me."[45]

As Election Day approached, McCollum was able to whittle down Nelson's lead but never could overtake him. The final tally was closer than many predicted: Nelson, 52 percent, McCollum, 47 percent. At Nelson's victory party, he noted that he had known McCollum since high school and still considered him a friend but, in the same breath, told his supporters that his victory was a rejection of "in-your-face . . . politics, excessive partisanship, and ideological rigidity."[46] That comment could be considered a critique of McCollum's impeachment role.

McCollum, in his concession speech, told supporters that his had been "a campaign of ideas" and that "we will prevail in the long run." One GOP strategist, though, countered that McCollum "never gave voters a clear idea of who he was, and he was running against someone that people at least thought was on their side against insurance companies."[47]

Overall, it appears that McCollum lost primarily because he had to fight an uphill battle for name recognition outside his own district. The campaign did not revolve around Bill Clinton; and impeachment, significant as it may have been as a background issue, and important as it was for McCollum in raising money from the Party faithful, was not the determining factor. As noted previously, if he had chosen instead to run again for his congressional seat, he would have been in the section of this chapter entitled "The Safe Seats."

James Rogan

Impeachment probably affected the Rogan race more than most, even though, as in the other races, it was not a front-and-center issue. Rogan's first concern was not what the Democrats might do to him, but the back-lash he might face from Republicans for pushing impeachment:

> For almost all of us, certainly for me, we viewed it as an act of political suicide. . . . The polls told us that a vast majority of high-propensity Republican voters around the country said they were going to hold this against us. The pollsters and the pundits were telling us, "If you vote to impeachment him, you will cost the House the Republican majority that you worked for for forty years." We all believed we'd face primary chal-lenges.
>
> I thought I was gonna get beat in 2000. I didn't think I was going to get beat by a Democrat; I thought I was going to be beaten in a primary. I thought I would go home to my Republican clubs and have these angry hordes of Republicans shaking their fists at me, telling me, "What have you done? You've destroyed our chance to hold the House. You've ruined our majority. We've worked forty years to get this majority. You've thrown it away. Look at what you've done to us!" I thought I'd be taken out in the primary. I wasn't worried about the Democrats; I was worried about the Republicans.[48]

Rogan, though, believed he had acted appropriately in the impeach-ment. When he was a District Attorney, he used to instruct juries on the meaning of "reasonable doubt." He would always tell juries not to convict unless they were "satisfied beyond a reasonable doubt to a moral certainty" that the accused was guilty. He applied that standard to his role in the impeachment: "Let me tell you what reasonable doubt means to me. It means you can look yourself in the mirror tomorrow, a year from tomorrow, a hundred years from tomorrow and say, I did the right thing. I will be able to look myself in the mirror every day remaining in my life and know that we did the right thing."[49]

If he had voted no on impeachment, the consequences would have been catastrophic, he felt. Future presidents would be able to commit the same offenses without fear of reprisal. They would have precedent as an argument. It would have been established that perjury, subornation of perjury, and obstruction of justice are not impeachable offenses. Imagining a future situation, he said,

> When was that established, Mr. President? Why, that was established by a Republican Congress in 1998-1999. Can you imagine that? I mean, what kind of legacy would that be for me to leave to my country to tell every future President of the United States that I'm going to make perjury, subornation of perjury, and obstruction of justice—by precedent—a non-impeachable offense because I'm worried about my re-election? If I were going to take that approach, I don't deserve to be here. It's much better for me to leave, and I wasn't prepared to give that as a gift to a President who, in the future, shows disrespect for the Constitution or the rule of law. I wasn't going to do that.[50]

Rogan, and everyone else, knew that he was going to be the most vulnerable of all the Managers. A GOP consultant noted, "Demography, more than impeachment, is Rogan's problem." His district, which had favored Republicans 44-43 percent in 1993, had switched to a 44-37 Democratic tilt by the 2000 election. President Clinton had won the district by eight points in 1996; Democratic Governor Gray Davis took it by seventeen points in 1998.[51] Even without the impeachment controversy, Rogan would have had an uphill struggle. Yet he remained philosophical: "If I lose my race next year," he mused to a reporter from *The Hill*, "you guys are going to be calling me the day after the election and saying, 'Don't you think this has to do with impeachment?' And if the answer is yes, what better reason to lose than standing up for the Constitution and your oath of office?"[52]

The long knives came out immediately. The day before the Senate voted to acquit, entertainment mogul David Geffen, who resided in Rogan's district, spoke for the Hollywood elite: "Many of us are looking forward to spending time and money and effort to defeating James Rogan."[53] And a California Democratic Party spokesman commented icily, "Rogan is on the endangered species list. . . . He'll need an oxygen tank to survive. . . . He's going to find himself in a boat looking for a life raft." Three metaphors in one statement—obviously an attempt to empha- size a point. The spokesman had reason to crow because a Democratic Party poll found that only 34 percent of Rogan's constituents were intending to vote for him again, 55 percent disagreed with his stand on impeachment, and his job approval rating was only 45 percent. Rogan responded, "I'm not afraid to lose. That's liberating for a politician. . . . You battle-scarred cynical guys don't know quite what to do with a politi- cian who puts his finger to the wind and says, 'Yeah, it's blowing this way and it may cost me my reelection, but I'm going to do what I think is right.'"[54]

In an interview with the *Los Angeles Times* about two weeks after the end of the Senate trial, Rogan did not apologize for his Manager role. In fact, he lauded the effort and challenged any opponent to use it as an issue:

> I hope my opponent, whoever that might be, tries to make impeachment an issue because that is a debate I want to have. We are going to talk about a president who used his power and influence to decimate the sexual harassment laws as they apply in the country, a president who used his power and influence to perjure himself and obstruct justice. I want to find the Democrat out there, the liberal out there, the person who wants to step up to the plate against me who is going to mouth piety on fighting for women's rights and sexual harassment laws but then takes a pass when it is his guy who does it.
>
> I put my political career on the line to defend those laws even when it wasn't popular to do it. So, let's have that debate. If anybody expects me to back down or apologize for standing up for the law and the constitution in this area, they don't know me very well.[55]

Even a Democratic activist in Rogan's district confessed, "In this day and age of politicians not giving straight answers, Rogan gets points for sticking with what he did to Clinton, and defending it."[56]

Rogan's concern that he would be put out to pasture by his own Party was unrealized. Instead, he was considered a hero, not only among California Republicans but also among Republicans nationwide. In March 1999, California Party leaders urged him to run against Senator Dianne Feinstein rather than seek reelection in his district. When he attended a Republican state convention in Sacramento, he was treated like a conquering hero. According to one reporter, "They gave him standing ovations, mobbed him for autographs, posted signs and stickers throughout the convention hotel hailing him, and singled him out for praise in a party resolution. 'Congressman Rogan,' the resolution said, 'unselfishly subordinated his personal, political interest to the public interest by, as he states, "doing what is right.""[57]

Rogan contemplated making the Senate run, but, tempting as it was, he decided by the end of April not to pursue it. At that point, he was not even sure he would run for reelection to the House. "Ultimately, it became apparent to me the Republican Party can do without me as a Senate candidate," he related in an interview. "I'm not sure my two little 6-year-old girls can do without a dad at home for the next two years."[58] His decision not to try for the Senate disappointed Party activists, but within the next few months, he did decide to seek reelection to his House seat.

The Democrats recruited state Senator Adam Schiff to run against Rogan. They had met politically before; Rogan had beaten Schiff twice for a state Assemblyman seat. Neither candidate made impeachment a focus of the campaign, but Rogan did have a ready answer whenever anyone questioned him about his impeachment role: "I voted four times to elect Al Gore president of the United States." He confided, "That's how I intend to spin it to the Democrats." While impeachment was not part of either candidate's stump speech, both used it extensively in attracting financial support. Conservatives nationwide received mail from Rogan that highlighted his stand on impeachment and reminded them that "Bill Clinton wants to make an example of me for standing up for the Constitution and the rule of law." Schiff, meanwhile, employed Senator Barbara Boxer for a fundraising letter that accused Rogan of "disregarding the Constitution and all precedent" in an effort "to bring down our twice-elected president."[59]

Playing the impeachment card publicly was troublesome for the Democrats. As one Party activist worried, "If we talk too much about impeachment, we could hurt Schiff with the people who don't want to hear about it anymore. We could also crank up all the conservatives to give even more money to Rogan." On the Republican side, one California lawmaker stated his rationale for not worrying about how people perceived Rogan, impeachment or not: "People will always respect someone who stands on principle," he asserted. "Some people say that Jim is a polarizing figure, but you know what? That's what they used to say about Ronald Reagan."[60]

The financial appeals worked for both sides. By mid-October of 2000, analysts estimated that Rogan would pull in nearly $6 million and Schiff about $5 million, making this the most expensive House race in American history. Rogan's donor list grew from 3,000 names in the 1998 election to 50,000, with donations coming from forty-six states. He even held fundraisers in places like Nebraska. For the Democrats, Hollywood liberals headed the donor list. Norman Lear and David Geffen hosted a fundraiser for Schiff that took in nearly $100,000. Another Schiff fundraiser featured none other than Bill Clinton as the host.[61]

The race concentrated on issues such as HMO reform, gun control, and aid to education. A typical Schiff ad critiqued Rogan for not voting to hire 100,000 new teachers. Rogan responded, "They can spend a billion dollars against me for all I care. They can't hide the fact they have bred failed public schools for poor and minority children for 50 years."[62] The race also grew more vituperative as it progressed. Schiff, in an indirect reference toward the impeachment imbroglio, accused Rogan of "ignoring local issues to play a partisan national role." Rogan returned fire, charging Schiff with lying about both of their records.[63] He called Schiff "a less than mediocre state senator," "the teachers' union's biggest shill," and a "weasel mouth." He decried Schiff's ploy of portraying him "as hating children, seniors, the world, and everything that's good and decent in America."[64]

Rogan also tried hard to connect with the Armenian community in his district. Armenian Americans comprise 15 percent of the electorate in California's 27th Congressional District, a higher percentage of Armenian Americans than in any other district in the country. There are seven Armenian newspapers and three Armenian cable television channels. Schiff targeted what he considered to be Rogan's neglect of Armenian issues.[65] Rogan, though, had been concentrating on the Armenian community. His sole overseas trip as a Congressman had been to Armenia in September 1999. In August 2000, he took up the cause of a congressional resolution to label as "genocide" the massacres of Armenians (possibly as many as 1.5 million) that occurred from 1915 to 1923 under the old Ottoman Empire, now modern Turkey.[66] The October House vote on the resolution was canceled, however, after Turkey objected and President Clinton sent a letter to House GOP leaders, "urging them 'in the strongest terms' not to bring it to the floor." Rogan said he was "saddened" by that decision, yet he was pleased at how far the resolution had progressed. A spokesman for the National Republican Congressional Committee commented that Rogan was "confident the Armenian American community will realize that this resolution would never have had a prayer were it not for him."[67]

Throughout the race, when it came to the impeachment and the possibility of losing the election because of it, Rogan held firmly to his message of integrity. In December 1999, he said, "If the voters of my district want to punish me for doing what I think is right, even if it is not popular, I am prepared to accept their judgment. That makes life ulcer-free."[68] One month later, he stated, "People may not agree with me on every issue, but they cannot accuse me of political cowardice."[69] In June 2000, he commented, "People at the end of the day want their leader to do what they think is right; and not what they think is going to get them re-elected. Well, I gave at the office on that one. And on November 7th, the folks here can decide whether they want a congressman like that. If they don't, I will come home and thank them very much for the privilege."[70] And as the election season swept into full gear in September 2000, he had this to say: "If I lose this race, it will be because I cast a vote for impeachment in a district and a climate where it was horribly unpopular. But there are some things more important than job security."[71]

When all the votes were counted, Rogan came up short. He received only 44 percent, while Schiff got 53 percent. Demographics explains a large part of the loss, but one cannot help but believe that without impeachment looming over the contest, the final tally would have been much closer. Whether Rogan could have won the district again, minus impeachment, after two extremely narrow victories in previous years, is an open question. With impeachment, however, it was all but impossible.

Rogan, in his heart, knew this might happen. Perhaps that is why he spoke about the possibility so often. But in a February 2000 interview, he explained that he always kept a consistent perspective:

> I was told at the time it [impeachment] would probably cost me my reelection. It still may cost me my reelection. That would make me nervous if I approached this job in a totally secular view that everything I've acquired is the result of my own doing and that this job belonged to me and now, having done what I thought was right, somebody was trying to take away that which is mine. I don't approach the job from that perspective. I am here because the Lord has given me the privilege of serving my country in Congress. It's a temporary privilege; I don't get to keep this forever. It doesn't belong to me. I have no claim to it. It belongs to the voters of the 27th District. They own the job, but they don't own my conscience. I was not prepared to sacrifice that to hang onto this job. I am not prepared to make that sacrifice today. If the voters turn me out of office because I did what I thought was right, I will leave here with only one feeling in my heart—a great feeling of grati-

tude that they gave me the opportunity to serve Congress and to serve my country. So that's sort of—in a nutshell—my philo-sophical take on this entire thing from A to Z.[72]

Chapter Fifteen Endnotes

[1] Richard L. Berke and James Bennet, "Clinton Vows Strong Drive to Win a House Majority, Advisers Say," *The New York Times*, 11 February 1999, A1.

[2] Timothy J. Burger, "Payback Can Bite, GOP Pols Warn Prez," *New York Daily News*, 12 February 1999, 6.

[3] Berke and Bennet, "Clinton Vows Strong Drive."

[4] Burger, "Payback Can Bite."

[5] Katharine Q. Seelye, "Republicans Respond Angrily to Reports of Clinton Vow," *The New York Times*, 12 February 1999, A23.

[6] "Barr Reacts to Reports of Clinton Retribution Plan"; available at http://www.house.gov/barr/p_021199.html; accessed 26 January 2000.

[7] Seelye, "Republicans Respond Angrily."

[8] Alison Mitchell, "GOP Fundraisers Take a Lesson from Clinton," *The New York Times*, 25 March 1999, A28.

[9] Robert Schlesinger, "Impeachment Made Managers Folk Heroes," *The Hill*, 12 January 2000, 9.

[10] Timothy J. Burger, "Impeach Managers Enjoying New Clout," *New York Daily News*, 6 June 1999, 26.

[11] Ralph Z. Hallow, "Impeachment of Clinton May Aid GOP After All," *The Washington Times*, 25 June 1999.

[12] Anne E. Kornblut, "On Impeachment Issue, a Bipartisan Pact: A Year before Campaign Heats Up, Few Candidates Want to Discuss the Past," *The Boston Globe*, 5 September 1999, A17.

[13] Robert Schlesinger, "Impeachment's Ghost Still Haunts 2000 Campaign as Presidential Hopefuls Deal with Clinton Fatigue," *The Hill*, 12 January 2000, 5.

[14] Ibid.

[15] Charles Krauthammer, "The Clinton Effect," *The Washington Post*, 18 August 2000, A43.

[16] Hyde interview.

[17] Mary Jacoby, "McCollum Uses Impeachment in Fundraising Letter," *St. Petersburg Times*, 27 January 2000, 1A.

[18] Thomas M. DeFrank, "Wounded Hyde May Call It Quits," *New York Daily News*, 28 February 1999, 18.

[19] Sensenbrenner interview.

[20] Gekas interview.

[21] Buyer interview.

[22] Larry MacIntyre, "Editorial: Character Flaw Worth Preserving," *The Indianapolis Star*, 17 February 1999, A14.

[23] Penny Bender, "Bryant Has No Regrets," *Gannett News Service*, 13 February 1999.

[24] Ibid.

[25] Jackson Baker, "Bryant Still Eyeing Governorship," *The Memphis Flyer*, November 25-December 1, 1999.

[26] Cannon interview.

[27] Michael Powell, "Managers' Special: Independent Women's Forum Honors House Impeachment Crew," *The Washington Post*, 21 April 1999, C01.

[28] Graham interview.

[29] Schlesinger, "Impeachment Made Managers Folk Heroes."

[30] Rick Lyman, "The President's Trial: The Future: In One Arkansas District, a Backlash," *The New York Times*, 8 February 1999, A21.

[31] "Rep. Hutchinson to Run Unopposed," *Roll Call*, 10 April 2000, 27.

[32] Chabot interview.

[33] Dave Boyer, "Bush Gains Momentum on Tour of Vital States," *The Washington Times*, 31 July 2000.

[34] Tom Squitieri, "Impeachment Finances Key California Race," *USA Today*, 18 August 1999.

[35] Barr interview.

[36] Rebecca Carr, "Barr Will Pitch $2 Million Battle for House Seat," *The Atlanta Journal and Constitution*, 17 December 1999, 5E.

[37] Whitt, "Team Hopes Softer Image Makes Voters Smile."

[38] David Pendered, "Barr: You Don't Send Me to Washington to Smile," *The Atlanta Journal and Constitution*, 22 October 2000.

[39] Larry Lipman, "GOP Staves Off Democratic Attack on Seats," *The Palm Beach Post*, 8 November 2000, 11A.

[40] McCollum interview.

[41] Brian E. Crowley, "Republicans Pin US Senate Hopes on McCollum: Candidate Rose from Obscurity during Clinton Impeachment," *The Palm Beach Post*, 10 September 2000, 1A.

[42] Ibid.

[43] Ibid.

[44] Steve Bousquet, "Republicans' Grip on Senate Seat Looking Weak," *The Miami Herald*, 19 September 2000, 1A.

[45] Steve Bousquet, "Clinton's Revenge Is My Defeat, McCollum Tells Political Backers," *The Miami Herald*, 5 October 2000, 5B.

[46] Mark Hollis, "Race for Mack's Seat Surprisingly Close," *Fort Lauderdale Sun-Sentinel*, 8 November 2000, 1A.

[47] Brian E. Crowley, "Nelson Wins in Quick Count," *The Palm Beach Post*, 8 November 2000, 9A.

[48] Rogan interview.

[49] Ibid.

[50] Ibid.

[51] Matthew Rees, "Rogan's Run," *The Weekly Standard*, 9 October 2000, 16-17.

[52] Schlesinger, "Impeachment Made Managers Folk Heroes."

[53] Berke and Bennet, "Clinton Vows Strong Drive to Win a House Majority."

[54] George Skelton, "Rogan Becomes Democrats' Dartboard," *Los Angeles Times*, 18 February 1999, A3.

[55] Bob Rector, "Glendale Republican Talks about Impeachment and His Own Political Career," *Los Angeles Times*, 28 February 1999, B17.

[56] Dick Polman, "Blood Lust over Congressional Race in California Already Fills the Air," *The Houston Chronicle*, 10 October 1999, A6.

[57] Bill Ainsworth, "Republican Test: Find Feinstein Challenger," *The San Diego Union-Tribune*, 6 March 1999, A1.

[58] Mark Z. Barabak and Cathleen Decker, "Rogan Rules Out Senate Bid," *Los Angeles Times*, 28 April 1999, A3.

[59] Squitieri, "Impeachment Finances Key California Race."

[60] Polman, "Blood Lust over Congressional Race in California."

[61] Rees, "Rogan's Run," 16; Ruth Marcus and Juliet Eilperin, "Battle for House Fuels Cash Race: Vulnerable Incumbents, Rivals Raising Funds at Record Pace," *The Washington Post*, 11 August 1999, A1.

[62] Juliet Eilperin, "Democrats Go on Attack Early with TV Ads in 6 House Races," *The Washington Post*, 26 August 2000, A7.

[63] Laura Mecoy, "Road to House Majority May Run through California," *The Sacramento Bee*, 2 October 2000, A1.

[64] Rees, "Rogan's Run," 18.

[65] Ibid., 16.

[66] Steven Mufson, "Local Politics Is Global as Hill Turns to Armenia," *The Washington Post*, 9 October 2000, A1.

[67] Juliet Eilperin and Steven Mufson, "Hastert Withdraws 'Genocide' Resolution: Clinton Plea, Ties with Turkey Cited," *The Washington Post*, 20 October 2000, A4.

[68] Sean Scully, "Most Prosecutors Safe One Year after Impeachment," *The Washington Times*, 22 December 1999.

[69] Patrick McGreevy, "I-Word in the Air as Rogan Seeks Reelection to House," *Los Angeles Times*, 9 January 2000.

70 "Specter of Impeachment Haunts Rep. Jim Rogan's Re-election Effort," 2 June 2000; available at http://www.cnn.com/2000/ALLPOLITICS/stories/06/02/cal.race/index.html; accessed 1 September 2000.

71 Gail Russell Chaddock, "House Races Go National: In Close Contests, Issues and Fundraising Extend Far Beyond a District's Boundaries," *The Christian Science Monitor*, 14 September 2000, 20.

72 Rogan interview.

CONCLUSION

Principle or Partisanship?

"Well, I think doing the job has changed me for the better. I think it has made me more knowledgeable, more able, probably a little more wise." Thus began the so-called "exit interview" of President Bill Clinton by *Esquire* magazine just prior to the 2000 elections. He had labored "under a virtually unprecedented barrage of attack, both political and personal," he lamented. But there was a silver lining because "it helped me to develop a certain discipline and a certain humility."[1] Some questioned the humility of the interviewee just by looking at the cover picture on that particular *Esquire*. There was the President, sitting in a chair, with what appeared to be a smug look on his face. And his words— unprecedented barrage of attack, both political and personal—by implication put the blame on his political opponents, not on his own actions that led to the myriad investigations during his two terms.

The President then took a shot at the Republican Congress:

> I think that in breaking the back of the Gingrich revolution and cutting through a lot of the meanness and antipathy toward the government per se that existed—which I think also Oklahoma City had a lot to do with, breaking the back—I think that it's much harder to, at least overtly, practice the politics of division than it was. The president is supposed to be a unifying force, not just in rhetoric but in fact.[2]

First, he associated the Republican-controlled Congress with "meanness" and "antipathy toward the government." Then he linked the bombing of the Oklahoma City Federal Building with the spirit of that Congress, and he rejoiced that now it was harder to "practice the politics of division." Last of all, he pointed to himself as a unifying force in the country. So, in effect, it could be said that he celebrated the demise of the politics of division by practicing it. And in what way was he a unifying force for the country? The impeachment was the outgrowth of his actions. Did it unify the country?

Later in the interview, he made these statements:

> I basically sort of convinced myself, and I still believe, that most of what happened to me politically was the cost of doing business, at the end of a twenty-year period of very increasingly negative, vitriolic politics, propagated mostly, but not entirely, by the far Right and their alliance with the Republican Party— which is not to say we [the Democrats] were blameless. . . . But mostly they generated it, beginning really in the late seventies, the basic attempt to delegitimize and de-Americanize your opponent. . . .
>
> The Republicans were trying to precipitate this great constitutional crisis for political advantage. And the American people knew things were rocking along pretty well in our country and they didn't want their government to go away. And they certainly didn't deserve to have their president disappear or become diverted.[3]

In the President's view, then, the Right and the Republican Party had been vitriolic and negative for the past twenty years and had to shoulder the blame for the poisoned political climate. In addition, he said the Republicans created the impeachment for their partisan advancement. One wonders how Ronald Reagan, who led the nation for eight of those twenty years, can be considered vitriolic and negative. His contribution to the politics of the 1980s was to point the way toward hope. His hallmark was his optimism. And what political advantage did the Republicans believe they were going to achieve by impeaching a popular President? As the previous chapters have shown, most of the Managers swam against the tide in pushing for impeachment—a tide that existed within their own Party as well as among the Democrats and the general public. They firmly believed the Party might suffer a backlash for proceeding, yet they also believed that they had to proceed for the sake of the Constitution and the rule of law.

Clinton's questioner then noted that the Republicans were trying to make the 2000 elections a referendum on him personally. "Well, they can't," the President responded, "for two reasons. One is, unlike them, I have apologized to the American people for what I did wrong, and most Americans think I paid a pretty high price." The implication was that the Republicans, and the Managers in particular, owed the American people an apology for their actions. "That's the first thing," he continued. "The second thing is, most people know that what they did was not about morality or truth or the law, it was about politics and power and didn't have anything to do with them or their welfare; it had to do with the Republicans and *their* welfare." That statement dismissed every argument the Managers made concerning the rule of law, the crimes of perjury and obstruction of justice, and the consequences to the constitutional system of allowing those criminal actions to go unpunished. In Clinton's estimation, their attempt to bring accountability was about politics and nothing else. Then he was even more explicit: "They never apologized to the country for impeachment, they never apologized for all the things they've done."[4]

One comes away from that interview with the distinct impression that the President did not do anything even remotely related to a high crime or misdemeanor, but that the Republicans were the real culprits who should apologize to the country for their dastardly deeds. One year earlier, President Clinton had even predicted that his stand against impeachment would be viewed as a noble *defense* of the Constitution— certainly the antithesis of the message coming from the House Managers.[5]

For some conservatives, this attitude, coupled with the Senate acquittal, demonstrated a reversal of gigantic proportions in the culture of the country. Paul Weyrich, President of the conservative Free Congress Foundation, shortly after the Senate trial ended, sounded a mournful tone. "You don't have to go back 40 or 50 years to think of a time when a president would have been driven from office for doing what Clinton did," he commented. "Indeed, it might have still happened even 10 years ago. John Tower, President Bush's nominee for secretary of defense, was defeated on charges of personal conduct in 1989. Then, there seemed to be a connection between personal character and service in office. We owe the late Senator Tower an apology. In the current climate, he would be celebrated as the right man for the job." He concluded,

> What this means in plain English is that the efforts to return some semblance of moral order to the nation through the political process have failed. If there really were a "moral majority" in the country, Clinton would have been driven from office a year ago . . . It is clear that we now live in a hostile culture. Any nation that finds a Bill Clinton more popular after his trial than before is a nation that Alexis DeTocqueville would not recognize.[6]

While it was easy for conservatives to be pessimistic, there were still some signs of moral conscience in the electorate on the first anniversary of the historic House vote for impeachment. A *USA Today*/CNN/Gallup Poll showed that the percentage of the population that approved of the House vote had risen from 35 percent to 50 percent. Moreover, 42 percent of Americans polled now disapproved of the Senate acquittal, while only 29 percent had disagreed with it at the time. Opined Dee Dee Myers, former Clinton press secretary, "It may be a function of people no longer being faced with the real possibility (of Clinton's removal), and so they can express their lingering disgust with the events without any real consequences." Stephen Hess of the Brookings Institution agreed: "Now they are saying we can look at what he's really like. He really is a scoundrel. He really did lie to us. He really did perjure himself. This poll reflects that now that that's over, now that the crisis is past, we can express our disdain for what this man put us through."[7]

Another poll indicated that the Clinton impeachment was not merely an inconsequential matter in the minds of the American people. A *USA Weekend*-Newseum poll in December 1999 revealed that the Clinton impeachment ranked ahead of President Nixon's resignation, the assassinations of Martin Luther King, Jr., and Robert Kennedy, the explosion of the Space Shuttle *Challenger*, and the Cuban Missile Crisis as a top news story of the twentieth century.[8] Meanwhile, a *NewsMax.com*/Zogby International poll that came out simultaneously with the others mentioned above found that "two-thirds of Americans want Congress to consider a second round of impeachment proceedings against Bill Clinton for possibly swapping United States military secrets to China in exchange for campaign cash."[9] Despite their distaste for impeachment, it still was conceivable that the American public could be roused to support the action if traitorous activity could be confirmed.

All of this evidence points to a growing acceptance that perhaps the House Managers were not partisan in their endeavor—that principle might have been their motivation. The motives of some Democrats, meanwhile, are becoming clearer. As revealed in Peter Baker's book, *The Breach*, there was a concerted partisan effort to paint the Republicans as the outrageous partisans. Baker, a *Washington Post* reporter, notes that when lawyers for the two sides had come to agreement on which parts of the Starr Report would not be released to the public, Julian Epstein, chief counsel for the Democrats, was not pleased. As Baker relates,

> They had to have differences. They had to have split votes. The whole premise governing the Democratic strategy was to paint the Republicans as unfair, to make a case that they were being partisan. After the public backlash against the salacious material in the Starr report, Epstein particularly wanted to have some disagreements so that the Democrats could say the Republicans were only interested in putting out smut—never

mind that most Democrats voted along with the GOP majority to release the original Starr report, all equally ignorant of what it might contain.[10]

Baker notes that "with harmony threatening to break out," Epstein told the Democratic lawyers to go back to the materials and come up with redactions with which the Republicans could not agree, redactions that would gut the case against the President. They did so. The Republicans, when faced with these additional materials that Democrats said could not be released, had to vote against those redactions. "That gave the Democrats all they needed to parade out to the cameras and complain that they were being railroaded, as liberal congressman Barney Frank of Massachusetts proceeded to do during the first available break. 'There's no bipartisanship,' Frank huffed to reporters waiting outside the closed doors. 'They're just deciding what they want to do and doing it.'"[11] Epstein's stated goal at one point during the Judiciary Committee hearings was to make sure the public looked upon them as the way *not* to conduct hearings. As Baker explains, "The last thing they wanted were television cameras showing the public a deliberate and thoughtful process . . . Their goal was to make it look more political."[12]

Another example was the strategy that Richard Gephardt, the Democratic minority leader in the House, followed in the opening of the impeachment inquiry. He knew that Democrats could not oppose the inquiry directly without appearing partisan, so his answer "was to draft a Democratic version of an inquiry resolution that would give his members political cover—one that would make it look as if the Democrats were taking the matter seriously but would restrict the process in such a way that the Republicans would be sure to reject it. If Gephardt could get a party-line vote out of it, he would make Republican 'partisanship' the issue. Win by losing."[13]

As the Democrats continued to work on their own inquiry proposal, some of them worried that the proposal was getting perilously close to what Republicans could accept. James Carville, the President's most vociferous defender, grew alarmed at the prospect: "If the Republicans agreed to the Democratic plan, it would destroy Carville's whole line of attack—and by extension the president's defense. His entire argument was that the impeachment drive was a partisan witch-hunt; a bipartisan agreement would remove all the arrows from his quiver."[14]

Did Republicans demonstrate partisanship? Certainly—but not the type suggested by the Democrats. Republican partisanship was the opposite of the public accusations. Some Republicans, fearing for the future success of their Party, sought to run away from the impeachment. It was only the overwhelming evidence in the Starr materials that forced some of them in the House, against their wishes, to vote for articles of impeachment. In the Senate, it was the fear of a public backlash that led to a truncated trial without live witnesses, thus dooming any hope the Managers might have had to sway the minds of those struggling with their consciences. Partisanship existed, but not the variety of which the Democrats loudly complained. Instead, Republicans showed partisanship in their preference for a weakened President Clinton rather than a strong President Gore.

Into the midst of these different brands of partisanship strode the House Managers, proclaiming that they were standing for principle. They were mocked for taking on a lost cause. They were derided for trying to bring a popular President to the bar of public accountability. As they exited the Senate after losing the vote, they seemed dispirited. David Schippers, the Managers' chief investigative counsel, tells what happened next:

> We all left together, led by Hyde, to go back to the Rayburn Building. It was necessary for us to walk from the Senate side of the Capitol, through the great Rotunda, and out the doors on the House side. As we walked through the Senate corridor on the way to the Rotunda, we met several uniformed Capitol Police. Every one of them had a word of gratitude or encouragement. "God bless you guys," or "We're proud to know you," or just "Thank you." That helped raise our spirits, but what waited for us in the Rotunda was amazing.

The Rotunda was crowded with tourists and visitors who had wanted to be present during the impeachment vote. A roped-off passage through the center of the room had been erected for our passage. The first one to appear in the Rotunda was Henry Hyde, followed by the other Managers, some staffers, and me. As Hyde appeared, first one and then a few others began to clap. By the time we reached the center of the room, everyone in the Rotunda was applauding those thirteen beaten warriors. Some people reached over the barrier to shake Hyde's hand. Suddenly, every one of us began to walk a little faster and with a spring in our step. I looked at the Managers and saw that they were smiling, where a minute earlier they had been downcast. All along they knew that, come what may, they were honorably performing their constitutional duty. Now they realized that the great unpolled American people knew it, too. As usual, Chairman Henry Hyde was right: "Don't ever underestimate the American people."[15]

One dictionary definition of a hero is "a man admired for his achievements and noble qualities and considered a model or ideal." It is unfashionable in our age of anti-heroes to call anyone heroic. It seems naïve to believe that some people actually rise above their circumstances for altruistic reasons. We are too sophisticated to believe any such thing. Everyone is out for himself; we all look out for number one; principles are useful in our speeches, but deadly if we try to put them into practice. We make snide comments about those who remind us of lofty ideals. We assume they do not really mean what they say. This book contains significant portions of speeches made by thirteen men who prosecuted a President. The cynical among the readers of these pages will laugh at the mere suggestion that these men really meant what they said. But . . . what if they were serious and not merely making speeches for their own self-advancement? What if they truly were concerned about the rule of law and the principles of right conduct and constitutionalism? If one grants that possibility, then we might be looking at true heroes after all. Perhaps one measure of true heroism is that it is not recognized until the event that inspired the heroism recedes further into the past. As the current generation passes and the Clinton impeachment becomes just another one of those events that fills a space in the history texts, will future generations look upon these men as heroes? Will they acknowledge their noble qualities and consider them as models or ideals?

It is perhaps fitting to end this book with an insight from the leader of the Manager team, Henry Hyde, who declared in his closing argument before the Senate,

> To the House Managers, I say your devotion to duty and the Constitution has set an example that is a victory for humanity. Charles de Gaulle once said that France would not be true to herself unless she was engaged in some great enterprise. That is true of us all. Do we spend our short lives as consumers, space occupiers, clock watchers, as spectators, or in the service of some great enterprise?
>
> I believe, being a Senator, being a Congressman, and struggling with all our might for equal justice for all, is a great enterprise. It is our great enterprise. And to my House Managers, your great enterprise was not to *speak* truth to power, but to *shout* it. And now let us all take our place in history on the side of honor and, oh, yes: Let right be done.[16]

Conclusion Endnotes

[1] Michael Paterniti, "Bill Clinton: The Exit Interview," *Esquire* [on-line edition]; available at http://www.esquire.com/features/articles/001026_mfr_clinton_1.html; accessed 30 October 2000.

[2] Ibid.

[3] Ibid.

[4] Ibid.

[5] Bill Sammon, "A Year Later Americans Warm to Impeachment: House Managers Take Comfort in Poll," *The Washington Times*, 18 December 1999, A1.

[6] Paul Weyrich, "Down to Survival for Conservatives," *The Houston Chronicle*, 28 February 1999, Outlook Section, 1.

[7] Laurence McQuillan, "Public Changes Mind on Impeachment," *USA Today*, 17 December 1999.

[8] Carl Limbacher, "Century-End Poll: Clinton's Impeachment More Important than Nixon's Resignation," *NewsMax.com*, 26 December 1999; available at http://www.newsmax.com/showinsidecover.shtml?a=1999/12/26/121609; accessed 24 January 2000.

[9] "Poll: Two-thirds of Americans Want New Impeachment Review," *NewsMax.com*, 21 December 1999; available at http://www.newsmax.com/articles/?a=1999/12/20/215921; accessed 24 January 2000.

[10] Baker, *The Breach*, 101.

[11] Ibid., 102.

[12] Ibid., 164.

[13] Ibid., 115.

[14] Ibid., 126.

[15] Schippers, *Sellout*, 281-82.

[16] Closing Argument of Hon. Henry Hyde, Senate Impeachment Trial of President Clinton, 8 February 1999.

Index